Health and Medicine
among the
Latter-day Saints

Health/Medicine and the Faith Traditions

Edited by James P. Wind and Martin E. Marty

The series Health/Medicine and the Faith Traditions
explores the ways in which major religions
relate to the questions of human well-being.
It issues from Project Ten, an interfaith program
of The Park Ridge Center for the Study of
Health, Faith, and Ethics.

Barbara Hofmaier, Book Editor

The Park Ridge Center
is a corporation of the Lutheran General Health System.

The Park Ridge Center
676 N. St. Clair, Suite 450
Chicago, Illinois 60611

Health and Medicine among the Latter-day Saints

SCIENCE, SENSE, AND SCRIPTURE

Lester E. Bush, Jr.

*for Gene Outka —
with Best Wishes,
John Bush*

Crossroad • New York

1993

The Crossroad Publishing Company
370 Lexington Avenue, New York, NY 10017

Copyright © 1993 by the Lutheran General Health System

Printed in the United States of America

Library of Congress Cataloging-in-Publication Data

Bush, Lester E.
    Health and medicine among the Latter-Day Saints : science, sense, and scripture / Lester E. Bush, Jr.
        p.   cm. — (Health/medicine and the faith traditions)
    Includes bibliographical references and index.
    ISBN 0-8245-1219-7
    1. Hygiene, Mormon.   2. Health—Religious aspects—Mormon Church.
3. Medicine—Religious aspects—Mormon Church.   4. Spiritual
healing.   5. Church of Jesus Christ of Latter-Day Saints–
–Membership.   6. Mormon Church—Membership.   I. Title.   II. Series.
BX8643.H8B87   1992
261.5'61'088283—dc20   92-30023
                                                            CIP

Contents

Foreword

Readers of all twelve volumes in this Health/Medicine and the Faith Traditions series are likely to have had experiences similar to mine as I have helped charter, edit, study, and introduce each book. Typical readers are likely to be positively related to one or another of the faith traditions. They will recognize, as I do, that when readers wish to become acquainted with a religion that is not their own, some will chiefly find some points of contact; more will discover analogies; still more will experience a great sense of distance; and almost everyone will know some bewilderments in the face of "the other."

Thus those who have studied the Reformed, Lutheran, Anglican, and Methodist traditions, and who belong to one of these, will mainly find points of contact among them. When Catholics read Protestant or Christians read Jewish books, they will find analogies in understandings of care and cure, illness and health. That is: at many points there will be similarities within the differences, and at others differences within the similarities. When any of these "Westerners" approach, for example, the Native American, the Muslim, and even more the Hindu traditions, they need greater resources out of which to express empathy and to find understanding.

If readers belong to the 8 percent of the American people who, when asked, list "no religious preference" or "no religion" as their self-description—and mean it—these books will be encounters with something alien in every case. Readers who are not without religious identification but are quite indifferent to the claims of faith may persist in reading out of curiosity or the desire for knowledge that will help them relate, perhaps with medical interests in mind, to persons in the tradition being described.

Several books strike those outside their traditions as being most bewildering if not almost impossible to crack and decode. Americans who consider their faith tradition to be classical and orthodox and who then read about faiths that grew on this continent regularly report on this decoding problem when they deal with Christian Science and Adventism. In the present case, I expect to hear about difficulties with the Latter-day Saints. Sociologist Peter Berger speaks of certain faith communities as being "cognitive minorities." That is, their members move freely within the culture, but as a group they see things differently than do all their neighbors. They interpret reality in distinctive ways. (Given the rapid growth of the Latter-day Saints, one is tempted to ask: how long will they make up a "cognitive minority"?)

In the chapters that follow, Lester Bush will do little to diminish the distance between readers of this faith community and others, except insofar as he provides information and demonstrates the logic by which one Latter-day Saint teaching follows or connects with another. I have guided dissertations by scholars among the Saints, have been their guests, have participated in their scholarly societies. Yet here, almost from page one, I find that, as in those several other cases, the integral character of Mormonism, that which provides vision and wholeness to those who share it, is precisely what keeps me—as a representative non-Mormon ("Gentile," to them)—at a distance.

Yet one can—and, I would say, one *must*—begin to cross the boundaries that define that distance. Mormons are among the fastest growing faiths in the nation, even though American religious and cultural niches often are already filled and their residents resistant. And Mormons are experiencing even greater gains elsewhere. If one force is growing while others languish, or even growing at the expense of others, even prudentially one will want to know why. Do you arm yourself against such groups, as nineteenth-century non-Mormons did against the hated Saints in America? Do you take lessons from their more nearly acceptable descendants? How does one serve them, as fellow citizens, or as physician or nurse; how is one served by them, as patient?

Because some of the Mormon positions color political choices, particularly in areas where the church is strong, it is important to understand the views commonly held. Why no fluoridation of water in Utah? Why is it foolish to be pro "prochoice" in Mormon domains and still hope to be elected to public office? Why did the Equal Rights Amendment face such opposition by the Mormon church? What chance do homosexuals have in the Mormon Kingdom?

Also, since Mormons have attained a good reputation for so many of their practices, it has become even more important to learn about the context out of which those positive practices grow. Thus, as Bush points out, there are some differences—not dramatic and perhaps not permanent, yet real and empirically testable—in longevity, in health, and in apparent well-being within the Mormon population compared to the citizenry at large. What is their secret? Can one learn from them without first having adopted their worldview? Can their "behavioral minority" status be severed from their "cognitive minority" position?

In pursuit of answers to some of these questions, most readers will find sufficient impulse to read and then get caught up in the world of Mormons as outlined by Lester Bush. It becomes clear almost at once that Mormons are not merely a church. They are a people. They own identifying symbols and follow practices that put greater distance between "mainstream" Christians than the distance between one and another of almost any of these Christian groups. Bush's fascinating description of the always-to-be-worn "garment" gives hint of the elaborate and intricate array of nuances that follows.

Early on, a note cites non-Mormon scholar Jan Shipps to the effect that Mormonism is "a new religious tradition." Shipps has taught some of us to see that the Latter-day Saints do something as radical to the Christian biblical tradition as Christians did when they took over the whole canon of the Jews, called it "the Old Testament," reinterpreted everything in the received tradition, and added writings of their own. The Mormons consider themselves Christian—though most Christians have had trouble embracing them for this self-description. Yet the first elements of the Mormon worldview immediately represent drastic departures from Christian and Jewish outlooks, and the later elements of the faith lie at even further distances than the first.

Accepting Joseph Smith as a prophet of God and the *Book of Mormon* as an authentic revelation is part of that first word. As Bush makes clear, there is also a second differentiating theme: monotheism gets challenged by poly- or pantheisms in Mormon revelation. All the old landmarks seem to be lost; new ones take their place.

Bush, only the second physician in this series of writers, does not spend a great deal of time preparing us for the workup on Mormonism that follows. Some might have chosen to build a bridge by first showing all the likenesses between it and anything else. Bush finds it more efficient and clarifying to begin right in the middle of things, or, better, at the end of things: with "death and dying." In those themes come the testings of what any tradition has been about. Whoever is having a first encounter with Mormonism will already in this chapter recognize how intact, apparently enclosed, and inaccessible that faith may be to others. Its temple rites differ from anything commonly established in the other faiths. Reason from the end of earthly existence, Bush seems to be saying, and the rest of Mormonism will make more sense.

But what about the book's larger audience, the people *within* the Mormon tradition? Why should Mormons find Bush's very coherent presentation useful? Certainly what he talks about must be the subject of any number of books with which they are already familiar? Certainly not. As with other books in the series, this is a pioneering work that sets out to gather the strands of a tradition, to braid and synthesize them and set them forth sympathetically but not uncritically. Of course, with thousands of pages having been written on almost every Mormon topic herein, one does not expect to find the wholly new here. But it is one thing to be given restrictions on alcohol, tobacco, and hot drinks on one day; then to have a marriage manual placed in one's hands the next; and further, to have the story of Barney Clark and the implantation of an artificial organ told as a Mormon tale the next. And it is another thing to see how all these connect, how they interrelate and grow out of a single source, the fundamental religious vision of Joseph Smith and his successors.

The Mormon tradition is particularly interesting because it, more readily than most, is open to new revelation, to development of views, to progress and change. Some of the changes came in response to vicissitudes that faced the Saints in their Utah territory or with the advent of modern technology. Some seem to be responses born of a need to satisfy the interests of constituencies. In any case, Bush shows in what ways the Mormons have kept accommodating themselves to new circumstances and in what ways they have been resistant.

The author is not promoting an ideology or overpushing a thesis. Sometimes a chapter ends with observations about how much Mormonism has adapted and how many distinctives it is losing. Another chapter ends with a caution against seeing Mormonism as ready to dissolve into the background and blend into the woodwork. A double process of adapting and resisting goes on; that should be no surprise, because it tends to go on in most faiths. The Mormon leadership, however, is so bold and articulate about the development that it provides a good case example to those who want to study change within more subtle communities.

Mormonism, these pages remind us, is sometimes called the most American of the religions. The scenes in its holy book are set in this hemisphere, and its sacred writings say good things about the American Ways. Studying this tradition from Lester Bush's vantage may inform the Saints about how and why they got where they are and about what issues of illness and health will have to do with their general progress. It will inform the rest of us about neighbors, fellow citizens, people who care about care and who would cure and be cured—while pursuing ways which set them apart in a culture that generally bids people to blur and blend their ways. Here, then, is an intact tradition worth studying, expounded by one of those rare individuals who is equally at home in the "health/medicine" and "faith" aspects of that dynamic tradition.

Martin E. Marty

Preface

The "afterclap" of Puritanism—in Emerson's pithy characterization—which emerged in early-nineteenth-century New York to become the Church of Jesus Christ of Later-day Saints has been the subject of a remarkable amount of recent scholarly study. This can be attributed both to the highly publicized growth of the church and to a consensus that, despite its self-conscious "peculiarness," Mormonism (as the tradition popularly came to be known) is and always has been, in the words of sociologist Thomas F. O'Dea, "the most American of religions."[1] It also reflects the profusion of primary source material available on the Mormons, courtesy of the diligence with which they recorded their century-and-a-half journey to date.

At the request of the Park Ridge Center for the Study of Health, Faith, and Ethics, the present monograph is added to this growing body of "Mormon studies," representing an innovative nineteenth-century American religion in the Center's illuminating survey of health and medicine among the faith traditions. As with other contributions to this series, the present work addresses ten common themes of concern: dying, passages, well-being, healing, suffering, madness, sexuality, caring, dignity, and morality.

In approaching this task I have faced several times over the embarrassment of riches in Mormon source materials noted in Lawrence Foster's study of religion and sexuality.[2] Thousands of articles have appeared in official church publications over the years bearing on the issues at hand, and relevant entries in journals and other manuscript sources total many times that number. Buried as these references are amidst hundreds of thousands of pages of minimally indexed materials, they afford a challenging if rewarding opportunity for research into the Mormon point of view. There are data enough to support book-length treatments of most of the themes covered in this study. As what can be only an introduction to these subjects, the present work is based primarily on a review of most officially published Mormon sources, supplemented where possible by journal or diary accounts that shed light on the published record.

Certain aspects of the tradition of the Latter-day Saints (LDS) require this survey to be somewhat different from others in this series. Despite the homogeneous stereotype many hold of the Mormons, a significant spectrum of views exists within the church, which can be understood only in the context of the often unrecognized diversity of the past. Projections that fail to take this into account would almost surely prove erroneous. On the other hand, in taking a developmental approach one embarks on a charged journey. Analyses like the present work are believed by many church leaders to be the province of the official church, which typically entrusts doctrinal commentary to men within the leadership whose purpose is to build faith and substantiate established views. Moreover, the historical record passes through terrain which ofttimes proves unexpected. These factors have led me to an approach more documentary than interpretive.

Most important aspects of the story here recounted—for example, that relating to LDS healing practices and the Mormon health code—have not previously been addressed in print in any depth. I therefore have chosen to develop in detail the doctrinal history necessary to illuminate the complexity of the record, a complexity as likely to be unfamiliar to Mormon readers as to others. Furthermore, the tradition accords great weight to the guidance of the church's senior presiding authority—the First Presidency—which consists of a president and, generally, two counselors.[3] Because of the importance attached to *exactly* what the First Presidency has said, and the practical unavailability of virtually all but their most current guidance, I often have quoted their "statements" with minimal paraphrase. Moreover, it is only within this monograph that even an LDS reader would be likely to find the text of the vast majority of previous health-related official guidance. Non-Mormon readers may wish to pass more quickly through some of the historical and documentary detail than those within the tradition would be inclined to do.

Finally, while I have, where warranted, drawn a number of analytic conclusions, in general it has seemed preferable to allow so specific a record to speak for itself.

A brief word is in order about organization. The ten themes selected for study by the Park Ridge Center are fundamental to all religions. Not all, however, have received equal attention in Mormon thought. Aspects of dying, well-being, healing, and sexuality—issues of the here and now—have generated volumes of discussion within the church. More abstract concerns like suffering and passages have been less frequently addressed. Accordingly the latter will be considered in the chapters on well-being and dying, respectively, within which context they more often are mentioned. Dignity and morality are treated jointly from the broader standpoint of personal agency (or, as termed by Mormons, "free agency") vis-à-vis institutional authority. While morality extends for most Mormons well beyond medically related concerns, the medical-ethical record on this point affords a particularly instructive case study. As this particular discussion to some extent recapitulates the record on specific issues in Mormon medical history, it has been made the final chapter. Those unfamiliar with the Mormon tradition will profit from an early reading of this chapter—perhaps following their reading of Chapter 1 on the Mormon context—because it provides important perspective on the sources of and limits on authoritative guidance within the church.

Finally, I wish to acknowledge the tremendous help provided in this project by my friend Gregory Prince, who has shared generously his time, unpublished research, and remarkable private library, and to thank as well the Park Ridge Center, and especially James Wind, for many helpful suggestions and considerable patience. Above all, I wish to thank my wife, Yvonne, for support and encouragement beyond any reasonable expectation.

·1·

On the Mormon Context

The Church of Jesus Christ of Latter-day Saints was organized in 1830 in the "burned-over district" of upstate New York.[1] Its founding elder was a twenty-five-year-old farmer and one-time seeker of hidden treasure named Joseph Smith (1805–1844). Smith preached a restoration of primitive Christianity and divinely bestowed authority, and he offered as evidence of his prophetic call the *Book of Mormon*, a theological narrative set against the backdrop of ancient America and translated, he said, from a set of inscribed "golden plates," the location of which was revealed to him in a vision.

Smith's scriptural treasure presented itself as an abridgment of what principally was the religious history of the inhabitants of ancient America. Prepared about 400 C.E. by the last of a long series of prophets, a man named Mormon (thus the title of the *Book of Mormon* and, shortly, the popular name of the new believers), this record implied that contemporary American Indians were descendants of two small groups that had left Jerusalem just before its destruction by Nebuchadnezzar in 587 B.C.E. A righteous line within one of the groups maintained a Bible-like prophetic tradition which at the time the book was compiled was about to come to a violent end.

Beyond the light it apparently shed on the popular question of Indian origins, Smith's record addressed a number of more traditional religious concerns. The title page enumerated the most salient purposes of the work: "to shew unto the remnant of the House of Israel how great things the Lord hath done for their fathers; and that they may know the covenants of the Lord, that they are not cast off forever; and also to the convincing of the Jew and Gentile that Jesus is the Christ, the Eternal God, manifesting himself to all nations." Implicit throughout was the message that urgency should attend the proclamation of this restored Word, for it was only to come forth in the very "last days."

The physical structure of the new scripture was reassuringly consistent with the established yardstick of the day, the Authorized (King James) Ver-

1

sion of the Bible. Divided into a series of "books" bearing the names of their prophetic authors (the Books of Alma, Mosiah, Helamen, and so on) and cast in a prose style clearly indebted to that of the King James Bible, the narrative consisted of a relatively sparse multi-century military and religious history interspersed with detailed texts of a number of visions, prophecies, and sermons. Within this body of inspired writing were to be found answers to many pressing theological and practical questions—including, providentially, those posed by deist and rationalist critics of the Bible.

Anchored by this 600-page "restoration of the fullness of the gospel" and guided by an ongoing series of revelations, Joseph Smith and his followers set out to reestablish fully the ancient order of things—in anticipation of Christ's imminent millennial return. In the process Smith led his growing band of primitivist seekers on a complex odyssey which, over a period of nearly two decades, eventually led to the Great Salt Lake Valley of the mountain West.

From New York the group first moved simultaneously to the Western Reserve of Ohio (temporary headquarters of the church) and western Missouri (the site designated by the Mormon prophet as Zion, the New Jerusalem to which Christ shortly would come to usher in the millennium), and thence to Illinois on the Mississippi, where Joseph Smith was killed in 1844. It was from Illinois that his successor, Brigham Young (1801–1877), led the Mormon pioneers of 1847 to their safe haven in the West.

Not long after announcing the Restoration, Joseph Smith began to depart from his initial primitivist notions—to the alienation of some of his earlier followers—and soon developed a hierarchical style of leadership, with himself as undisputed leader and sole spokesman for God. In the process he moved distinctly away from the many traditional Protestant notions that permeate the earliest Mormon writings. Eventually Smith's restoration combined the New Testament ideals of communitarianism, apostolic witness, and guidance by the Holy Spirit at both individual and institutional levels; the Old Testament models of a gathering of believers, prophets, and polygyny; and some of his own innovations, including an increasingly stratified priesthood of all adult male believers. Ultimately emerging from this inspiration was, in the words of historian Jan Shipps's recent study, an authentically new religious tradition.[2]

However far-reaching the religious implications of these early years, the secular experience was often anything but promising. Primitivist converts grew increasingly concerned over the concentration of power in the person of Joseph Smith, a concern reinforced by the publication of a quasi-creedal collection of his revelations and teachings in 1835 (as the *Doctrine and*

Covenants of the Church of the Latter Day Saints) and by the failure of communitarian and other financial initiatives in Ohio. In 1837 the prophet was forced to flee the state amidst a schism over his leadership, which included the apostasy of a third of his recently constituted presiding Quorum of Twelve Apostles (also known as the Quorum of the Twelve).

Meanwhile, in Missouri, at a time when religious claims and doctrinal innovations were beginning to move the new church away from American religious and social norms, gathering converts swelled the Mormon community to the point of dominance over other local institutions. This led to a series of confrontations with their neighbors, resulting first in the expulsion of the Latter-day Saints from the site of their anticipated millennial Zion and ultimately in an 1838 "extermination order" by the state governor which drove them from the state altogether.

Reestablished in a sparsely settled area of Illinois, the Mormons enjoyed several years of relative peace and constructed the city-state of Nauvoo, to which some sixteen thousand saints gathered. This was the period of Joseph Smith's most expansive theological innovation, as he elaborated on earlier texts and tenets and introduced some of Mormonism's most distinctive doctrines: the plurality of gods, humankind's potential godhood, exaltation (salvation) of the dead through vicarious ordinances, secret (though not uncommon) temple ceremonies with a promise of eternal family relationships, and the practice of "celestial" or plural marriage. It was this latter practice, more than any other, that led to schism within the Nauvoo community and ultimately to the prophet's murder in 1844.

With the death of Joseph Smith, the most theologically dramatic phase of Mormon history came to a close. Nearly all the church's canonized revelations date from this foundational period, as do records of the singular visitations (to Joseph Smith) of John the Baptist, apostles Peter, James, and John, and Old Testament prophets Moses, Elias, and Elijah—most transferring "keys" which were said to allow the latter-day resumption of priestly ordinances and offices. Moreover, while all succeeding Mormon presidents also have been recognized as "prophets, seers, and revelators," only Smith undertook to write and translate sacred texts. These included, in addition to the *Book of Mormon*, a reworking of the Authorized Version of the Bible and a rendition of an Egyptian funerary text said by Smith to have derived from the writings of the Patriarch Abraham.

Within three years of the prophet's martyrdom Brigham Young led the first Mormon pioneers to the conclusion of their journey, the valley of the Great Salt Lake. Perhaps half the Nauvoo-area Mormon community accepted the leadership claims of the Quorum of the Twelve, with Young at its head, and followed this vanguard. Many who remained behind affiliated with various other "Mormon" groups, some still extant today, which accepted the earlier restorationaist claims of Joseph Smith but rejected the theology of the Nauvoo period. By far the largest of these, the Reorganized (in 1860) Church of Jesus Christ of Latter Day Saints has turned to the direct descendants of Joseph Smith for their prophetic leadership. Headquartered in Independence, Missouri (Smith's original Zion), the Reorganized Latter Day Saints (RLDS) now number several hundred thousand members worldwide.

To Brigham Young and the Twelve fell the enormous task of forging a temporal kingdom of God from America's western wilderness. Young's remarkable accomplishments in colonization are well known. Ultimately he located over 350 communities of Mormons in parts of what now constitute seven states. Pragmatism characterized his approach—as governor and as church president—to both secular and spiritual responsibilities.

Doctrinally Young deferred regularly and pointedly to his predecessor. Few aspects of Joseph Smith's legacy brought him more attention than did Mormon plural marriages. It fell to Young to oversee the official public acknowledgment (in 1852) of this controversial practice. Twenty-seven wives and 57 children further attest to his personal commitment to what came to be known as "the principle." One distinctive Mormon doctrine, of some recent notoriety, apparently did originate with Brigham Young. This was the notion that blacks, as descendants of Cain, should be denied the Mormon priesthood. Although this idea cannot be traced directly to Joseph Smith, Young may well have felt that it logically emerged from the prophet's doctrinal legacy.

Shored up by literally thousands of immigrating British and Scandinavian converts—products of the missionary activities of the Twelve during the Nauvoo years—the Utah church concerned itself principally with carving a new Zion out of the desert. With a few exceptions, these early pioneer years in the West were not concerned so much with theology as with the physical creation of Mormonism's kingdom of God. Nevertheless, the strongly theocratic Mormon political structure and the increasingly conspicuous polygamy of its social structure soon brought both the U.S. Army and the Congress into confrontation with the desert Saints.

The U.S.-Mormon contest of wills was marked by an extended series of encounters, beginning in 1851 with a string of antagonistic federal appointees to oversee the new territory. Other major milestones include the 1857 invasion of Utah by General A. S. Johnston and the U.S. Army, the passage of a series of increasingly severe antipolygamy measures—notably the Morrill (1862), Edmunds (1882), and Edmunds-Tucker (1887) acts—and ultimately the "polyg" raids by federal marshals which in the 1880s sent the Mormon leadership into either the underground or prison.

This confrontation was not resolved until 1890, when a church manifesto announced the abandonment of polygamy and a consciously undertaken "Americanization" process transformed the Utah judicial and political community into a reasonable semblance of that found elsewhere in America. These changes opened the way, in 1896, to Utah's statehood. The Americanization process continued throughout the next decade, largely as a result of the attention focused on Mormon beliefs and practices during the debate surrounding the seating of Mormon congressmen. In particular the hearings associated with seating Utah senator (and Mormon apostle) Reed Smoot led directly to the dismantling of virtually all vestiges of theocratic local government as well as to a Second Manifesto (1904) virtually ending the sub-rosa polygamous marriages that had continued in high church circles.

In retrospect Mormons in Utah for the last five decades of the nineteenth century can be said to have waged a holy struggle on two fronts: against a hostile natural environment as pioneers further colonized the Great Basin, and against a U.S. government increasingly determined to abolish Mormon theocracy and polygamy. As noted, the first struggle was won. The second, however, was lost.

The decades immediately surrounding the turn of the century saw the reconsideration of many Mormon beliefs and practices and a redefinition of what, as a practical matter, it meant to be a Mormon. Beyond the relatively conspicuous case of polygamy, there were other, more subtle but nonetheless important theological revisions which removed some of the radical edges of the Nauvoo and early Utah legacy. Millennialism and the notion of "gathering" were deemphasized if not discarded. The jurisdiction of church courts was redefined to exclude nonecclesiastical issues, and court sanctions were limited to purely ecclesiastical actions (for example, excommunication). The People's Party, political organ of the church, was disbanded and members were instructed to support one of the major national parties.

Finally, significant organizational changes were made and a formal "church program" implemented. Building on autonomous adult and youth programs instituted in the nineteenth century, the new approach included an increasingly centralized administration and curriculum, and standardization of both schedules for congregational (ward) meetings and the criteria for "good standing" as members. Also at this time, the scope of responsibility and age criteria for entry into the lower levels of the Mormon priesthood were redefined and clarified.

In short, momentous changes accompanied the church's entry into the twentieth century. As will be seen, these pivotal decades also saw important shifts in thinking more directly related to health and medicine. Changes in perspective on the role of the temple influenced both the Mormon view of death and the LDS health record. The perspectives on madness, therapeutics, and healing ordinances also shifted markedly, with long-term implications for church thinking. Finally, and especially during the period 1910–1920, shifts in societal values in the area of personal morality caused the church to take a much more active role in promoting standards of behavior. These developments are addressed more fully in the chapters that follow.

The twentieth century has seen a general continuation and amplification of turn-of-the-century developments. Though modernist and fundamentalist challenges as well as the Great Depression all had an impact on the church or its programs, the overall trend has been toward increasing centralization and increasing accommodation to (the moderate to conservative side of) mainstream American values.

In the absence of the once anticipated millennialist gathering, an aggressive missionary program has undertaken the task of carrying Mormonism into the world. By 1961 annual conversions exceeded church growth through births for the first time in a century. This was no small achievement. Although birth rates admittedly had been well below the maximal fertility levels of the nineteenth century, death rates had plummeted as well, so net natural growth remained high. The total membership, moreover, itself had quadrupled between 1900 and 1950; in absolute terms, therefore, natural growth was at an all-time high.) This continuing natural growth, combined with a significantly expanded proselyting effort (pressed forward by over 43,000 full-time missionaries, with a quarter-million annual conversions), has generated one of the highest overall growth rates of any major denomination in America. Present church membership increases by over 4 percent a year and doubles about every fifteen years.

A growing internationalism has followed inevitably from the church's vigorous missionary efforts. Nearly 40 percent of a worldwide membership now approaching 8 million (in some 17,500 congregations) presently reside outside the United States. Important modifications of the Mormon worldview have followed. The abandonment of the church's priesthood restriction on blacks, for example, was related by church president Spencer Kimball to his concerns over the growth of the church in Brazil. More broadly, a concern for the health and welfare of an emerging Third-World membership has led to shifts in the leadership's thinking on humanitarian aid to developing countries.

The general liberalization of American social values over the past few decades also has had a demonstrable, if sometimes delayed or muted, impact on Mormon thinking. While conspicuously evident in the area of civil rights, equally far-reaching effects will be seen on a number of medical ethical issues. This may, in part, also be a by-product of missionary successes in the United States, as the majority of Latter-day Saints in the U.S. now reside outside the Mormon heartland and therefore are less exposed to its many ancillary "Mormon" cultural influences.

The twentieth century thus has seen Mormonism evolve from an innovative "peculiar people" to an increasingly structured, quintessential American religion. Though now devoid of many of its more colorful (or radical) aspects, it maintains as central tenets ideals that arose during its earliest days: prophetic leadership, an open canon, humankind's potential godhood and the plurality of gods, the potential exaltation of all humankind through vicarious ordinances, and continuity of family association past mortal life.

At present the church is dealing with several important issues. Salient among these are the challenges of administering an organization experiencing rapid growth; responding to a growing body of Third-World converts; and (especially in the U.S.) insuring the integrity of the LDS heritage and message in the face of the pressures inherent in an increasingly pluralistic society.

Mormonism has survived, even prospered, in the face of many serious challenges in the past. Viewing such challenges as only to be expected given the unique responsibility and authority with which it has been entrusted, church leaders have ever remained confident that a solution to any significant problem ultimately will be provided. The record to date substantiates their belief. As in the past, such solutions undoubtedly will reflect both reliance on the revelatory enlightenment of an authoritative hierarchy on the one hand and accommodation to the demands of social, economic, and political realities on the other.

As noted in the Preface, readers who are unfamiliar with the Mormon tradition may wish to turn now to Chapter 8, which provides important perspective on the sources of and limits on authoritative guidance within the Mormon church.

· 2 ·

On Death and Dying

If sociologist Peter Berger is correct that the "power of religion depends, in the last resort, upon the credibility of the banners it puts in the hands of men as they stand before death, or more accurately they walk inevitably toward it,"[1] Joseph Smith and his initial band of disciples early developed a solid foundation for enduring success. At a time in American history when family and friends seemed rather to be running to their graves, the Mormon prophet unfolded what historian Klaus Hansen has labeled a "brilliantly conceived ritualization of [death's] meaning" that effectively countered its destructive and demoralizing impact. So successful was this effort, writes Hansen, that "there can be no doubt that the vitality of Mormonism derived to a large extent from [it]."[2]

It was, moreover, in the context of individual deaths that early developments in Mormon thinking on the nature of God and humanity were often first evident. Funeral sermons brought new light and reassurance to the bereaved and shaped the Mormon view of the eternities. As Joseph Smith explained in one memorial sermon,

> All men know that they must die. And it is important that we should understand the reasons and causes of our exposure to the vicissitudes of life and of death, and the designs and purposes of God in our coming into the world, our suffering here, and our departure hence. What is the object of our coming into existence, then dying and falling away, to be here no more? It is but reasonable to suppose that God would reveal something in reference to the matter, and it is a subject we ought to study more than any other.[3]

When fully developed, the resulting theology influenced the Mormon views of both dying and living. This chapter thus not only deals with issues immediately surrounding death in Mormon society but also provides essential doctrinal context for much of the later discussion of well-being, healing, madness, and sexuality. In this foundational chapter we look first at the

9

Mormon view of the eternities and the perceived role of the institutional church in the eternal scheme. We then turn to more practical matters of the here and now: autopsies, funerals, burial, and the emotionally charged issues of suicide, euthanasia, and the prolongation of life.

COVENANTS AND GUARANTEES

Joseph Smith and his followers, like their Christian contemporaries, sought and found solace in the face of death through a vision of rest and reward in the eternal hereafter. They believed that the atoning sacrifice of Jesus Christ vouchsafed for humankind a universal resurrection, albeit to markedly different circumstances. Resurrected saints would find their rest in the presence of God, while sinners would agonize in hell.

Although an implicit equation of "saint" with "baptized believer" can be found in both New Testament and *Book of Mormon* texts, the latter extended salvation somewhat further. Those who died in childhood—in Joseph Smith's day, about a third of all children—were deemed "alive in Christ." Having died before reaching an age at which they could be held accountable, they were said incapable of committing sin—and thus not in need of baptism to be counted among the saints. The age of accountability initially was not specified, though at the time common law exempted those below seven or eight from criminal liability. In 1831 a revelation formally set the ecclesiastical age of accountability at eight years. Salvation also was extended to those who died "without the law." The *Book of Mormon* held that they, too, were exempt from punishment because, there having been "no law given," no condemnation could be made.[4]

Like religious seekers before and since, converts to Mormonism sought tangible assurances of their postmortal standing. The *Book of Mormon,* however, suggested nothing like the Calvinist guarantee of election and implicitly rejected a predestinarian view. On the other hand, it did afford seekers a divinely authenticated text which implicitly responded to skeptics who found fault with biblical proof texts. More important, it provided the basis on which a claim of divinely bestowed religious authority could be built. If the *Book of Mormon* restored the "fullness" of the primitive gospel long since lost, it likely also heralded the return of the authentic apostolic priesthood long sought by Christian restorationists.

The foundational Mormon scriptures spoke of elders, teachers, and priests, and it was these terms that the Mormons initially adopted for the offices in their restored priesthood. From the outset both elders and priests were empowererd to perform the essential saving ordinance of baptism.

Then an early revelation encouraging the Saints to move to Ohio promised among other things that there they would be further "endowed with power from on High."[5] A few months after the requested move, several men were ordained to a newly announced "high" (later, "Melchizidek") priesthood. They became Mormonism's first "high priests" (with loose biblical and *Book of Mormon* precedents) and soon were advised by Smith—"the Prophet"— that their office had the power "to seal up [ritually to guarantee] the Saints unto eternal life."[6] Thereafter those holding the high priesthood began to seal up (for example, through a prayerful pronouncement) deserving individuals and congregations "to eternal life," ostensibly ensuring their celestial reward. Although a momentous step in asserting earthly authority to perform exalting ordinances which would be ratified in heaven, this proved only the first step in a remarkable progression of increasingly ritualized sealing ordinances aimed at guaranteeing even more dramatic celestial rewards.

A year after moving to Ohio, Joseph Smith organized a "school of the prophets" for his growing flock. Admission to this school, which was held in the upper room of a general store, required by revelatory decree a ritual washing of the feet (and sometimes hands or face) "according to the practice recorded in the 13th chapter of John's Gospel" (in which Christ washes the feet of his disciples and instructs them "to wash one another's feet"). The ritual washing cleansed initiates "from the blood of this generation" and again "sealed [them] up unto eternal life."[7]

Several months later Joseph Smith announced further revelatory instruction to build "a house" in which this school would be conducted, and in which God "design[ed] to endow those whom I have chosen with power from on high."[8] Although in a sense a predictable step in an ongoing process, this also marks a major milestone. This "house of God" was to become the first of what soon will number fifty Mormon temples; within it for the first time Joseph Smith combined sacred ordinance with sacred space.

By the time the Kirtland (Ohio) temple was dedicated early in 1836, Smith already had introduced key aspects of what came to be termed the "Kirtland endowment." In retrospect the ceremonial aspects of the associated temple rite were rather limited, involving washings and anointings introduced and practiced in the preparatory school of the prophets. These included an initial bathing in "pure water," then in "whiskey, perfumed with cinnamon," followed by a copious anointing of the head with "holy oil." (The basis for the use of whiskey is unknown, though by this time a divine health code— discussed in Chapter 3—had commended "strong drink" for the washing of the body; the "holy oil" was said to be "the same kind of oil and [the application] in the man[ner] that were Moses and Aaron, and those who stood before the Lord in ancient days.")[9] The final step, sometimes performed in a separate meeting, was a ritual washing of the feet. These rituals were designed to purify worthy members for the promised endowment that would follow. The endowment itself was viewed both as the pentecost experienced by members at the dedicatory ceremonies of the temple and as a fuller subsequent bestowal of personal charismatic gifts (healing, prophecy, speaking in tongues).

As with virtually all other aspects of the early Restoration, the endowment was traced to biblical antecedents. This is well illustrated in the instructions Joseph Smith gave to a new presiding council, the Quorum of the Twelve, just prior to the completion of the temple. They were "not to go to other nations till you receive your endowments," he instructed. "Tarry at Kirtland until you are endowed with power from on high. You need a fountain of wisdom, knowledge and intelligence such as you never had . . . that wisdom, that intelligence, and that power, which characterized the ancient saints, and now characterizes the inhabitants of the upper world."[10] The New Testament prototype was Christ's instruction to his apostles to "tarry ye in the city of Jerusalem, until ye be endued [endowed] with power from on high" (Luke 24:49).

After instituting these extensive preparatory rituals, Smith announced that he had completed the organization of the church and that members "had passed through all the necessary ceremonies."[11] A few days later another vision changed his mind, but the markedly expanded ritual that eventually ensued was not introduced until the Saints reached Nauvoo several years later. The purifying rituals performed in Kirtland later came to be labeled the "Kirtland endowment," but it was in Nauvoo, Illinois, site of Mormonism's second completed temple, that the "endowment" first came to refer to an ordinance per se. Moreover, the gift bestowed through this latter ritual was neither pentecostal experience nor this-worldly power, but rather assurances about the life to come. As Mormon theology had progressed substantially beyond that of the Kirtland years, these assurances could be considerable.

The earliest Mormons apparently understood their foundational scriptures as endorsing the absolutist views of both contemporary Protestant and Catholic belief: an all-powerful God of spirit had created *ex nihilo* the earth and all that was in it.[12] From this rather conventional starting point, Joseph Smith unfolded an expanding vision of the relationship of God and humankind and of their roles in the eternities. Smith's teachings on this subject increasingly set the early Saints theologically apart from their Christian neighbors, and they remain to the present day among the most distinctive of the tenets of Mormonism.

Initial steps were relatively modest. Humankind was said to have existed prior to the creation of the world, not just as a notion in the mind of God but as material "spirits." God as well was held to be a tangible being. (Eventually it was explained that all spirit was "matter," albeit of a "finer" or "purer" type.)[13] In this premortal state—which Mormons term the "preexistence," the spirits of humankind were said to have chosen voluntarily to come to earth for the purpose of obtaining bodies of "flesh and blood" and to demonstrate their worthiness to return to the presence of God.

In Joseph Smith's unfolding view, the reward held out for those who succeeded in their earthly test soon exceeded by far the expectations of other Christians. An early (1832) revelation promised that those who received "celestial glory receive of God's fulness and of his glory, becoming gods, even the sons of God," while another added that all that the "Father hath shall be given" and that the saints could be "made equal with him." Over the next decade this cryptic message expanded into several interrelated concepts, which collectively were given their most forceful expression in an 1844 funeral discourse. Thought by many to be Smith's greatest sermon, the fourfold message of his remarks was (1) that there were many gods, (2) that the gods existed one above another back into the eternities, (3) that God once was in the same circumstance that man now is, and (4) that men could become gods.[14] It was in this latter quest that Mormon temples were held essential.

In Nauvoo, Smith once again introduced his close associates to a ritual intended for use in a temple being built in the city. The new ceremony, which incorporated the Kirtland ordinances and was said to be a restoration of an ancient biblical practice, became known as the Nauvoo endowment— or, ever since that time, simply as "the endowment." Displacing all other sealings to eternal life, the Nauvoo endowment promised participants singularly exalted status in the life hereafter. It marked the completion of what Klaus Hansen termed the Mormon ritualization of the problem of death.

Although the modern church views many aspects of the Nauvoo endowment as both sacred and secret, church leaders have been willing to provide some insights into this capstone Mormon ritual. The ceremonies previously instituted at Kirtland were retained as an "initiatory" portion of the new Nauvoo endowment. To these were added, as Brigham Young later explained, new instruction in the "ordinances . . . which are necessary . . . to walk back to the presence of the Father, passing the angels who stand as sentinels, being enabled to give them the key words, the signs and tokens, pertaining to the Holy Priesthood."[15] Recognizably Masonic in some of its symbolism, the instructions, words, tokens, and signs spoken of by Young were incorporated into a symbolic reenactment of Joseph Smith's revision of the creation and expulsion narratives of Genesis.[16] Initiates attired themselves in symbolic clothing and participated directly in the ceremony. Thereafter, those who had "received their endowments" wore a distinctive undergarment as a reminder of the covenants that had been made.[17] Additionally, as is discussed more fully below, the Saints began to bury their previously endowed dead in the clothing worn during the ceremony, thereby tying this ritual even more firmly to the life hereafter.

The covenants made in the endowment ceremony, as explained by later apostle James Talmage, included a "promise to observe the law of strict virtue and charity, to be charitable, benevolent, tolerant and pure; to devote both talent and material means to the spread of truth and the uplifting of the race; to maintain devotion to the cause of truth; and to seek in every way to contribute to the great preparation that the earth may be made ready to receive her King,—the Lord Jesus Christ."[18]

In return for this commitment, the Saints believed they had an unprecedented promise from the Lord. Conditional on their continued faithfulness, they were assured future status as gods and goddesses. In addition, once having received their endowments, a husband and wife could be "sealed" in marriage for "time and all eternity" (that is, beyond the grave) and have their children sealed eternally to them as well. Collectively these promises offered immense hope and reassurance to families rent asunder by untimely deaths, and to all came the message that indeed even the most humbled and oppressed could achieve a personal station spectacularly beyond anything the world had to offer.

The Nauvoo endowment, with only modest changes, continues to the present day as the capstone ordinance of Mormonism. Currently some 5 million endowments (including those for the dead, explained below) are performed in Mormon temples each year. A "second endowment" also was introduced in Nauvoo, with the even greater guarantee that those so endowed would become gods almost regardless of later sins, albeit after a suitable period of divine punishment. By the early twentieth century, the promise of this penultimate ordinance had become so qualified that it offered little beyond that already implicit in the "first" endowment. The frequency with which it was performed dropped dramatically, from as many as several hundred annually to a mere handful a year in the late twentieth century.[19]

Once the endowment and sealing were obtained, there initially was relatively little doctrinal incentive to return again to the temple. Circumstances eventually changed: emphasis on ordinance work for the dead (discussed below) expanded greatly, and now regular temple attendance is a virtual prerequisite to good standing in LDS congregations even remotely near a temple. Thus continued "worthiness" to enter the temple has become a major factor in the lives of most Latter-day Saints.

Joseph Smith taught that this-worldly ordinances were essential for "salvation" (through baptism) and "exaltation" to godhood (through the endowment) of both those living and dead. Building on a cryptic New Testament reference to baptism "for the dead" (1 Corinthians 15:29), he instituted the practice of proxy baptism for deceased family members (and some close friends) who it was believed would have accepted the Mormon gospel had they had the opportunity. A proxy endowment also was mentioned by Smith but was not formally begun until temples were opened in Utah several decades later. Proxy sealings (of families) as well began in Utah temples, though increasingly those without demonstrably worthy ancestors chose rather to be sealed (by "adoption") to living or deceased church leaders.

In the 1890s church president Wilford Woodruff ended the practice of adoption to leading brethren and redirected proxy work almost exclusively toward ancestors (including those about whose attitudes or worthiness nothing could be inferred). Within a year the Genealogical Society of Utah came into being, under church auspices, and through it the well-known Mormon commitment to genealogy. Over the next several decades, members increasingly were encouraged to search out their ancestors and perform proxy temple work for them. This significantly increased temple attendance. It also led to the creation of the most extensive genealogical data bank in the world (well over 2 billion names on file) and made possible some landmark recent medical studies on the inheritance of cancer.[20]

By the mid twentieth century, and despite substantial growth in membership, the pool of identified ancestors began to dwindle. In response the church initiated a "name extraction program" in 1962 which now finds suitable candidates for proxy work in almost any population records (for example, cemetery or census data) without concern for lineage or ancestry. This has provided such an enormous reservoir of names for temple work that members now have a near-unending requirement to participate. To date some 100 million vicarious endowments have been performed in an effort which, it is believed, will extend into the millennium—where overlooked worthy forebears will be able to insure their ordinances are accomplished.

The growing emphasis on temple attendance has been facilitated by several developments, including discontinuance (in 1891) of a requirement that the church president himself endorse every temple participant, lengthening the time that a "temple recommend" (that is, an authorization to enter the temple) is valid, from six months to a year (1949), and the granting of access to all temples on the basis of a single temple recommend (1963). More important still has been the construction of some thirty-four temples outside the Mormon West—well over half in various places abroad.

The expanded place of "temple work" (as it is termed) among the Latter-day Saints has allowed those performing vicarious ordinances regularly to experience anew the endowment and to vocalize on behalf of others their own previously made covenants. It also has afforded a mechanism whereby the church can shape the personal practices of devout members and allow local leaders recurring insight into the degree to which individual members adhere to church principles.

Eligibility for participation in the endowment always has required a tangible demonstration of commitment to the principles of the gospel. For the many years when temples were found only in the Mormon West, this commitment included a willingness to gather to the "heart of Zion." Beyond this, members were expected to pay a full tithe (10 percent of personal—generally agricultural—"increase") and avoid flagrant violation of revealed counsel against the use of tobacco and alcohol.

Those seeking to enter the temple in the twentieth century have had to comply with a much expanded (and, since 1934, explicitly written) list of worthiness measures. Fuller adherence to the LDS health code is now required, including total abstinence from coffee, tea, tobacco, and alcohol (discussed in Chapter 3), as is payment to the church of a full tithe (currently defined as 10 percent of gross income).

Members also are expected to be free of an expanding list of "immoral practices," which most recently was extended in 1982 to include "impure" acts *within* the bonds of marriage.[21]

Additionally, "recommends" are conditional: those endowed must continue to wear temple-associated undergarments day and night, a measure intended to serve both as a physical tie to the endowment and as a physical barrier to immodesty and immorality. For decades, until the 1920s, the garment was exceptionally well suited to the latter purpose. A slightly (symbolically) modified one-piece union suit, it extended from ankle and wrist to neck. The "modern" garment, which displaced the original some sixty years ago, has sleeves shortened to mid-upper arm, and legs to knee length, and in 1980 became available in a two-piece version (in part because of physical challenges the one-piece version posed to those with handicaps). Worn unmodified, as the church requires, both the one- and two-piece garment remain a substantial incentive to conservative attire. Neither sleeve-less dresses, for example, nor Bermuda shorts can be worn without exposing the garment, which is considered unacceptable.

There are very few circumstances when garments legitimately can be modified or set aside. They need not be worn during sports or while swimming, and alterations occasionally have been authorized to allow service personnel to comply with a mandatory dress code. (Indeed, since 1987 a brown two-piece garment, of slightly different design, has been available to active-duty military personnel for just this reason.) Hospitalized Mormons also are excused from wearing their garments when a hospital gown would be more appropriate for medical reasons. The decision to set aside the garment while in hospital, however, is particularly problematic for some. Very early in church history, the garment came to be viewed as a shield against disease and injury, and to the present day faith-promoting accounts circulate of injuries unexpectedly minimized or avoided in areas of the body physically covered by the garment.

PROJECTIONS ACROSS THE VEIL

The Mormon view of the hereafter vouchsafed by the sealing authority introduced in 1831, and later associated with temple ritual, was initially sketchy and conventional. Relevant *Book of Mormon* passages, said to derive ultimately from the lost perspective of early Old Testament times and prophets, conveyed a New Testament perspective already accepted by Mormon converts as scriptural. Death in both sources (as then understood) merely marked the separation of the spirit from the physical, earthly body which was consigned to the grave. The spirits of the righteous—those who had accepted the gospel message, been baptized, and remained faithful to the end—went to the "paradise of God" to rest in his presence. The spirits of the wicked suffered the "hell" of a "spiritual death," in which they were barred from the presence of God and remained subject to the devil and his angels. Ultimately, after a millenium, the spirits of all were to be "delivered up," and "by the power of the resurrection of the Holy One of Israel" body and spirit were to be reunited to form an "immortal soul." In this state each was to give account before the "judgment-seat" of God, following which the righteous would inherit the kingdom of God and "their joy shall be full forever." The wicked were to be banished "unto everlasting fire . . . and their torment is as a lake of fire and brimstone, whose flame ascendeth up forever and ever and has no end."[22]

Very soon after the formal organization of the church, this rather undifferentiated founding vision began to be refined and expanded in a manner already current among contemporary Universalists. Late in 1830, Smith announced a revelation which explained that the "endless" or "eternal" punishment of the damned was to be understood metaphorically. This was "God's punishment" (God being "Endless" and "Eternal"), not punishment without end. Though the idea already may have been familiar to recent converts, it now carried a reassuring divine seal.[23]

Then, in 1832, the Prophet reported two additional revelations offering further hope to saint as well as sinner.[24] His new vision of the eternities revealed three major kingdoms in heaven, all clothed in glory, albeit to different degrees. Perhaps most novel was that labeled the "telestial" kingdom, ultimate destination of the wicked who had been "thrust down to hell" at the time of their death. Here would be found the "liars, and sorcerers, and adulterers, and whoremongers" as well as those "who would not be gathered with the saints"—in short, the sinners of the world. Even such as these, the Prophet reported, would after suffering "the wrath of Almighty God" bow their knees, be forgiven, and receive a heavenly reward.

Above this kingdom in glory was a "terrestrial" kingdom, which awaited those "who received not the testimony of Jesus in the flesh, but afterwards received it [in the preresurrection spirit world]." This was the destiny of "honorable men . . . who were blinded by the craftiness of men."

At the apex was the "celestial kingdom," destination of the saints, who would receive "all things," be made "priests and kings," and "dwell in the presence of God and his Christ forever and ever."

In an analogy apparently inspired by 1 Corinthians (15:41–42), the relative glory of the three heavenly kingdoms was likened to the physical heavens. The glory of the terrestrial kingdom differed from that of the celestial "as that of the moon differs from the sun," while the telestial stood in a similar relationship to the terrestrial, "even as the stars differ from that of the glory of the moon." The labels *celestial* and *terrestrial* seem also to derive from the passage in Corinthians.

Telestial is a term more uniquely Mormon, although it suggests some knowledge of the Greek behind the Pauline text. The clearest indication of this is found in another revelation later that year, which also parallels Corinthians. In this second revelation, a series of resurrections is described, which seemingly relate to the various heavenly kingdoms. The righteous, those who "are Christ's," will be resurrected first according to this account, and will join with Christ in his millennial rule. Second will come those who are "Christ's at his coming," the "good men" who had been deceived who will also return for the millennium where they "might receive the gospel, and be judged according to men in the flesh." These groups are clearly those previously identified as destined for the celestial and terrestial kingdoms, respectively. Finally "the rest of the dead" were to come forth penitent after having been "cast down to hell and suffer[ing] the wrath of Almighty God" for the duration of the millennium. Then will all be presented "unto the Father, spotless." (The parallel Corinthians account [15:23–24]—though with a different apparent message—says in speaking of the resurrection, "Christ the firstfruits; afterward they that are Christ's at his coming. Then cometh the end [Greek, *telos*], when he shall deliver up the kingdom to God." As understood by the early Mormons, therefore, "the rest" who came at "the end" were destined for the telestial kingdom.)[25]

While initially the celestial kingdom of early Mormondom was in some ways the familiar heaven of contemporary Christianity, to which the label *celestial* was popularly applied, it soon came to represent much more. It was here that those who had remained faithful to the end would "receive of God's fulness and of his glory, and become gods, even the sons of God."

At the other extreme, these same early revelations made clear that by the end of the millennium only a relative handful would be "filthy still," candidates to be cast into an "outer darkness" totally bereft of any glory whatever (a place akin to the traditional Christian hell). These were those who had "denied the Holy Spirit after having received it" and "denied the Only Begotten Son of the Father," thereby becoming partakers in the shedding of his blood. Another 1831 revelation implied that those who shed innocent blood directly by committing murder also were to be included here. Labeled "sons of perdition," this unfortunate group was to "go away into the lake of fire and brimstone, with the devil and his angels . . . into everlasting punishment, where their worm dieth not, and the fire is not quenched which is their torment." Their end was to be revealed to no man "except to them who are made partakers thereof."[26]

Joseph Smith added little further to this basic (and later canonized) outline of life hereafter. In 1843 another revelation briefly addressed the question of heaven but only clarified that there were gradations within even the "celestial glory" (*Doctrine and Covenants* [hereafter cited as *D&C*] 131). Two additional visions that touch on the subject, one attributed to Joseph Smith and the other to early-twentieth-century church president Joseph F. Smith, were accepted into the church canon in 1976—the first such additions in the twentieth century. Joseph Smith's vision, in 1836, was primarily an affirmation that children who died before age eight and all who lived before who would have received the gospel, had they had the chance (including his deceased brother Alvin, seen in the vision), were "heirs of the celestial kingdom." Joseph did mention the "beautiful streets of that kingdom, which had the appearance of being paved with gold" (*D&C* 137).

Joseph F. Smith's 1918 vision dealt with Christ's visit to the spirits of the dead while his body was in the tomb; it explained that "faithful elders of this dispensation, when they depart from mortal life, continue their labors in the preaching of the gospel of repentance and redemption . . . among those who are in darkness and under the bondage of sin in the great world of the spirits of the dead" (*D&C* 138). In a sense this vision ratified beliefs already held at the popular level based on a wealth of personal visions and dreams reported by individual Saints.

Nineteenth-century journals as well as LDS periodicals of the day abound with accounts of those who, often near death, experienced at least some of a now familiar constellation associated with "near-death experiences": a sense of being outside (sometimes hovering above) one's body, a "being of light," encounters with deceased relatives or friends, and the notion that it was necessary (sometimes by choice) that they return to mortality. Typically LDS accounts included distinctively Mormon elements. Frequently Joseph Smith or Brigham Young, or some other prominent church leader, was encountered. An organized—sometimes recognizably LDS—social structure might be seen, and many of the people encountered were earnestly involved in typically Mormon endeavors, such as missionary, genealogical, or other temple-related work. Women, if seen at work, more often were in a domestic role. Clothing generally was white, as worn in the temple, and occasionally was the unique temple clothing itself.[27]

Cumulatively the hereafter of the Latter-day Saints came to be—and is still—understood in concrete earthly terms: with buildings under construction, rooms still incomplete, and an organization along family and LDS social lines. Indeed it was authoritatively taught that this heavenly venue is earth itself, albeit a paradisical earth in a dimension not visible to mortal eyes.[28] A veil is said to have fallen over our eyes at birth, preventing a view of the spirit world. Within the temple a literal veil, symbolic of the veil separating mortals from the spirit world, is lifted or separated as part of the depiction of the exaltation promised in the endowment. Mormons, drawing on this imagery, frequently speak of deceased relatives as having "crossed the veil," or they may say, when feeling especially near to a departed loved one, that the veil is "very thin.")

The altogether physical nature of this view is completely compatible with Mormonism's literalistic understanding of the anticipated resurrection. Following Ezekiel (37:7–8), Joseph F. Smith's 1918 vision recounted that "sleeping dust was to be restored unto its perfect frame, bone to his bone, and the sinews and the flesh upon them, the spirit and the body to be united never again to be divided" (*D&C* 138:17). This basic understanding can be traced to Joseph Smith and his nineteenth-century successors, and many Saints still believe that the very particles of which the body was composed at the time of death will be reconstituted at the time of resurrection. Only the blood, which is said to have conferred mortality, will be missing. Instead "spirit" will course through the veins of an immortal, resurrected being.[29]

Easily the most dramatic depiction of such a resurrection comes from a turn-of-the-century Mormon farmer who reported a truly singular episode. The account of Zeke Johnson literally fleshed out the imagery of his Old Testament namesake:

> As I was plowing around I noticed that my plow had turned out the skeleton of a small child. The skull and the backbone, most of the bones of course were decayed and gone. . . . As I was looking at that little skeleton that I had plowed out and wondering, all of a sudden to my surprise I saw the bones begin to wiggle and they began to change position and to take different color and within a minute there lay a beautiful little skeleton. It was a perfect little skeleton.
>
> Then I saw the inner parts of the natural body coming in—the entriles, etc. I saw the flesh coming on and I saw the skin come on the body when the inner parts of the body was complete. A beautiful head of hair adorned the top of the head, it had a beautiful crystal decoration in the hair. It was combed beautifully and parted on one side. In about a half a minute after the hair was on the head, the child raised up on her feet. She was lying a little on her left side with her back toward me. Because of this I wasn't able to discern the sex of the child, but as she raised up, a beautiful robe came down over her left shoulder and I saw it must be a girl.
>
> She looked at me and I looked at her and for a quarter of a minute we just looked at each other smiling. Then [in] my ambition to get hold of her, I says, "Oh, you beautiful child," and I reached as if I would embrace her and she disappeared.[30]

Historically church leaders were untroubled by the notion that the dust of the deceased might have been scattered "to the corners of the earth." It still would be literally reclaimed. More recently, nuclear war and the discovery of DNA has led many educated Mormons to conclude that knowledge of the genetic sequence is all that God will require to effect the promised resurrection.

Perhaps the most troublesome aspect of the resurrection has been the status of those who die as children. It is assumed that humankind is resurrected in the general physical circumstance (albeit in perfected health) that obtained at death. There has been some disagreement, however, on the appearance of the spirit during the period after death put prior to resurrection. Some personal visions of the spirit world have included recognizable children. Others report seeing the adult spirits of those who died in infancy. The predominant view now seems to be that all spirits are "adult," as they presumably were before birth, but that they may appear as children in visions to make themselves recognizable to those who knew them as children before death.[31]

More problematic still for Mormon commentators has been the circumstance of the resurrected body of those who died in infancy. Joseph Smith apparently taught that the body did *not* grow further after resurrection and thus that a mature spirit would forever be housed in the body of a child or infant. Brigham Young felt it more likely that the resurrected body, though perhaps that of an infant at the time of resurrection, would grow to adulthood. For many generations LDS parents, grieving the loss of a child, have found solace in the Young-inspired belief that they will eventually be able to raise their child in the life hereafter. Given the adult status of the spirit, problems still remain—though Young believed the spirit must again be amenable to compression as he felt it must have been at birth. While not definitively resolved, the question does reveal much about the literal-mindedness of LDS thought.[32]

PASSAGES AND THE PLAN OF SALVATION

The anthropomorphism implicit in the Mormon view was understood quite literally. God was viewed—in the words of one influential early writer—as of the same "species" as humans, with all of the physical and emotional attributes of a human being. In this context, the pre-earthly origin of spirits (viewed by Smith as *physical* entities, composed of exceptionally pure "matter") came to be understood as analogous to earthly birth (they had gestated in the "womb" of a heavenly mother). Unorganized "intelligence," rather than these individualized spirits, were said to have coexisted with God (or, the gods) forever; and some of this "intelligence" came together within the heavenly womb to constitute the spirit.[33]

The spirit, like the human analogue, was believed to have matured to the point of readiness to undertake the earthly experience, in which it would acquire its nonspiritual earthly body and grow further through the various challenges of mortal life. The acquisition of a physical body of flesh and blood was considered essential to further progression. Not only was the body of spirit, alone, unable to experience many of the physical qualities of life, it was said to be incapable of reproduction. Since those destined for godhood were themselves expected to bring forth spirit-children—and then create a world in which they would experience mortality—acquisition of an "earthly tabernacle" was absolutely essential.

Not all spirits successfully completed their premortal probation. Fully a third were said to have joined Lucifer in a great "war in heaven" (as alluded to in Revelation 12:7–8). At issue was the desire of Lucifer and his followers to abridge human "free agency" (freedom to make choices). As a result of this rebellion, Lucifer and the others were cast out and so came to earth without physical bodies. They are said to exist now as the devil and his evil spirits, their goal to corrupt humankind and attempt to possess the coveted physical bodies of men and women. They are the source of worldly sin and temptation, the prime movers behind all evil.

Although the spirits of men and women are believed to come to earth innately good and "pure," the challenge posed by these evil influences is too great for humankind to remain sufficiently worthy to return to the presence of God. Only a "plan of redemption" or "salvation" instituted by God makes a return possible. This plan necessitated the voluntary, redeeming sacrifice of Christ, and faith, repentance, essential ordinance work, and righteous living by those desiring salvation and exaltation. Baptism by one in authority is said to cleanse those baptized of previous sins and implies repentance and a commitment to Christ-like living in the future. This repentance and commitment is reaffirmed after baptism when one partakes periodically (generally weekly) of a sacrament of bread and water emblematic of Christ's sacrifice of flesh and blood. (The latter, termed simply "the sacrament" within Mormonism, is essentially analogous to the Lord's Supper or Holy Communion of other Christian communities.)

The mandatory passages through which Mormons believe they must pass during their sojourn on earth are in the strictest sense limited to the three ordinances also performed for the dead: baptism by one in authority (at age eight, or at the time of conversion), with an associated "laying on of hands" for "the gift of the Holy Ghost"; the endowment (now at age nineteen, if a proselyting mission is about to begin, or otherwise usually just before marriage); and "sealing" in eternal or celestial marriage. For many years the final step of celestial marriage was only believed exalting if the marriage was polygamous. This belief largely disappeared early in the twentieth century, shortly after federal pressure brought an end to the practice of "plural marriage."[34]

Though not viewed in the same light, several other major milestones are regarded as important to an individual's good standing within the church. Nearly all Mormon infants are named and blessed in a brief, nonmandatory ordinance which formally enters them into the records of the church. For most of the twentieth century boys in good standing, following baptism at age eight, have been ordained to a "lesser" (Aaronic) priesthood when they are twelve and progress to Aaronic priesthood offices of somewhat greater authority and responsibility at ages fourteen and sixteen. At age nineteen young men are expected to go on a two-year mission. At the beginning of the mission they are ordained to the higher (Melchizedek) priesthood: this ordination is also a prerequisite to receiving the endowment and being sealed for "time and eternity" in marriage. While a mission is not mandatory, about a third of LDS young men choose to go (the percent was much smaller before 1960). Those who don't, if they remain active in the church, eventually are ordained to the higher priesthood and become eligible to receive temple ordinances.

Young women, being ineligible for the priesthood, have no major milestones after baptism until they are about to be married. Like young men they are expected to participate in church-related, age-specific classes and activities which have varied over the years and now extend from age two throughout life. A small but growing number of women now go on missions, for which they are eligible on reaching age twenty-one. They may receive their temple endowment at that time, but the vast majority of LDS women receive their endowments at the time of marriage, just before being sealed to their husband. A woman (or man) whose spouse is not eligible for the endowment is allowed the endowment only if the spouse consents in writing. Policy on this point has varied over the years. The incurred obligation for those endowed to wear, thenceforward, a very conservative, if not peculiar, undergarment has led in the past to serious problems for some women married to nonbelievers. Those now authorizing endowments to women in "part member families" are specifically instructed to first satisfy themselves that problems will not result.[35]

Finally, as adults Mormons are expected to be very involved in a multitude of congregational meetings and other activities and to participate in their children's own ordinances, as well as vicarious temple work for the dead. Excepting only the dedication of the grave, however, there are no further true ordinances of passage in Mormon adult life.

THE EXPERIENCE OF DEATH

Within a year of the organization of the church, Joseph Smith announced a revelation in which the Lord promised that "those that die in me shall not taste of death, for it shall be sweet unto them; and they that die not in me, wo unto them, for their death is bitter." "Thou shalt live in love," the faithful were admonished, "insomuch that thou shalt weep for the loss of them that die, and more especially for those that have not hope of a glorious resurrection."[36]

While recognizing the legitimate sadness that accompanies the loss of loved ones, succeeding church leaders sought to emphasize the perceived positive side of death, which they characterized as both a rebirth and a victory. Deaths among the elderly especially have provided from the earliest years a popular context for the celebration of relevant LDS theology. A full life, well-lived, has been extolled in many an LDS funeral, and listeners enjoined to contemplate the promised reward awaiting the departed.

A discussion several years ago of LDS mourning customs highlighted this perspective. On the basis of several years' observations of Mormon funerals and graveside rituals, the author concluded they somewhat resembled the church service accompanying the departure of missionaries on their mission: "Here is a group of loved ones, not hard-faced and stoical, not blank and numb, but sensitized. There is apparent grief, but not despair. There is warmth and promise." His anecdotal "impressions" of the LDS response to death convey an almost stereotypical view of how things should be:

—The ancient mother who cheerfully sews her own white [temple] burial clothes.

—The widely known speaker who tapes his own funeral sermon and sparkles it with his verve for life.

—A gathering, as death hovers close, to appoint a celestial mailman. Messages to be delivered to loved ones on the other side. "Give my love to Mother," or "Tell Aunt Martha we're doing fine." Here is absent the curious etiquette that forbids that even a husband and wife use the word "death" when one knows clearly that one is on his deathbed. . . .

—Addressing the deceased at the funeral or gravesite as if she or he is present. . . .

—The sense of mission in the military. Facing death is the price of Christ's way.

—The music which resembles a hymnal rhapsody rather than the darkening dirge. . . .

—The jibe of [former church leader] J. Golden Kimball: "I can't wait to die to see if all this stuff we've been teaching is true," combined with the sober testimony, "When I meet my Father, I know he will understand me, and that is more than you have been able to do."

—Prompt and some would say sudden remarriage. Joseph Smith followed the early custom of thinking marriage within three months was unkind to the memory of the dead but reversed himself when he counseled his Brother Hyrum to marry "without delay."[37]

Deaths among the elderly, however, were for most of the nineteenth century much less frequent than those among infants and children, deaths which elicited a quite different response.

Notwithstanding the doctrinal promise that assured exaltation, and a belief that children might yet be raised in the eternities, early Mormon diarists show these losses, especially when unexpected, to have been a source of immense grief. "Thus died my only son," wrote one anguished father, "and one too on whom I had placed my own name and was truly the dearest object of my heart."[38] And another:

> His age was two years, nine months and eight days. He was a very bright and intelligent little boy. His death was the greatest sorrow trial to us that we ever had, it was months before we got reconciled. And I almost complained of the Lord for taking him from us for I could not think why he should be taken when I felt in my heart that we were trying harder than ever before to do right in all things and keep the commandments of the Lord.[39]

When asked why so many innocent children are taken away, Joseph Smith responded that the world had grown so wicked that "the Lord takes many away even in infancy that they may escape the envy of man, the sorrows & evils of this present world & they were two [sic] pure & to [sic] lovly to live on Earth. Therefore if rightly considered, instead of morning [sic] we have reason to rejoice, as they are deliverd from evil & we shall soon have them again."[40] While bereaved parents seemed to prefer that their children remain to earn their own exaltation, they typically continued to place their faith in a God whose ways they could not comprehend. The private response of those losing children in the present day hasn't been studied systematically, but one senses that things are not much different now. An initial sense of shock, loss, and often even betrayal is eventually assuaged by a decision to continue to trust in God and a knowledge that the child is alive and well in another sphere, where ultimately he or she will be reunited with the family.[41]

By far the most theologically problematic deaths have been those of young adults, especially parents of young children. This was true for nineteenth-century Saints and remains so today. As previously noted, a nineteenth-century solution, particularly when younger men died, was to conclude they were "needed" to further the work of the priesthood "on the other side." Typically this was said to be missionary work among the spirits of the departed. The loss of a young mother was not so easily explained, though an unspecified "need" often was invoked. This rationale is still sometimes heard today, though there is ambivalence among those who reflect on the emotional damage often inflicted on the surviving familiy. One young LDS mother dying of cancer, for example, wrote a moving message to be read at her funeral asking that no one "reassure" her family that she had more important work to do than raising her children. She was sure that such reassurance would only compound a difficult problem. In the end, most Mormons probably would apply even more widely the sentiments expressed by Gordon B. Hinckley, of the First Presidency, at memorial services for 27 miners killed in a 1984 fire in southern Utah. Acknowledging that the aftereffects of the tragedy would be felt by the families involved "for years and years," Hinckley simply concluded that "no human can understand why such catastrophes occur." "Great as is the present tragedy," he continued, "it would be even greater if it meant oblivion for those who are gone." Their families could be reassured that though their mortal bodies had expired, "the spirit lives on. They are as much individuals today as they were a week ago."[42]

AUTOPSIES, FUNERALS, BURIAL, AND CREMATION

Initially the funeral practices of the Mormons were not especially distinctive. The deceased typically died at home and was watched overnight in a traditional "wake" to insure that no sign of life was missed.[43] The body was washed, prepared for burial, and placed in a coffin at home as well and transported to the cemetery or family plot for burial by the family. Services were held in the church or at the graveside, but in either event a dedicatory prayer generally was given at the grave site (though not until 1976 was this prayer officially designated a "priesthood ordinance"). In pioneer Utah it became common practice to bury the dead facing east, apparently in anticipation of their rising to meet Christ at his second coming.[44]

The form of the funeral service itself—which continues little changed to the present—was similar to contemporary Protestant practice. It consisted of prayers, hymns, and sermons, some of the earliest of which, as noted, ushered in new dimensions in LDS theology. With the added flexibility that followed the advent of embalming later in the century, funeral services typically were moved to Sunday afternoons, a practice discarded by the church only within the last few decades. (Sunday funeral services now are discouraged.) Initially, of course, the hardships of forced relocations led to some burials, especially of infants, with almost no ceremony at all.

By midcentury LDS funerals had acquired a few distinctive attributes. Following the introduction of the Nauvoo temple endowment, deceased saints who had received their endowments were buried in their temple robes—symbolic of both their commitment and guarantees (that is, their covenants). At this time American society was abandoning the use of funeral shrouds in favor of burial in the Sunday best. Mormons followed a third path, rich with ritual overtones. The use of temple attire as burial clothing remains to this day a unique aspect of LDS funeral practices. Although never made doctrinally mandatory, and without expressly defined theological implications, this custom has assumed great importance within the Mormon community. Detailed official guidance has been issued on appropriate funeral preparations for those previously endowed as well as on eligibility (for example, deceased excommunicants are debarred, though not "lapsed" Mormons who have not been officially cut off). Considerable attention is devoted to insuring the availability of appropriate clothing to all those who might have to prepare for the funeral of one who has been "endowed."

Through their use of this unique burial attire, Mormon families symbolically imply the eternal commitment of the loved one to the exalting temple ritual (which is performed, it could be said, in these "funeral robes") and to the continuation of their family unit into the eternities. In the process another American tradition is preserved, long since gone from society at large. It often remains the responsibility of the immediate family to clothe the body in the temple robes, and thus some direct contact with the deceased is assured.

Brigham Young provided a characteristically good-humored but no-nonsense statement of things in 1877 in the instructions he left for his own funeral, a model in many ways for ceremonies thereafter:

> I, Brigham Young, wish my funeral services to be conducted after the following manner:
> When I breathe my last I wish my friends to put my body in as clean and wholesome state as can conveniently be done, and preserve the same for one, two, three, or four days, or as long as my body can be preserved in a good condition.
> I want my coffin made of plump 1¼ inch redwood boards, not scrimped in length, but two inches longer than I would measure, and from two to three inches wider than is commonly made for a person of my breadth and size, and deep enough to place me on a little comfortable cotton bed with a good suitable pillow in size and quality. My body dressed in Temple clothing and laid nicely into my coffin, and the coffin to have the appearance that if I wanted to turn a little to the right or left I should have plenty of room to do so; the lid can be made crowning.
> At my interment I wish all of my family present that can be conveniently, and the male members to wear no crepe on their hats or their coats; the

females to buy no black bonnets, nor black dresses, nor black veils; but if
they have them they are at liberty to wear them.

The services may be permitted, as singing and a prayer offered, and if
any of my friends wish to say a few words, and really desire, do so.

After a description of the vault into which he wished the coffin to be placed
(and covered with "nice, fine, dry earth") Brigham concluded: "There let
my earthly house or tabernacle rest in peace and have a good sleep until
the morning of the first resurrection; no crying nor mourning with any one,
that I have done my work faithfully and in good faith."[45]

Although the Salt Lake tabernacle was draped in black, in accordance
with Young's wishes none of the four thousand persons who marched to his
grave was dressed in mourning clothes. Among those in attendance was
apostle and eventual church president Wilford Woodruff, who several years
later penned his own instructions. At his death he also wished "my body
washed clean and clothed in clean white linen, according to the order of the
Holy Priesthood, and put into a plain, decent coffin, made of native wood,
with plenty of room." He as well instructed that he did not wish "any black
made use of about my coffin, or about the vehicle that conveys my body to
the grave." He did not "wish my family or friends to wear any badge of
mourning for me at my funeral or afterwards, for, if I am true and faithful
unto death, there will be no necessity for any one to mourn me. I have no
directions to give concerning the services of my funeral, any further than it
would be pleasing to me for as many of the Presidency and Twelve Apostles
who may be present to speak as may be thought wisdom. Their speech will
be to the living."

Reflecting the, by this time, well-developed belief in the proximity of the
"spirit world," Woodruff then added, "If the laws and customs of the spirit
world will permit, I should wish to attend my funeral myself, but I shall
be governed by the counsel I receive in the spirit world." He concluded,
characteristically, with a request that "a plain marble slab [be] put at the
head of my grave, stating my name and age, and [that] I died in the faith of
the Gospel of Christ and in the fellowship of the Saints."[46]

Later Mormon leaders were largely successful in directing funeral practices along similar lines. A turn-of-the-century LDS guide to funeral etiquette commended the "strong sentiment which has set in amongst our
people against the assuming of mourning garments and especially that
abomination, a widow's cap and veil." Though on the right track, the Saints
were further encouraged to discard "all mourning stationery, mourning
cards and all such practices." Choirs should discontinue any remaining "traditions of the world in singing mournful hymns and doleful music" at funer-

als. The music should "express rather the hope of the future than the gloom of the present." A particularly graphic indicator of thinking in the last years of the century was the copious *white* funeral bunting first used at memorial services held in the Salt Lake Tabernacle about 1888. Within two decades the white bunting was in turn displaced by flowers.

Recognizing that death could nonetheless leave loved ones surrounded "with every physical and mental power of depression," friends were enjoined to impart "encouragment, good cheer and bright thoughts," and the bereaved advised against "retiring from all pleasure and social life for a certain length of time."[47]

In discouraging a conspicuously somber response to death, the church leadership was helped by a similar trend in the country generally. They also hoped that the funeral experience would retain its simplicity. This unfortunately ran counter to a broader move toward what church leaders saw as "show and ostentation." The LDS guide to funeral etiquette mentioned above condemned the "often very extravagant" use of carriages and flowers among the faithful. While believing nothing to be "more acceptable and beautiful in time of sorrow than flowers," the growing notion that this was a mandatory prerequisite to attendance at a funeral was found especially objectionable. A few years later this point was addressed more emphatically by church president Joseph F. Smith, who condemned the "profusion of flowers, the expensive dress, and . . . ornaments of gold in the form of rings and other jewelry used in decorating the dead." He particularly decried the request of some that the deceased not initially be clothed in their temple clothing, that they rather might be viewed "in this finery."[48]

Overall the goal of twentieth-century church leaders that funeral services remain "simple" and "expressive of hope, life and resurrection"[49] has been achieved. A comparative study of Utah funeral customs in 1939 noted that while floral gifts were "unusually numerous" at LDS funerals, the service was "not one of pomp, ceremony, or show." It consisted, as earlier and as still today, of prayers, musical numbers, and several speakers who—in a subtle though perhaps significant change from the foundational years—dwelt more on the "meritorious life of the deceased" than on the life hereafter. Since midcentury local leaders have received official (though rather generalized) guidance on the specifics of the funeral service. It is to be patterned after the Sunday sacrament meeting, "simple, with brief sermons and music centered on the gospel."[50]

Recently there has been some concern among church leaders that funerals have become less reverent and too often introduce alterations into the "approved simple agenda." Specific concerns include the use of family members as speakers in the service who "tell things that would be appropriate at a family reunion or at some other family gathering but not on an occasion that should be sacred and solemn." If family members did speak, it was felt they had an "obligation to speak with reverence and to teach principles of the gospel." Also to be discouraged was any obligatory practice of filing by an open casket to conclude the funeral service. A simple family prayer was felt appropriate when the casket was closed, but not additional talks or musical numbers.

These concerns led to a general address in 1988 by a senior apostle who reiterated official guidance on the funeral service issued in 1972. The earlier guidance had requested that

> henceforth all funerals conducted under the auspices of the officials of the church follow the general format of the sacrament meeting with respect to music, speaking, and prayers. Music should be used at the beginning of the service prior to the opening prayer and possibly after the invocation also; as in our Sunday meetings. The closing portion of the funeral likewise should follow our customary pattern of having a final musical number immediately before the concluding prayer. Where feasible, a choir could very well be used on the musical program.
>
> With respect to speaking, it should be kept in mind that funeral services provide an excellent opportunity for teaching the basic doctrines . . . in a positive manner. . . . Following these suggestions will help to keep our services in line with our established pattern and will avoid practices now so commonly followed elsewhere.[51]

Nineteenth-century Mormons, like nearly all their Christian contemporaries, saw burial as the appropriate means of disposing of the bodies of the dead. They no doubt believed, as many do today, that the symbolism of the ordinance of baptism presupposed interment in the earth at death.[52] However, aside from the incorporation into funeral sermons or graveside prayers of such biblical aphorisms as "Dust thou art, and unto dust shalt thou return," commentators seem not to have felt the subject one that required discussion.

Autopsies also occasionally were performed from early pioneer years without any apparent doctrinal ill ease or response. As these sometimes were performed by respected, church-appointed midwives (who also could serve as undertakers),[53] implicit sanction is even suggested. It is only within the past decade, however, that the church has publicized officially this point of view. Until 1989 the church's statement included a concern that "any organs that are removed during an autopsy should be replaced, as far as practical, before burial," but the most recent guidance is limited to a brief statement that "an autopsy may be performed if the family of the deceased gives consent and if the autopsy complies with the law."[54]

A subject that has received more attention is cremation, which first became a national fashion late in the nineteenth century partly because of its alleged "hygienic" advantages over burying. This movement received occasional sympathetic attention in church periodicals, which were also supportive of other aspects of the new scientific medicine. In 1884, for example, James Talmage—eventually a highly influential shaper of church beliefs—summarized in a lengthy essay, "The Disposal of the Dead," the many perceived public health advantages of cremation. Nearly all derived from the "matter of general acceptance, that no dead body is ever placed in the soil without polluting the earth, the air, and the water above and about it." Perhaps the most arresting point made was that through cremation "the horrible catastrophe of burying alive would be averted." (In this he touched on an exquisite national anxiety which also received occasional treatment in the late-nineteenth-century Mormon press. Although it seems not to have been a pressing issue in Utah, at least one LDS apostle provided in his will that he not be buried for several days, to avoid just this possbility.) Talmage's nonjudgmental conclusion was that "whether the disassociation process [of the body] occupy ten, fifty, or more years in the grave of corruption, or as many minutes in the warm and rosy bed of the crematorium, yet in either instance the inevitable decree is obeyed: 'Dust thou art, and unto dust shalt thou return.'"[55]

Hygienic and other arguments notwithstanding, in practice church leaders and the Mormon community for the most part rejected cremation as an alternative to traditional burial. Indeed, well into the twentieth century a large segment of Mormon society even eschewed use of hardwood or metal caskets, or cement vaults, as impediments to the return of the body to the earth. No clear formal statement of belief was issued on the subject, however, so occasional cremations also took place. Eventually, the church through its official *Handbook of Instructions* advised, in 1940, that "the Church has never encouraged cremation as a proper method of disposing of the remains of the dead. It is ocnsidered proper to consign them to the earth. That has always been the custom. The attitude taken is that nothing should be done that is destructive of the body; that should be left to nature. Where bodies are cremated, no prayer should be offered during or following the cremation ceremony."[56]

The church did not reject all innovations in the handling of the dead, however, nor did all Mormons reject the more progressive ideas sweeping the country at large. Talmage's comments above illustrate this point, but he was not unique. Not long before the 1940 *Handbook* counsel on burial, for example, the LDS Relief Society magazine carried an editorial endorsement of mausoleums, labeling them a "better method of taking care of the dead at a price that is not inconsistent with our general progress towards higher ideals."[57] This coincided with both a national movement toward the use of mausoleums, and the construction of the Salt Lake Memorial Mausoleum, whose services were regularly advertised in the Relief Society's journal.

More significant, embalming had been introduced into the community some years earlier without significant controversy. Beyond providing for some flexibility in the scheduling of funeral services, this development aligned the Mormon community with a natonal trend toward increasing reliance on professional morticians, rather than the family, in the preparation of the remains of loved ones.

All of this was, of course, partially motivated by the same public health concerns voiced in support of cremation. These concerns eventually led to regulations, within Utah as elsewhere, controlling the practice of embalming and the handling of bodies in general. One result has been the development in some areas of legal barriers which prevent Mormon families from themselves clothing their dead in temple robes. The church has responded to this development with a significant deemphasis in instruction to the Relief Society, for example, on the preparation of the dead for burial, and with general guidance accommodating to the new circumstances:

> In some areas only a licensed mortician, or his employee is allowed to handle a deceased body. Where such a regulation exists, a member of the family or an appropriate person assigned by the bishop or Relief Society president may carefully look over the clothing after the body is dressed to make sure that it has been properly placed on the body. Morticians have always been willing to cooperate in this matter. Some morticians permit a family member or an assigned person to be present at the time the temple clothing is placed on the body of the deceased person.[58]

When allowed, family members who have received their temple endowments may still dress the deceased, or families may request dressing service from the church. In the latter case, an endowed person of the same sex is selected to perform this function.

With the passage of time—and the growth of the international church—advice on cremation has softened. Although cremation was still explicitly discouraged as late as 1968, local leaders were then advised that "the decision is left with the family. Local laws must be observed. If bodies are to be cremated, funeral services may be held in the usual way, but the disposition of the ashes usually makes unnecessary the offering of graveside or dedicatory prayers." Guidance in 1963 had made clear that "temple garments and robes should be removed before the body is cremated," but by 1976 this counsel was reversed: "deceased persons should remain fully dressed in their temple clothing at the time cremation takes place."[59]

The present official guidance on cremation, published in 1989, is the most positively worded to date: "Generally, cremation is not encouraged. However, in some countries, the law requires it. The family of the deceased must decide whether to cremate the body, taking into account any laws governing burial or cremation. Where possible the body of a deceased member who has been endowed should be dressed in temple clothing when the body is cremated. A funeral service may be held if the ashes are buried or deposited in a mausoleum."[60]

SUICIDE, EUTHANASIA, AND PROLONGATION OF LIFE

Joseph Smith is credited with saying that if people only knew how wonderful heaven would be, they would kill themselves to get there.[61] In LDS theology, however, had they done so their prospects would dim considerably. Suicide long has been regarded as akin to the "shedding of innocent blood," the latter an unforgivable sin foreclosing any heavenly reward.

During most of the nineteenth century *self-murder*, as it was then termed, was not a sufficiently common problem among Mormons to warrant much discussion. Toward the end of the century national attention focused on an apparent rise in suicides in the U.S. (allegedly up 35 percent between 1860 and the 1890s) and in Europe. This concern was reflected in commentary in Utah, and in 1886 the First Presidency addressed the subject for the first time in a general "epistle" issued in October:

> There is [an] evil that is growing amongst the peoples of the world that is not unfelt amidst the Latter-day Saints. It is the crime of self-murder. Suicide should be made odious among the people of God, it should be emphasized as a deadly sin, and no undue feelings of tenderness toward the unfortunate dead, or of sympathy towards the living bereaved, should prevent us denouncing it as a crime against God and humanity, against the Creator and the creature. . . . [I]n many countries especial pains have been taken to discourage it, by refusal to bury in consecrated ground, by indignities offered to the lifeless remains, or by such lack of funereal observances as would produce a peculiar and horrifying effect upon the survivors. Now, while not advocating measures of this description, we do not think that the same laudations and panegyrics should be pronounced over the self-murderer as are so freely uttered over the faithful Saint who

has gone to his eternal rest. There is a difference in their death, and that difference should be impressed upon the living, unless the deceased, at the time of the rash act, was in such a mental condition as not to be wholly responsible for his actions; but again, if this condition be the result of sin, of departure from God's laws, then the unfortunate one, like the inebriate, is not altogether free from the responsibility of acts committed while in this state of mental derangement; if he is not censurable for the act itself, he is for the causes that induced it. In such cases the mantle of charity must not be stretched so widely, in our desire to protect our erring friends, as to reflect dishonor on the work of God, or contempt for the principles of the everlasting Gospel. . . .[62]

A number of the "indignities" visited on the remains were graphically identified in articles in church periodicals a few years later. Among the more sensational were those said to be used in France, including "exposing in the public morgue the naked body of the victim" "hanging the body by the feet" and then dragging it through the streets, tying it face down on a hurdle which was pulled behind a dung cart, and other like actions. It was reported that the first of these measures had immediately checked an "epidemic" then current.[63]

In practice the Mormon response to suicide was, as indicated by the First Presidency, generally restrained and in accordance with a broader tradition which limited the religious entitlements of the deceased. Published LDS guidance on the "funerals of suicides" advised that suicide was "self-murder, and therefore, anyone committing this crime should not expect a public and honorable funeral." Such a person "should be buried privately and without ostentation, and certainly the funeral services should be conducted without the authorities of the Church lending their presence to the funeral."[64] It was further clarified several years later that vicarious temple work usually could not be performed on behalf of those who committed suicide, apparently on the grounds that the act rendered an individual "ineligible for eternal salvation." Only with "good evidence" of insanity could vicarious temple work be performed.[65]

While Mormonism retains to the present day its strong views on suicide per se, in recent decades a much less judgmental view has emerged with regard to its victims. As a consequence restrictions on funeral services have been eliminated, and a decision made to allow vicarious temple work for those who allegedly had committed suicide (and murder, as well as those who had been excommunicated) on the grounds that the circumstance was often "hearsay" and that judgments might best be left "in the hands of the Lord." Finally, it also has been determined recently that an endowed person who has committed suicide may be buried in temple clothing, unless he or she was excommunicated at the time. (The transformation of suicide from being primarily a moral issue to being primarily a mental health issue is discussed more fully in *Chapter 5*.)[66]

One facet of the early suicide discussion had a late-twentieth-century ring to it. Prominent turn-of-the-century "eastern" physicians were said to advocate suicide in some cases of serious illness. A few even endorsed active intervention to bring about a "humane and just" conclusion "in cases of hopeless insanity, in diseases incurable, and in cases where persons were victims of fatal accidents." This latter view, especially, on gaining some momentum in the early twentieth century, drew sharp editorial condemnation from the church. The "divine requirement" was "Thou shalt not kill":

> Anything that relieves the conscience of man from its duty to preserve life, even in extremity, would be most dangerous to the welfare of our highest and best civilization. Once let it enter the heart of man that there are exceptions to this divine requirement, and the lines marking off justifiable causes would become more and more indistinct, until human life would cease to have that sacred and binding obligation upon a human conscience that it has today.[67]

The LDS view, however, stopped far short of advocating medical intervention at all costs. Though divinely encouraged to protect their health and heal their sick, Mormons were early advised by revelation that occasionally people were "appointed to death" (*D&C* 42:48). Beyond ameliorating to some extent the harsh fact of death, this view placed limits, in theory and in practice, on the heroics felt appropriate in terminal illnesses. In an 1842 case that received some notoriety in London, a faithful sister died after a brief illness in which treatment was limited to anointing "with oil in the name of the Lord, . . . sage tea and Cayenne pepper, [and] leeches." The coroner, believing this a possible case of manslaughter, convened a jury. Although a verdict of "natural death" resulted, the coroner expressed to the press "a hope that the present inquiry would act as caution to [the Mormons] how they acted in such cases for the future." The Saints were neither intimidated nor dismayed; they reprinted a critical London account of the episode in their own official journal with a hyperbolic editorial observing that "what gives deep interest to the fact [of the death] and adds solemnity to the scene is that she died a 'natural *death!!!!!*.'" Among the litany of "unnatural" alternatives offered was "the privilege of being killed through the administration of the learned medical faculty."[68]

Given Mormon antipathy to the heroic orthodox medicine of the day (discussed in Chapter 3), this episode perhaps somewhat overstates the case.

Nonetheless, nineteenth-century Mormon healing efforts can hardly be termed aggressive. Per revelatory instruction the sick were treated with fasting, prayer, anointing with oil, and the administration of herbs and mild food; faced with traumatic final illnesses, faithful members were comfortable discontinuing all measures but those designed to ameliorate suffering. Later in the century it became common in especially painful or hopeless cases to replace healing blessing with a quasi-ordinance to speed the illness to its final conclusion. Confronting a sister who had "cancer in the breast which was Eating her Vitals & rotting her flesh," Brigham Young together with other church leaders, for example, "dedicated her to God for her death & burial"—and in about twelve hours she was dead. During church president John Taylor's final illness, he also was "dedicated" to the Lord "either to live, or to go hence as the Lord Willed." Taylor died the following day.[69]

If anything, this variant practice grew with the passage of time, until it came into conflict with early-twentieth-century leadership efforts to standardize healing practices within the church. In this latter setting the First Presidency issued a formal statement, in 1922, "On Dedicating the Sick and the Suffering to the Lord." In this they advised,

> The custom which is growing in the Church to dedicate those who appear to be beyond recovery, to the Lord, has no place among the ordinances of the Church. The Lord has instructed us, where people are sick, to call in the elders, two or more, who should pray for and lay their hands upon them in the name of the Lord; and "if they die," says the Lord, "they shall die unto me; and if they live, they shall live unto me." No possible advantage can result from dedicating faithful members of the Church prior to their death. Their membership in the Church, their devotion to the faith which they have espoused, are sufficient guarantee, so far as their future welfare is concerned.[70]

This technically remains the position of the church to the present. Unquestionably nothing akin to "last rites" ever developed within the LDS tradition, as the necessary saving ordinances are believed to be limited to baptism and the temple rituals. However, the practice of blessing those with a terminal illness that they will be released from suffering never has come to an end. Though little now is written on the subject, anecdotes continue to circulate in the community about present-day blessings and the promised outcome that has followed.[71]

Understandably, then, there never has been any felt obligation to take heroic steps to prolong life. Recent years have seen some further discussion of this subject, reflecting both the advent of unprecedented life support systems and renewed national attention to the question of euthanasia. For the most part this discussion has been oral rather than written, and it reveals strong differences among LDS practitioners in attitudes toward *passive* euthanasia (the withholding of lifesaving measures). By contrast, the withholding of *heroic* active measures is still viewed by most as an acceptable option, and Utah has joined many other states in enacting "living will" legislation to allow patients some measure of prior control over this decision. From 1974 to 1989 official church guidance on the subject was limited to a brief statement on "prolonging life":

> Because of its belief in the dignity of life, the Church opposes euthanasia. In addition to faith in the Lord, members should call upon recognized and licensed medical practitioners to assist in reversing conditions that threaten life. When dying becomes inevitable, it should be considered a blessing and a purposeful part of mortality.

This perspective received added emphasis with the addition in 1989 of the explicit advice that "members should not feel obligated to extend mortal life by means that are unreasonable. These judgments are best made by family members after receiving wise and competent medical advice and seeking divine guidance through fasting and prayer." At this same time new guidance on euthanasia was added, warning that "a person who participates in euthanasia—deliberately putting to death a person suffering from incurable conditions of disease—violates the commandments of God."[72]

The few LDS practitioners who have ventured into print on this subject generally feel that because each case is different no detailed general guidelines will or should be issued by the church. Believing that families whose prayerful study suggests passive euthanasia is an appropriate course should have no obstacle to the implementation of their wishes, they oppose restricting legislation.[73]

One thoughtful LDS "decision tree" has been proposed which probably comes close to crystallizing the present view of most Mormons on this difficult subject. Discussing a hypothetical case of a comatose four-year-old with significant and apparently permanent brain damage secondary to respiratory failure, who was able to breathe unassisted but incapable of voluntarily taking nourishment, the authors proposed that the following steps be taken by the parents in deciding the best course of action:

1. Information was to be acquired about options and consequences, and values clarified.

2. Directly relevant scriptures or authoritative statements were to be sought. The authors considered there were none.

3. The needs of others, particularly those of the immediate and extended family, were to be analyzed. In the hypothetical case, these would have been affected adversely through the demands inherent in institutional care for the child.

4. The needs of the comatose child were to be evaluated. The authors' tentative assessment here recapitulated much that has been covered in the present chapter:

> [The child had] acquired a mortal body and a firm place in a family [the parents having been sealed in the temple] with the potential of being together forever. Baptism, the priesthood, celestial marriage, and fatherhood can all come in the next life [through vicarious temple ordinances for the dead]. Since [the child's] physical condition makes it impossible for him to use his body to express thoughts or concepts, such communication would need to come from the Spirit. We would expect to fast and pray earnestly that the Father would, if He wills it, make known to us [the child's] feelings. Barring a direct manifestation to the contrary, we would feel to release [the child's] spirit, since his condition simultaneously denies him both any conscious experience of mortality and the progression available to disembodied spirits.

The decision was to be evaluated through discussions "with the extended family, the bishop, the children, the doctors, and, if necessary, to seek confirmation again through the Spirit that it is the correct, or at least an acceptable decision." They continue,

> If this evaluation turned up significant doubts or hesitations, we think we would feel very free to select another option since other options are reversible. We could institutionalize him for short periods to give us breaks from home care or begin with institutionalization and switch to home care when we ran out of money. But death is an irrevocable decision. We can imagine few things as agonizing as watching a beloved son or daughter suffer and die. But perhaps it really would be worse to see one of our children neither live nor die.[74]

·3·

On Being Well and Suffering

Prepare to die, is not the exhortation in this church and kingdom; but prepare to live is the word with us, and improve all we can in this life that we may be the better prepared to enjoy a better life hereafter, wherein we may enjoy a more exalted condition of intelligence, wisdom, light, knowledge, power, glory, and exaltation. Then let us seek to extend the present life to the uttermost, by observing every law of health.[1]

This exhortation was offered by Brigham Young in 1865, and indeed, few things are more widely known about Mormons than their refusal for health reasons to use tobacco, alcohol, tea, and coffee. This abstemiousness derives from a health code believed by them to be divinely revealed. It also reflects a remarkable attitude within Mormonism about the inseparability of things physical and things spiritual. To give counsel on being well has been seen within the tradition as part of the core responsibility of an inspired leadership. To an almost equal extent a personal effort to be well is viewed by members as essential to both *spiritual* and physical well-being. In tracing the record on this subject, the present chapter gives an indication of what this commitment has meant over time, both for church counsel and for the achievement of individual good health.

HEALTH THEN

By modern standards nineteenth-century America was an unhealthy place indeed. At the time of the Mormon restoration, infants were twenty times more likely to die before age one—and thirty times more likely to die before adulthood—than an infant born today. Fully a third of children failed to survive childhood. Even having reached adulthood, Americans remained nearly three times as likely to die at most ages than those of the same age today. All in all, U.S. death rates then were far worse than those now found in the most medically backward countries in the world.

41

In retrospect it is easy to identify the basis for these grave facts. Less than a score of killer diseases probably accounted for 75–80 percent of all deaths from colonial times to the early years of the twentieth century. In essence, this handful of mortal ailments was responsible for most of the difference between nineteenth-century mortality rates and those of the "healthy" modern world. Cholera, diphtheria, dysentery, gastroenteritis in infancy, malaria, measles, meningitis, pneumonia, scarlet fever and erysipelas, smallpox, tuberculosis, typhoid fever, whooping cough, and yellow fever were perhaps the most devastating of these diseases, physically and socially, but in some settings others such as scurvy and tetanus took a considerable toll. Parasitic and nutritional disorders, while generally not in themselves mortal risks, rendered large segments of society less able to fend off the effects of more lethal diseases.

The early Mormon record was essentially indistinguishable from that of contemporaries in similar circumstances.[2] Circumstances, however, could vary widely. Communities with large numbers of children—such as the youthful, near-maximal-fertility Saints—tended to have higher overall death rates because of the disproportionate childhood toll. The almost universally contaminated water supply was the major culprit here, with an infant's second summer (first off the breast) a notoriously dangerous period. Cemetery and sexton records from early Mormon communities confirm the expected. Childhood deaths below age twelve accounted for two-thirds of total deaths (versus only 2–3 percent today), with a preponderance coming during the hot months of summer and early fall (during which 75–85 percent of all community deaths were among the young). Endemic waterborne diseases like dysentery, gastroenteritis, and typhoid fever dominate all other causes of death, but epidemics of measles, diphtheria, whooping cough, and other droplet-borne (that is, respiratory) diseases also took a heavy toll. During one especially bad two-year period (1879–80) diphtheria alone accounted for 25 percent and 32 percent of all Salt Lake City deaths.

To a very limited extent the adverse effects of high birth rates on total mortality were offset by the relative absence of the elderly in early Mormon communities. Amost two-thirds of the *adult* LDS community in Kirtland, Ohio, were in their twenties or thirties; less than 5 percent were over sixty. Death rates in the older LDS population—a population that grew slowly but steadily throughout the century—were, of course, substantially higher than that of younger adults. Surprisingly, however, their record was not so dissimilar from the modern day. In one carefully studied LDS community in southern Utah, life expectancy in the period from 1861 to 1880 was, for those age twenty, a remarkable seventy-one years for men and sixty-seven years for women.[3] ("Unexpected" longevity among adults was true nationally as well. Without a cigarette industry, substantially lower rates of cancer and heart disease to some extent offset deaths from infectious diseases in this age group.)

Immigrants were at especially high risk for local health problems until they were "seasoned" (that is, until survivors gained a degree of immunity to local diseases through nonfatal infection). Early Mormon communities, because of their several moves to heavily malarious frontier areas, and because of a continuing influx of converts, always were composed predominantly of newcomers, and they suffered accordingly. On the other hand, later isolation in the intermountain West spared them the ravages of a number of major Eastern plagues. Cholera, which had decimated both an 1833 Mormon expeditionary group in Missouri and departing pioneers in 1848–49, could not readily follow the Saints to the desert West, and Mormon isolation also afforded protection, for the most part, from the most serious strains of smallpox; in combination with other geographical features, isolation also freed most LDS communities from their long-standing nemesis, malaria.

Under circumstances of extraordinary privation, those of all ages—but especially infants—were likely victims of a host of diseases. The Mormons' semiforced departure from Nauvoo to a harsh Winter Quarters on the Missouri led to death rates three to four times higher than that experienced at any other time. Perhaps a third of children born at Winter Quarters died—mostly of diarrheal disease—before their first birthday. Scurvy also took a major toll, as virtually the entire community developed a profound vitamin-C deficiency before the end of the first winter.

Overall Mormon death rates in Nauvoo probably were in the lower twenties per thousand, at a time when some frontier communities considered 20 per 1,000 the best that could be expected. But death rates rose spectacularly during the early phase of the exodus, to about 80 per 1,000, a level comparable to that of the worst epidemic years in Eastern coastal cities. Once established in the Salt Lake valley, deaths again declined to Nauvoo levels. Then, as elsewhere, with continuing population growth, these rates climbed slowly from the low twenties in 1860 to the mid twenties in the 1880s—despite a declining proportion of the population in the vulnerable years of childhood. More people simply led to greater contamination of water supplies and greater risk of contagious exposure. After 1869 a transcontinental railroad facilitated the westerly movement of disease along with its human hosts. For the same reason infant mortality also increased during the early decades in Utah, from around 155 deaths per 1,000 to about 170 per 1,000 (this, in contrast to a present-day figure of 10 infant deaths per 1,000).

DISEASE CAUSALITY

Mormons seem always to have viewed most disease in naturalistic terms. This meant, in the 1830s, that most adult illness generally was believed directly or indirectly related to an overabundance of internal stimulation—either gastrointestinal or nervous. (Resulting concerns about dietary and beverage stimulants are discussed in the section below.) Those weakened by such stimulation were vulnerable to a myriad of fevers said to arise *de novo* from atmospheric miasma or putrefying organic matter. With time, fevers came to be understood more as primary, rather than secondary, agents of disease, characterized by Mormons with the same matter-of-factness that they did other local flora and fauna. As one church leader wrote from the settlements in Missouri, "Here sickness comes, and where does it not? The ague and fever; the chill fever, a kind of cold plague, and other diseases, prey on emigrants till they are thoroughly seasoned to the climate. Here death puts an end to life, and so it does all over the globe."[4]

There were occasions, however, when Mormons viewed disease in distinctly unnatural terms—as a manifestation of evil spirits. The spirits of those cast down during the "war in heaven," in addition to seeking to thwart the plan of salvation through the enticement of humankind to sin, were said to seek every opportunity to take possession of the physical bodies which they had been denied. The spirits of evil people since departed also were believed to linger in their former dwellings. Typically, these spirits were said to inflict illness of a psychiatric sort (discussed in Chapter 5), but their effect could be physical as well.

Joseph Smith once explained that physical relapses suffered by his own child were traceable to the house in which the Smiths were staying. It formerly had been a public house, he said, occupied by wicked people, and the devil still considered that "it belonged to him." As a result he had caused the child's affliction. The Prophet also attributed early deaths in the malarious Nauvoo area to "disembodied spirits" still hanging around cabins (former "dens of iniquity") into which the Saints had moved for temporary shelter. "When the righteous took possession of their old houses, all combined to kill the new inhabitants, and hence so much sickness."[5] Brigham Young held a similar view, as evidenced by his explanation for the unprecedented illness and death experienced at Winter Quarters: "Some times in sickness & weakness the spirit of deavels get possession of the body whare the spirit of man is pure & overcomes it. . . . Some children are killed in this way for the devil is making war with every thing that has A tabernacle [i.e., a body] esspecially the Saints."[6]

Rare to begin with, demonic explanations for physical illness did not survive the advent of scientific medicine. The infrequent reference to demons thereafter referred to primarily emotional disorders. All other disease was characterized in the increasingly sophisticated language of contemporary medicine, indeed in language carried with remarkable frequency in official LDS periodicals. The "germ theory," the role of insect vectors, vitamin deficiencies, and the risk factors of cancer and cardiovascular disease—all have been the subject of scores of lessons and essays, which in content have been largely indistinguishable from contemporary secular sources.

THE PURPOSE OF SUFFERING

Notwithstanding the considerable persecution and grave illness that were part of Mormonism's early years, theological reflections on the role of suffering in the eternal scheme are not prominent in the tradition. Several themes nonetheless can be traced in the limited discussion to date. While all have persisted throughout Mormon history, the degree to which each is emphasized has varied. By far the most consistent notion is that suffering is intrinsic to the mortal experience, in essence an inescapable adjunct to the earthly sojourn "inherited" in a completely naturalistic sense—as was death—from Adam. In addition, suffering often has been viewed as a more active instrument in the hand of God, by which he both chastens the unrighteous and tests or strenghtens the Saints.

The idea that suffering (affliction) is implicit in mortality derives from a *Book of Mormon* prophet, Lehi, who taught that "it must needs be, that there is an opposition in all things." As explained by Lehi, and as generally understood within the church, were there not such opposition,

> righteousness could not be brought to pass, neither wickedness, neither holiness nor misery, neither good nor bad. Wherefore, all things must needs be a compound in one; wherefore, if it should be one body it must needs remain as dead, having no life neither death, nor corruption nor incorruption, happiness nor misery, neither sense nor insensibility.
>
> Wherefore, it must needs have been created for a thing of naught; wherefore there would have been no purpose in the end of creation. Wherefore, this thing must needs destroy the wisdom of God and his eternal purposes, and also the power, and the mercy, and the justice of God.

> And if ye shall say there is no law, ye shall also say there is no sin. If ye shall say there is no sin, ye shall also say there is no righteousness. And if there be no righteousness there be no happiness. And if there be no righteousness nor happiness there be no punishment nor misery. And if these things are not there is no God. And if there is no God we are not, neither the earth; for there could have been no creation of things, neither to act nor to be acted upon; wherefore, all things must have vanished away.[7]

Thus, if there is wellness, there must also be sickness.

Suffering as chastisement also was a scripturally based idea, derived from a myriad of biblical references. The Mormons were just one among many religious groups who labeled the 1832 cholera pandemic a worldwide visitation on the wicked. Even when the Latter-day faithful themselves were seized by this same plague—as happened to a third of a small Mormon expeditionary force organized in hopes of reclaiming Missouri properties— it was immediately pronounced a "consequence of the fractious and unruly spirits that had appeared among them."[8]

Soon, however, it was concluded that sometimes righteous living offered little protection. Following the Saints' first serious encounter with malaria in the newly founded city of Nauvoo, Joseph Smith explained that

> it is a false idea that the Saints will escape all the judgments, whilst the wicked suffer; for all flesh is subject to suffer, and "the righteous shall hardly escape;" still many of the Saints will escape, for the just shall live by faith; yet many of the righteous shall fall prey to disease, to pestilence, etc., by reason of the weakness of the flesh, and yet be saved in the Kingdom of God. So that it is an unhallowed principle to say that such and such have transgressed because they have been preyed upon by disease or death, for all flesh is subject to death; and the Savior has said, "Judge not, lest ye be judged."[9]

In later years disease—especially epidemic disease—was not often labeled chastisement except in apocalyptic discourse. A variant belief did persist in the notion that sin could have direct physical consequences. The effects of intemperance were long cast in this light, and sexually transmitted diseases continue at the popular level to be viewed as punishment for unchastity. In a sense this is reminiscent of the notion of disease as a natural consequence (that is, of nature) of any potential health risk, but in this case the relationship is seen as much more direct in the selection of victims than with other classes of disease. This distinction is more often implied than explicit, as in a 1974 *Church News* editorial that contrasted "herpes simplex Type 2, a venereal disease which is becoming pandemic in the United States," with various other strains of herpes, "most of them completely innocent and having no relationship to sinful relationships whatever."[10] Official church commentary on AIDS has most recently illustrated this point, with a clear distinction beng drawn between "innocent" victims and others.

A beneficent role for suffering in God's plan is another fairly persistent theme in Mormon discourse. The idea derives from such New Testament texts as "we must through much tribulation enter into the kingdom of God" (Acts 14:22) and "but we glory in tribulations also; knowing that tribulation worketh patience" (Romans 5:3); the latter in fact was cited by Joseph Smith in an epistle later canonized in LDS scripture. This theme was especially common during the difficult pioneer years when the Latter-day Saints were wont to compare themselves to saints tested in biblical times. It also was a particular favorite of those who emerged successfully from this ordeal. George Q. Cannon, for example, looked back on a long and distinguished career from his position in the First Presidency (the presiding authority of the church), and observed that afflictions "are necessary":

> It is necessary that we should be tempted, that we should be tried, that we should be purified, by going through these trials and passing through this furnace of affliction which this life furnishes. . . . I look back to the disagreeable parts of my life, that is, the parts that were thought to be disagreeable at the time, and I saw to myself, I thank God that I had these things to contend with.[11]

More recent LDS commentatary has been a little less willing to reach definitive conclusions about the purpose of suffering because, as one writer observed, "the question is a difficult one to resolve fully, especially as God himself has never seen fit to give a completely satisfying, rational explanation."[12] And the emphasis has returned to suffering as a natural part of mortality. In this view, the primary concern is with one's response to affliction, rather than with understanding per se. Most Mormons probably continue to believe that, up to a point, suffering can facilitate personal growth, of the sort they believe requisite to exaltation (and through which they believe God previously passed during his own mortality). Ultimately, however, most probably also agree with the author recently honored for her article "The Uses of Suffering," which appeared in the church's *Ensign* magazine. Acknowledging that some afflictions seem "far out of proportion to any concept of growth or testing of the sufferers" and indeed "transcend any rationalization," she forthrightly concludes that in such cases there are no easy answers. There is, however, the possibility of some indirect personal growth:

We who from love or obligation must watch such suffering cannot help but feel dismay at the seeming unfairness, the injustice of undeserved, overwhelming pain. Such suffering stirs our souls. But it also stretches our faith, tests our compassion, allows us necessary reexamination of our values, and teaches us that death, far from being a dreaded specter, can also come as a welcome friend, carrying our loved one to another sphere where life can again be meaningful and fulfilling.[13]

A WORD OF WISDOM

In retrospect, the most important Mormon response to matters of health and sickness came quite early. A divine guide to healthful living was announced by Joseph Smith in February 1833. Known as the "Word of Wisdom," this revelation was published as a broadsheet in December 1833 and made part of the first edition of the *Doctrine and Covenants* in 1835. As originally published, this "principle with promise" advised:

1. Behold, verily thus saith the Lord unto you, in consequence of evils and designs which do, and will exist in the hearts of conspiring men in the last days, I have warned you, and forewarn you, by giving unto you this word of wisdom by revelation, that insomuch as any man drinketh wine or strong drink among you, behold it is not good, neither meet in the sight of your Father, only in assembling yourselves together, to offer up your sacraments before him. And behold, this should be wine, yea, pure wine of the grape of the vine, [of] your own make. And again, strong drinks are not for the belly, but for the washing of your bodies. And again, tobacco is not for the body, neither for the belly; and is not good for man; but is an herb for bruises, and all sick cattle, to be used with judgment and skill. And again, hot drinks are not for the body, or belly.

2. And again, verily I say unto you, all wholesome herbs God hath ordained for the constitution, nature, and use of man.—Every herb in the season thereof. All these to be used with prudence and thanksgiving. Yea, flesh also of beasts and of the fowls of the air, I the Lord hath ordained for the use of man with thanksgiving. Nevertheless, they are to be used sparingly; and it is pleasing unto me, that they should not be used[,] only in times of winter or of cold, or famine. All grain is ordained for the use of man, and of beasts, to be the staff of life, not only for man, but for the beasts of the field, and the fowls of heaven, and all wild animals that run or creep on the earth; and these hath God made for the use of man only in times of famine, and excess hunger.

3. All grain is good for the food of man, as also the fruit of the vine, that which yieldeth fruit, whether in the ground or above the ground. Nevertheless wheat for man, and corn for the ox, and oats for the horse, and rye for the fowls, and for swine, and for all beasts of the field, and barley for all useful animals, and for mild drinks; as also other grain. And

all saints who remember to keep and do these saying, walking in obedience
to the commandments, shall receive health in their navel, and marrow to
their bones and shall find wisdom, and great treasures of knowledge, even
hidden treasures; and shall run and not be weary, and shall walk and not
faint; and I the Lord give unto them a promise, that the destroying angel
shall pass by them, as the children of Israel, and not slay them. Amen.

Sensitive to the varying popular attitudes then current, even within the
church, the first compilation of Smith's revelations added a brief word of
introduction explaining that what followed was

A word of wisdom for the benefit of the council of high priests, assembled in Kirtland, and church; and also the saints in Zion: to be sent greet-
ing: not by commandment, or constraint: but by revelation and the word
of wisdom: showing forth the order and will of God in the temporal salvation of all saints in the last days. Given for a principle with promise,
adapted to the capacity of the weak, and the weakest of all saints, who are
or can be called saints.

Eventually, in 1876, this introduction was included in the formal text of the
revelation, where it remains.

The circumstances that precipitated this guidance were not recorded at
the time. Much later it was said to be a response to the pipe smoking
and tobacco chewing of elders attending meetings at the Smith residence.
Whatever the triggering event, the text, which condemns in familiar language the five leading health risk factors of the day, was to some degree a
reflection of the times. It came during a period of unprecedented national
agitation on health-related matters that saw medical practitioners, no matter
how divergent their approaches to therapy, in broad agreement about the
profound dangers of certain beverage and dietary "stimulants."[14]

Alcohol was universally held to be the single most dangerous stimulant of
the day. Though initially the concern was directed almost exclusively to
distilled (or, as then termed, "strong") drinks, by 1830 many influential
authorities—and a temperance movement one million members strong—
also condemned the consumption of fermented drinks including cider, beer,
malt liquor, and wine. Sufficiently influential was this widespread condemnation that per capita alcohol consumption fell during the following decade by
an estimated two-thirds.

Tobacco, then principally chewed or smoked in pipes and cigars, probably
ranked in both conventional medical and botanic thinking as the second
severest health risk of the day. In addition to qualifying as a stimulant (as
then understood), it was considered a narcotic and poison, and by 1830 it

too was the target of a campaign, although of a lesser magnitude than that against alcohol.

Ranking somewhat behind tobacco as clear and present dangers were coffee and tea, or, as they were then popularly termed, "hot drinks." While there was more ambivalence on this subject, both beverages were viewed as mild stimulants requiring careful use. When brewed too strong or taken in large quantities, either could lead to serious illness; and for individuals of vulnerable "temperament" they were unhealthful even in moderation. The issue of temperature was itself believed important, perhaps even more so than the use of tea or coffee in and of themselves. Hot drinks of any sort were believed potentially quite injurious to the stomach and thereby to health in general. This applied to all liquids, including soup or even water. As in the cases of alcohol and tobacco, both botanic and orthodox physicians voiced these concerns. Many, and especially the health reformers, regularly delivered a four-point condemnation of alcohol, tobacco, coffee, and tea.

The fifth major risk factor of the day was meat, then reportedly consumed in prodigious quantities. Universally held to be more "stimulating" than fruits or vegetables, "flesh" was in turn subdivided as to risk. "Red" meats like beef, mutton, and pork were believed more stimulating than "white" meats like chicken and fish, and the meat of mature animals was believed more stimulating than that of the young. Although medical authorities often condemned what was perceived as excesses in meat consumption, they believed that some dietary meat was appropriate under certain circumstances. Generally speaking, a more stimulating diet (including meat) was useful when one was engaged in physically demanding work or when the body had to resist the cold of winter. A diet suitable under those circumstances could prove highly dangerous to a sedentary person, especially during warm months.

Some crusaders carried popular health reform well beyond the five principal risk factors and warned as well against spices, condiments, white bread, salt, and sex. Mainline medical authorities shared some of the concerns about spices and condiments, but primarily with regard only to the young or temperamentally vulnerable. (The use of stimulants as medicinals was a separate issue. In more profound states of exhaustion, as in the advanced stages of some diseases, powerful stimulants were regularly prescribed. And dietary or beverage tonics often were given to those emotionally or physically fatigued to prevent the development of more serious problems. Alcoholic beverages, coffee, and tea most often served this purpose. Tobacco, once a virtual panacea, was believed a specific remedy for a variety of problems. Its status as a therapeutic, however, eroded rapidly through the early decades of the nineteenth century.)

Thus, while in some aspects prescient in the warnings it offered Latter-day Saints of another century, Mormonism's early health code did not depart appreciably from the conventional wisdom of its day. And the LDS community responded to the new divine guidance much as might be expected. Predisposed to accept its basic message, they nevertheless showed considerable variation both in personal practices and in the community standard expected for good standing within the group. This variance reflected the differing contexts from which Mormon converts were drawn, as well as the fact that the Word of Wisdom was neither an absolute "commandment" nor the only divine instruction on the subject.

The *Book of Mormon* and Joseph Smith's subsequent revelations were believed to confirm, supplement, and occasionally correct the standard body of Christian canon already found in the Bible. The early Mormons thus accepted Old and New Testament precedents in many areas and usually found no inconsistency in their reading of ancient and modern scripture. This clearly was the case with the Word of Wisdom. The warnings on flesh, for example, were understood from the perspective of Paul's condemnation of those who required total abstinence from meat "which God hath created to be received with thanksgiving" (1 Timothy 4:3). This "doctrine of devils," as Paul labeled it, also was condemned—in very similar language—in latter-day revelation. In 1831, the Prophet announced that anyone who decreed absolute abstinence from meats "is not ordained of God; for, behold, the beasts of the field and the fowls of the air, and that which cometh of the earth, is ordained for the use of man for food and for raiment, and that he might have in abundance."[15]

Mormons also found further perspectives on alcohol. Though Leviticus (10:9) and Numbers (6:3) forbid the use of wine and strong drink to priests working in the tabernacle and to Nazarites, wine was a sacramental and celebratory drink in both Old and New Testament, and both wine and strong drink were endorsed medicinally. Indeed, the counsel of Proverbs (31:8) to "give strong drink unto him that is ready to perish, and wine unto those that be of heavy hearts," and Paul's advice (1 Timothy 5:23) to "use a little wine for thy stomach's sake and thine often infirmities" could as well have been lifted from nineteenth-century medical lore.

These additional scriptural precedents were comfortably accommodated by most of the leaders of the Latter-day Restoration. The Word of Wisdom itself advised that although ordinary use of wine was "not good," its use was appropriate in assembling yourselves together, to offer up your sacraments." Joseph Smith further looked to "the pattern set by our Savior Himself" in endorsing the use of wine at a wedding celebration, observing that "we feel disposed to patronize all the institutions of heaven."[16] Nor was there much concern about the use of stimulants medicinally. Notwithstanding the Word of Wisdom's narrow endorsement of alcohol only if topically applied, both alcohol and other proscribed "stimulants" were popular Mormon "remedies" throughout the nineteenth century.

With divine and human guidance in basic agreement, most early saints greatly reduced their usage of condemned items. Zebedee Coltrin, whose smoking at the School of the Prophets contributed to the revelation on health, recalled that twenty of the twenty-two elders who attended the school used tobacco—and that thereafter "all laid aside their pipes and use of tobacco."[17] Encouragement in this direction was found in spoken sermon, published article, and reprints from the non-Mormon press. And Mormons soon were noted for their general avoidance of coffee, tea, tobacco, and alcohol.

While adherence to the Word of Wisdom always has been strongly encouraged, the extent to which this has been *required* has varied dramatically. Initially attention was directed primarily at church officers. A year after the Word of Wisdom was announced, the church's High Council resolved that "no official member in this Church is worthy to hold an office, after having the Word of Wisdom properly taught him, and he, the official member, neglecting to comply with or obey it." Two years later the Seventies (a branch of the priesthood) in Kirtland resolved to discard the use of "ardent spirits of any kind," a commitment they felt necessary to reaffirm five months later.[18]

Soon attempts were made to mandate broader compliance. Two of the most important communities in the church, Kirtland, Ohio, and Far West, Missouri, voted, respectively, "to discountenance the use intirely of all liquors from the Church in Sickness & in health except wine at the Sacraments & for external Washing" and not to "fellowship any ordained member who will or does not observe the Word of *Wisdom according to its litteral reading.*"[19]

Throughout these early years, and notwithstanding the resolutions, Mormons continued to use wine on important occasions and regularly used proscribed items medicinally. Extensive use of wine, for example—both celebratory and sacramental—accompanied the dedication of the Kirtland temple, and wine is mentioned prominently in wedding celebrations of the day. Although a number of individuals were accused in church courts of violating the Word of Wisdom, this apparently was limited to cases involving drunkenness or some other major infraction as well. The defense of prominent Mormons accused in such cases clearly reflects the extent of acceptable usage. Oliver Cowdery, for example, justified his thrice daily use of tea during a Missouri winter for reasons of health.

During the Mormons' several-year sojourn in Nauvoo, Illinois, Joseph Smith led the church from its more restrictive initial view to a position of substantial tolerance on questions concerning the Word of Wisdom. A community brewery was approved, and ordinances passed that facilitated the sale of alcoholic beverages. The expressed rationale was often medicinal. An ordinance extending liquor licenses to ward representatives in early 1844, for example, went to some length to condemn the use of "distilled and fermented liquors . . . by persons in health." Individuals in less than optimal health—virtually the entire adult population—were a different story. The "aforesaid liquors are considered highly beneficial for medical and mechanical purposes, and may be safely employed for such uses, under the counsel of discreet persons."[20]

Whatever the rationale, the Prophet and other church leaders during these years clearly were comfortable drinking wine or beer on social occasions and using tea and coffee in their own homes. In one revealing encounter, Joseph Smith adjudicated the case of some brethren who had been drinking whiskey. On hearing their story, he concluded that "no evil had been done" and gave the offenders money with directions to "replenish the bottle to stimulate them in the fatigues of their sleepless journey." Another illustrative episode came in the hours prior to Joseph Smith's murder in the Carthage jail. He and other incarcerated leaders sent out for a pipe and tobacco to settle the stomach of one of the group, and a bottle of wine for all. Apostle (and later church president) John Taylor, who was there, responded to a report that the wine was taken as a sacrament: "It was no such thing; our spirits were generally dull and heavy, and it was sent for to revive us."[21]

In sum, by Joseph Smith's death the Mormons were not a "dry" community but one of moderation. He and his associates generally preferred not to "nip and tuck at the Word of Wisdom, but stress the integrity of one's heart." "Temperance in the extreme" was rejected, and there was no scandal associated with the public use of fermented drinks, coffee, tea, and tobacco. Although the Nauvoo temple was not completed until well after Joseph's death, it is clear that he would have endorsed the celebration held by faithful workers as they cleaned it up for formal dedication. A barrel of wine reserved for the occasion was brought out, and they "had a feast of cakes, pies, wine

&c., where we enjoyed ourselves with prayer, preaching, administering for healing, blessing children, and music and Dancing until near Midnight."[22]

This earliest phase in the history of the Word of Wisdom has been a source of discomfort to the twentieth-century church. Having eventually adopted a position of "temperance in the extreme," later church leaders chose to recast these formative years in the image of what ultimately was to follow. This notwithstanding, it is certainly true that the use of "stimulants" became much less an issue within the church during the 1840s—just as was true nationwide. Coffee, tea, tobacco, and alcohol were still considered potentially unhealthful in many circumstances, but probably in the same entirely discretionary sense that a modern Mormon would view high-calorie or high-cholesterol foods.

The move west did not appreciably change the perspective of the Nauvoo years. Indeed, church leaders recommended that Mormon pioneers include two pounds of coffee, five pounds of tea, and two-and-a-half gallons of alcohol among their supplies. And all these items were regularly used along the trail, both medicinally and socially.[23] Travelers who passed through Mormon country during the next few decades also found all still regularly in use, albeit at levels believed lower than elsewhere. Only liquor usage seemed dramatically lower than the national norm.

The later history of the Word of Wisdom can best be understood as two phases: 1850 to 1900, and 1900 to the present. During the first period, several retrenchments were undertaken, aimed at encouraging greater compliance with the health code. On occasion members or, more often, regional and local leaders were asked to commit to the discontinuance of the use of coffee, tea, tobacco, and alcohol, though by intent this commitment was never made mandatory. Typically the greatest attention was devoted to the youth, who it was hoped might grow up free of the habits of their elders. As a practical matter, however, even among church leaders there seems to have been no lasting shift in adherence, at least well into the 1880s. The usage among young people—especially of tobacco products—appeared if anything to increase toward the century's end.[24]

While it was hoped that obedience to the divine law would lead to the promised well-being, other concerns triggered the most extensive retrenchment efforts. By the last half of the century "stimulants" per se were no longer believed the basis for most ill health (if anything the perceived therapeutic value of alcohol, especially brandy, grew dramatically). Nor did the LDS experience, still dominated by infectious disease, reflect any appreciable advantage for even those who adhered most rigorously to the dietary code. What was clear, in the 1860s, was that too much of Zion's limited economic resource was lost to "gentiles" through expenditures on condemned items. Brigham Young, estimating that his followers were spending $100,000 a year on tobacco alone, therefore embarked on a several-year two-pronged crusade: (1) to promote greater adherence to the Word of Wisdom (as part of which he himself discontinued use of tobacco), and (2) to induce the Saints to produce their own tea, wine, and tobacco. Of these, wine production proved most successful. (In 1874, for example, a "wine mission" in southern Utah produced 100,000 gallons of wine.) Overall, however, church authorities remained very tolerant of those who failed to adhere to counsel, generally limiting formal action to cases involving the liquor trade or public intoxication. As was the case in Nauvoo (and Kirtland), completion of the first new Mormon temple in thirty years—in St. George, Utah, heart of the winemaking country—was marked by an extensive celebration of "wine & cakes."[25]

The 1880s brought an unprecedented federal anti-polygamy campaign which ultimately threatened the existence of the church. In this setting Mormon leaders again focused special attention on the Word of Wisdom, this time as a symbol of loyalty to the institution of the church and respect for the word of God. In essence adherence became for the first time a predominantly moral issue, a perspective that has continued to the present. Starting with the Quorum of the Twelve, which for the first time pledged strict personal compliance, Mormons again were enjoined to adhere to the health code. Those unwilling to do so were excluded from leadership positions in some communities and denied access to the prestigious "school of the prophets," a priesthood educational forum then being reestablished. The Relief Society (the LDS women's auxiliary) also extracted a pledge of compliance from its members.

This "reformation" largely ended just two years after it began when polygamous church leaders were forced underground. Nonetheless some modest net gains were made, though relapses abounded, as before, and, overall. Mormons continued extensive use of many condemned items. One lasting change came with a policy decision to end the "wine mission" and substitute water for wine in the sacrament. For a number of years thereafter both wine and water were used in the LDS sacrament service, depending on locale, but by 1900 water was used everywhere except in the temple (where sacramental wine continued in use until 1906).

As late as the presidency of Lorenzo Snow, who led the church from 1898 to 1901, hierarchal attitudes toward the Word of Wisdom were surprisingly varied. The First Presidency and Quorum of the Twelve were far from unanimous on such questions as whether more emphasis should be given to the warning against meat consumption (a point of particular emphasis in the 1860s and 1890s), how harshly the use of coffee and tea should be condemned, and whether beer—or at least Danish beer—should be condemned at all. (Narrowly read, beer is not part of the Word of Wisdom, which endorses barley "for mild drinks" and condemns only wine and distilled— "strong"—drink). Some senior leaders still used one questioned item or another, and even those who adhered strictly were not unanimous in believing mandatory compliance should be a precondition, for example, to temple attendance.[26]

The turn of the century brought a resurgent national temperance movement (culminating two decades later in Constitutional Prohibition), a new church president, and a renewed commitment to the principles of the Mormon health code. Under the administration of church president Joseph F. Smith (1901–18), who long had believed that revealed counsel should never be ignored, the use of wine in the temple finally was discontinued, and instruction issued that only those who would abstain from coffee, tea, tobacco, and alcohol would be ordained to the priesthood, sent on missions, admitted to the temple, or given leadership positions in local congregations. Eventually members involved in the sale or distribution of alcoholic beverages also were barred from church service, regardless of whether they used alcohol themselves (a restriction which lasted until midcentury). Implicit as well was a definitive deemphasis, which continues to the present, on the issue of meat consumption.

From at least the 1870s church leaders periodically considered and rejected the notion of legislating prohibition, largely because of a perceived conflict with the LDS commitment to "free agency." Joseph F. Smith did not share this perspective, and as church president he led the church into political activism on the issue. Official church support brought statewide prohibition to Utah in 1917.

Heber J. Grant, who succeeded Smith as church president in 1918, continued to emphasize absolute compliance with Word of Wisdom precepts. Special accommodations previously allowed those of advanced years and lifelong habits were no longer sanctioned. State legislation was aggressively and successfully supported which extended prohibition to tobacco products in 1921. Ecclesiastically, "liquor drinking" and "bootlegging" became grounds for excommunication. Tobacco prohibition proved unpopular, however, and was overturned in favor of controlled access in 1923. Thereafter, church leaders in 1929 successfully championed legislation to bar the advertisement of cigarettes on billboards, though the ban was declared unconstitutional just a few months later. Alcohol prohibition also soon ended in Utah, when the Twenty-first Amendment was enacted in 1933 (Utah having cast the decisive ratification vote *for* repeal).[27]

While prohibition is a long-dead subject, other legislation has drawn leadership attention. For decades church leaders opposed efforts to allow liquor by the drink in Utah, though this battle was largely lost in 1988 when minibottles were legalized. A formal stance was taken by the church in the early seventies, opposing the reduction of the legal drinking age in Washington State. Most recently the First Presidency in 1985 submitted their views to a U.S. Senate subcommittee hearing on alcoholism and drug abuse, in support of a ban or severe limitations on alcohol advertising.[28]

From the early twentieth century, the church's legislative activities were part of a larger moral and educational campaign—which continues little abated to the present day. Through slogan, song, and sermon, members—especially youth—were exhorted to abide by the Word of Wisdom. A content analysis shows this theme to have been dominant even among subjects addressed in the church leadership's important semiannual General Conferences (ranking 12th among 216 identified themes).[29] A content survey of editorials appearing in official LDS publications would have found the same emphasis continuing into recent years.

Although moral arguments figured prominently throughout these years, there was also a dominant new emphasis: "scientific support" for the Lord's counsel. From the very outset, of course, Mormons understood the Word of Wisdom to be fully sustained by respected medical principle, but rarely did they bother to explain the obvious by reference to contemporary authority. The advent of scientific medicine late in the nineteenth century, and its embrace by church leaders (discussed in Chapter 4), changed many things.

Turn-of-the-century LDS commentary, for example, could cite new evidence that coffee, tea, tobacco, and alcohol were either stimulating, narcotic, or poisonous. A recently discovered meat extract seemingly confirmed a stimulant factor there as well. Newly available data on death rates and scientific studies on experimental animals soon seemed to warrant entire books on the medical case for the Word of Wisdom. The church-published *Tobacco and Human Efficiency* (1918) was the first of a half dozen such works to appear over the next fifty years. Most influential of these was *The Word of Wisdom* by Apostle John Widtsoe and his wife, Leah, published in 1937 (with a revised edition in 1950).[30]

Ironically, prior to the last few decades, virtually all such writings have been based on new understanding subsequently proven to be to some degree in error. Despite implicitly undermining some key previous "evidence," however, each iteration in this progression has appeared to support even more solidly the LDS health code. In this setting, LDS writers have for over a century called attention to the new discoveries, and the prescience of Joseph Smith in anticipating "modern" medical wisdom 50, 100, or 150 years before its time.

Present-day writers most often now draw on sophisticated modern epidemiology research, which allows unprecedented insight into the relative risks of various personal and dietary habits. From the perspective of the Word of Wisdom, however, these latter studies allow a firm medical indictment only of tobacco and, for most people, immoderate use of alcohol. To make a categorical case against tea and coffee, LDS writers must still rely on much less definitive studies or popular but largely hypothetical concerns. Strict abstinence from the latter two therefore remain most often justified as symbolic of one's commitment to the church (with some expectation that one day a serious health risk will be demonstrated).

Attempts to extend more broadly the proscriptions of the Word of Wisdom, on the basis of principle, can be demonstrated throughout LDS history. In a sense, of course, anything alleged to be unhealthful could be deemed against the spirit of the Word of Wisdom. An eclectic collection of items have been so condemned, from hot soup, carbonation, white flour, and refined sugar to preservatives like sodium benzoate. Though some senior church leader at one time or another has condemned these and other items, there has been little popular or official support for these concerns.

Only foods containing true stimulants—for example, caffeine and related chemicals—have achieved a degree of quasi inclusion, "on principle," in the LDS health code. Almost from the beginning, an occasional LDS writer condemned the use of chocolate and cocoa. Since 1917 caffeine-containing soft drinks have received by far the greatest attention. Initial leadership concern centered on Coca-Cola and was based solely on the quantities of caffeine said to be present. In 1924, however, the Coca-Cola Company took exception to an apparent alliance between the church and the non-Mormon state health director of Utah against the dangers of Coke. Representatives were dispatched to meet with church president Heber J. Grant. They correctly persuaded him that Coca-Cola had only a fourth the caffeine of a comparable serving of coffee (rather than just the reverse, which the health director had claimed). As a result Grant, feeling "not the slightest desire to recommend that the people leave Coca Cola alone if this amount is absolutely harmless, which they claim it is," barred official church support for the anti-Coca-Cola campaign.[31]

Most visibly associated with the notion that *caffeine* should be the focus of church guidance on coffee and tea ("hot drinks") was Apostle John Widtsoe, who with others continued to crusade against caffeinated soft drinks (and, less emphatically, against chocolate and cocoa). Through his influence colas eventually were barred from most church institutions (for example, Brigham Young University), and their advertisement banned from official church periodicals. Consistent with this perspective, Widtsoe and, subsequently, the First Presidency also advised inquirers that the use of decaffeinated drinks (including "97 percent caffeine-free" coffee) was *not* in violation of the Word of Wisdom. Remarkably, this latter guidance, provided repeatedly by the First Presidency from the 1940s to the present, has yet to be officially published.[32]

To date the only official public guidance relating to the subject of caffeine-containing drinks was issued in 1972, on "Cola Drinks and the Word of Wisdom":

> The Word of Wisdom section 89 of the Doctrine and Covenants, remains as to terms and specifications as found in that section. There has been no official interpretation of that Word of Wisdom except that which was given by the Brethren in the very early days of the Church when it was declared that "hot drinks" meant tea and coffee.
>
> With reference to cola drinks, the Church has never officially taken a position on this matter, but the leaders of the Church have advised, and we do now specifically advise against the use of any drink containing harmful habit-forming drugs under circumstances that would result in acquiring the habit. Any beverage that contains ingredients harmful to the body should be avoided.[33]

Not surprisingly this statement was interpreted variously as both supporting and, more often, condemning the use of colas.

Current official guidance is even more succinct: "The only official interpretation of 'hot drinks' in the Word of Wisdom (*D&C* 89) is the statement that the term 'hot drinks' means tea and coffee. Members should not use any substance ['beverage," until 1989] that contains illegal drugs or other harmful or habit-forming ingredients."[34] And, anecdotally, large segments of the membership still find the official church view consistent with either their use or non-use of caffeine-containing soft drinks.

Regarding tobacco, alcohol, tea, and coffee, however, twentieth-century church leaders seem to have achieved a lasting level of compliance. Most survey data indicate overwhelming adherence to church counsel (with church-attending Mormons exceeding the 90 percent "abstinence" level). In comparison to others, Mormon men are only a fourth as likely as non-LDS men to smoke or use alcohol; and Mormon women only a fifth as likely.[35]

OTHER PREVENTIVE MEASURES

Though the Word of Wisdom dominates the LDS response to being well, it is only part of an extraordinary record of commitment to the maintenance of personal health. Prior even to the Word of Wisdom, Joseph Smith announced a revelation that briefly advised listeners to "cease to be idle; cease to be unclean; cease to find fault one with another; cease to sleep longer than is needful; retire to thy bed early, that ye may not be weary; arise early, that your bodies and your minds may be invigorated" (*D&C* 88:124). And, for over 150 years since that advice, Mormons have received a steady stream of concrete, church-sponsored guidance on issues of medical well-being. One can readily trace the progress of popular "scientific" thinking on preventive medicine through the pages of LDS periodicals.

Given the science of the day, the earliest guidance was at best of coincidental value. Severe corsets which may well have led to orthopedic problems were soundly condemned as causing tuberculosis or worse. Fruits or vegetables now known to be of value in preventing scurvy were recommended for this purpose among a host of others of no merit whatever. The tomato, a modestly useful addition to the frontier diet, was touted as a near miracle food. Rarely it was even suggested—for erroneous reasons—that water be boiled before consumption. More typical, unfortunately, was advice like that of Joseph Smith, who told immigrating converts that shallow wells in the lower parts of the city should be used in preference to river water, and that both were "more healthful to drink than spring water"—advice that in retrospect could hardly have been more medically off-target.[36]

Meaningful public health measures were rare. Attempts were made in Nauvoo to drain nearby swamps, in hopes of eliminating the fatal miasma believed to originate there. In the Salt Lake valley, a quarantine station was established to examine incoming immigrant parties. The quarantine could go well beyond a pro forma check. After an incoming company hid the fact of smallpox among its number, the First Presidency directed an extensive quarantine of all those potentially exposed to members of the group. It was further directed that "every locality of the disease be amply guarded by plain and abundant notices conspicuously posted at every approach thereto; and let there be no communication with the diseased, except by those who are not liable to the contagion."[37]

More generally, however, Mormons of the pioneer period were relaxed in their attitudes toward issues of personal and public health. When an 1855 "reformation" attempted among other things to promote weekly bathing, Brigham Young in presenting this goal forthrightly announced that it was not his practice, that he had tried it and found it "was not for everybody." This same year a frustrated Salt Lake City watermaster confronted Young over diverting through his hog pen the city creek that supplied virtually all the community's water. So far as Brother Brigham was concerned, "if he could drink his own filth he did not think others should complain."[38]

While the watermaster eventually prevailed, it was not because of public outrage, for this was a period, as a still imperfectly informed LDS physician later recalled, when

> the early settler could pile around him the offal and waste of living—the excreta from the pig-sty and out-house, the contents of the swill barrel could ferment alongside the larder—all these things could be had with little risk, for the "germs" were not [yet] present to . . . do their work of spreading contagion.[39]

In fact, as a locally assigned military surgeon correctly noted in the 1870s, the excessive childhood mortality of the day was in large part due to contamination of the well water used for drinking and culinary purposes by the "organic matters that settle down from the surface of the streets, yards, gutters, drains, water-closets, & etc., . . . and, as a consequence it becomes a purgative mixture, especially to strangers[,] and the amount of bowel disease, and deaths from its effects, is simply frightful, particularly among the children."[40]

With the emergence of scientific medicine late in the century, Mormon Utah and the rest of the nation slowly escaped from the grasp of the infectious diseases that so long had controlled life and death in America. The first substantial attempts to safeguard Salt Lake City's water supply were made and, more broadly, church-backed campaigns undertaken to improve sanitary conditions in Mormon communities. As part of this effort the First Presidency formally advised members:

> Much disease can be avoided by frequent ablutions, simple diet and the destruction or removal of all refuse. Cleanliness is part of godliness. Filth is obnoxious to the spirit of the Gospel. It is the breeding place for epidemics. Our bodies, our houses, our gardens and outhouses should all be kept free from uncleanly accumulations. Individual effort in this direction is a necessity, and this should be supplemented by organized regulations in the various wards (congregations) so that the atmosphere may not become charged with the germs of disease and death.[41]

The involvement of church leaders in public health matters further accelerated in the early twentieth century. (Voluntary) vaccination programs were supported and quarantine measures endorsed—even at the cost of impeding priesthood administrations to the sick. Access to the temple was restricted for those with apparently infectious diseases, and large tubs for literal ceremonial washings were replaced by a more hygienic symbolic gesture. Also for hygienic reasons, the traditional community sacramental cup was replaced by individual glass cuplets (and, years later, by small disposable paper cups).

At the community level several important church leaders, including later church president Heber J. Grant, became officers in the Utah Public Health Association (whose primary mission was tuberculosis control). One singularly successful combined church-community campaign was aimed at promoting the use of diphtheria toxin-antitoxin. An overall 80 percent reduction in diphtheria resulted, which transformed Salt Lake City's record from the worst in the West to one of the best. The church's Relief Society was also very involved in health promotion and worked actively to improve local milk supplies and to promote maternal and child health. For several entertaining years, it—along with other church and community health officials—sponsored a no-holds-barred "Swat the Fly" campaign, with generous rewards to those bringing in the most carcasses. (The grand winner brought in 707 quarts—by one estimate, over 9 million flies!) Less captivating but more effective in controlling the fly population were health department efforts—strongly supported through LDS publications—to eliminate cesspools and improve the sanitation of outhouses.[42]

Even well into the twentieth century, however, church-endorsed personal and public health insights could be strikingly imperfect. For decades LDS periodicals warned against the dangers of exhaled air, especially that which collected in unventilated bedrooms, and of the gaseous poisons that dissolved into drinking water left uncovered overnight. Equal attention was given to now archaic guidance on eating and bowel habits, and for a time Mormon girls could earn credits toward youth awards by, for one month, masticating their food "so thoroughly that it slips down without any visible effort at swallowing."[43] Mormons, for the sake of their health, also were encouraged for years to bathe in cold water, to dry with abrasive towels, and to wear as undergarments woolen long johns. Undergarments worn by women were to be supported solely from the shoulders. This curious guidance, though taken from Mormon sources, for the most part was simply "the latest" in popular health thinking. Indeed contemporary wisdom on underwear led to the relatively late claim that the temple undergarment itself—a slightly modified, shoulder-supported wrist-to-ankle union suit commonly made of wool—was clearly inspired in its prescient "physiologic" design.[44]

Although a lack of medical sophistication and an entrenched disposition to herbal remedies delayed meaningful reform in rural Utah, only rarely did Mormon belief itself obstruct public health progress. When this occurred, there usually was a perceived conflict with individual freedom of choice (or, as termed by Mormons, "free agency"). For example, compulsory vaccination of Utah school children was barred in 1901 by the Mormon-dominated state legislature, over the governor's veto. Though vaccination later was to become compulsory, for many years Utah had one of the highest rates of smallpox in the nation (albeit relatively low in comparison to nineteenth-century levels). Similar concerns delayed effective milk inspection. A vestige of this philosophy continues to the present in the continued refusal—through thirteen referenda over several decades—to allow fluoridation of Utah public water supplies.

Though health education continues to be an important function of current church manuals and periodicals, the high point in the member education program came in 1930, in the form of a 248-page lesson manual for adults on *Community Health and Hygiene*. Written by two professors at the University of Utah, this nationally commended handbook presented a forthright summary of the latest public health thinking on virtually every subject of community interest. In essence a university-level text, it has not been matched since in the relative sophistication of the health data provided.[45]

Although the church's more recent efforts at health education have not been as intensive or extensive as in the early decades of the twentieth century, the need today is probably somewhat less. And a substantial amount of health-related instruction continues to be provided, probably far more than is found in other denominations. When issues of particular note arise, the First Presidency in fact is now more likely to address them directly than was the case in the past. Several formal statements have been issued on immunization, including an endorsement of smallpox vaccination in 1900, support for the campaign against A-New Jersey (swine) influenza in 1976, and a broad statement of support for childhood immunizations in 1978. The latter, which remains the current position of the church, reads:

> Reports that increasing numbers of children are not being immunized against preventable childhood diseases deeply concern us. In the United States alone approximately 20 million children, 40 percent of those 14 years old or younger, have not been adequately immunized against polio,

measles, German measles (rubella), diphtheria, pertussis (whooping cough), mumps and tetanus.

Every parent who has agonized when these diseases have maimed or brought premature death to their children would join us, we are certain, in a plea to mobilize against these destroying diseases.

Immunization is such a simple, yet vital, matter and such a small price to pay for protection against these destroying diseases.

We urge members of The Church of Jesus Christ of Latter-day Saints to protect their own children through immunization. Then they may wish to join other public-spirited citizens in efforts to eradicate ignorance and apathy that have caused the disturbingly low levels of childhood immunization.

Failure to act could subject untold thousands to preventable lifelong physical or mental impairment, including paralysis, blindness, deafness, heart damage, and mental retardation.

Immunization campaigns in the United States and other nations, if successful, will end much needless suffering and erase the potential threat of epidemics. Such efforts are deserving of our full support.[46]

Perhaps second in significance to guidance on immunizations has been that on fluoridation. As noted earlier, Utah voters repeatedly have turned down propositions to fluoridate public water supplies. In conjunction with one of the more recent of the referenda (in 1972), the Presidency again chose not to endorse formally what opponents successfully portrayed as primarily a compulsory rather than public health program:

Questions are being asked regarding the Church's position on fluoridation of public water supplies to prevent tooth decay. As with other non-moral issues which may be under consideration or be brought before the voter by referendum, we reiterate the advice given by leaders of the church from time to time that it is the duty of every citizen to act in accordance with his or her convictions.

We have not in the past, nor do we now, seek to bring coercion or compulsion upon the church as to their actions. On the contrary, we have urged and do now urge that all citizens study the issue carefully and then act according to their honest conviction.[47]

As of 1985 only 2 percent of the Utah population had access to an optimally fluoridated water supply. On the other hand, nearly all physicians treating children prescribe topical or systemic fluorides, and about a third of Utah children have had dental sealants applied. These latter factors offset to some extent the disadvantages of not having a fluoridated water supply but still leave children in Utah with significantly more dental cavities than is the case nationally.[48]

HEALTH NOW

Like their nineteenth-century forebears, Mormons in some regards now do about as well medically as contemporaries in similar situations. Today, however, those in similar situations have exceptionally healthy life-styles— largely free of tobacco and alcohol, and with a lower-than-average incidence of several other demonstrated risk factors. Thus, in comparison to the national average, late-twentieth-century Mormons do extraordinarily well. On a number of counts, they do even better than currently can be explained.

Several factors are at play in this transformation in comparative health. By far the greatest factor was the identification nationally and elimination locally of the infectious diseases causing the overwhelming preponderance of nineteenth-century mortality—and against which Mormons had been as helpless as other Americans. In comparison to the stunning death rates of the nineteenth century, late-twentieth-century LDS health successes are only subtly greater than those of non-Mormons. Without the reduction of early crude death rates from the 30–40 per 1,000 range, to approximately a fourth that level now, LDS gains would not have emerged so clearly from the "background noise" of deaths from infectious disease.

A second major factor was the rise early in the twentieth century of the immensely powerful cigarette industry, a development that introduced by far the largest avoidable cause of twentieth-century adult mortality, alone now accounting for nearly a third of all cancer and heart deaths. The twentieth-century church's insistence on absolute adherence to aspects of the Word of Wisdom spared the large majority of Mormons an epidemic of tobacco-related diseases. In this context, mid- and late-twentieth-century LDS health did not so much get better; the health of others got worse.

Markedly reduced alcohol consumption among Mormons unquestionably has led also to much lower death rates from specific diseases like cirrhosis and cancer of the upper gastrointestinal tract. However, a net impact on overall mortality has yet to be demonstrated on this count, possibly because of a potentially offsetting impact on cardiovascular disease. Abstinence from coffee and tea has yet to be associated with any dramatic effect on Mormon health.

Other risk factors known to play a role in the development of various cancers are also less common among Mormons, in part for ecclesiastical reasons. These include age at first full-term pregnancy, number of sexual partners, and possibly amount of dietary fiber consumed. Potentially related Mormon health gains are noted below.

Finally, Mormons also may have profited through their adoption of the mountain West as a heartland. Westerners, and especially those in the inter-mountain region, have been shown to do somewhat better than average on a number of important counts, including a less sedentary life-style and somewhat less obesity, and—by inference—to suffer somewhat less cardio-vascular disease and stroke.[49] (Though there is a net gain in health, some lesser regional disadvantages also can be shown. Goiter was a serious re-gional problem well into the twentieth century, and rheumatic fever re-mained unusually common even later. Diseases related to sun-exposure, such as melanoma and cancer of the lip, remain a comparatively high risk in the region.)

For over a century Mormons have believed on the basis of scriptural promise that they enjoy above-average health. In fact the actual record prob-ably only began to match their expectations a half-century ago, about the time when a flawed study—by Mormons seeking validation of church teach-ings—asserted on the basis of published death rates that Mormons had about half the cancer incidence of those in six industrialized nations used for comparison, and much less heart, kidney, and lung disease. Mormons were said also to have substantially less nervous and digestive disease and only a small fraction of the expected incidence of tuberculosis and diabetes. Beyond the general unreliability of the diagnostic data, the comparisons failed to consider the unusually large proportion of young people in Mormon commu-nities who were not subject to death from the chronic diseases of adulthood. However, time would prove the author (coincidentally) correct with regard to cancer and heart disease, which were about to emerge as the leading killers of adult Americans.[50]

It was not until the 1970s that LDS health received serious epidemiologi-cal attention. Following James Enstrom's pioneering study of Mormon (and Seventh-day Adventist) cancer mortality, there have been over a score of scientifically responsible articles looking either directly at the health of Mormons (in California, Utah, and Canada), or somewhat more broadly, of Utahns (70 percent of whom are LDS).[51] Expectedly, these studies have shown Mormons to have a substantially lower-than-average incidence (less than half) of diseases associated with tobacco or alcohol: cancer of the gum and mouth, tongue, pharynx, lung, esophagus, bladder, and cervix (the latter being associated with tobacco use and with multiple sex partners, both low-incidence risk factors in LDS communities). Incidence rates also are significantly lower (by 15 to 50 percent, depending on gender and disease) for cardiovascular diseases, cirrhosis of the liver, and low-birth-weight infants.

Less readily explained on the basis of known risk factors is a 30–40 percent lower incidence of colon cancer and a 20–50 percent lower incidence of cancer of the stomach, pancreas, uterus, ovary, and prostate. Seventh-day Adventists, with a similar health code, attribute their comparably low colon cancer death rates to the vegetarianism of half their membership, but studies of Mormons show LDS meat consumption to be as high or higher than national averages. The fiber or fat content of LDS diets may eventually explain this finding. Only half of a 30-percent lower incidence of breast cancer in LDS women can be explained by a known risk factor—early childbearing—though less tobacco use may be a factor here. Similarly only half of the comparably lower levels of cardiovascular disease can be attributed to low levels of tobacco use among Mormons. An unusually low infant mortality rate among Mormons probably also involves factors beyond alcohol and tobacco use, and the low incidence of neural tube defects (for example, spina bifida) among Mormon babies remain equally unexplained.[52]

Especially intriguing are findings that attempt to correlate "activity level" (level of church involvement) among Mormons (and thereby compliance with church guidelines) with the incidence of various diseases.[53] Those conditions known to be associated with tobacco and alcohol are demonstrably much more common among less active (presumably less compliant) members. Intriguingly, there are other diseases in which Mormons as a group also do well—such as cancer of the colon and rectum, prostate, pancreas, ovary, and breast—which do not show this correlation with church activity. Equally curious, the incidence of other cancers—such as stomach cancer, leukemia, and lymphoma—for which there was no obvious risk factor that could be associated with the strength of LDS commitment are found to correlate with church activity. Clearly, it will be some time before all the demonstrated epidemiologic patterns can be fully explained.

The most recent and in some ways most striking study of Mormon health raises some interesting questions. This prospective 1989 study of religiously active Mormons in California found that middle-aged LDS high priests (the highest level of the lay priesthood) who were physically active and got proper sleep had mortality rates (standardized mortality ratios) dramatically below that expected in comparison to other white males: 68 percent less from cancer, 86 percent less from cardiovascular disease, and 78 percent less from all causes of death. As remarkable as were these findings, the author further found that the results could be replicated in a non-LDS comparison group composed of white, nonsmoking men who attended church weekly—despite, from the Mormon perspective, use by the latter group of alcohol (69 percent), coffee (82 percent), and tea (24 percent). Thus, while the comparatively excellent health of Mormons has been documented yet again, important questions remain concerning the reasons.[54]

Among the most definitive measures of good health is, of course, actual longevity. Reducing age-specific death rate by 50 percent—for example, from 2 (per 100) to 1—only increases survival for the year from 98 percent to 99 percent. As these are approximately the actual age-specific death rates for middle-aged people in the U.S., Mormon gains from one point of view are relatively slight. The cumulative effect, over twenty or thirty years, of this slight advantage can be considerable, however. Life table analysis of the LDS record suggests that in the U.S. life expectancy for Mormon males is about 5½ years longer than for non-Mormons, and for Mormon females about 3½ years. Religously active Mormons may fare better by two or so years. Continued national attention on risk factor reduction, however, is beginning to change the health of Americans in general, so it will be interesting to see how long the LDS differential remains. It well may be that distinctive Mormon health will prove a phenomenon unique to the twentieth century.[55]

· 4 ·

On Healing

The Mormon restoration occurred at a time in American history when urbanization and population growth were leading to unprecedented levels of death and disease. Would-be healers, unable to distinguish between early symptoms of benign everyday maladies and those of potentially fatal illnesses, were also (in retrospect) largely powerless to alter the natural course of disease. In this uncertain context, anxious sufferers, family, and friends turned to an increasing variety of practitioners and remedies. Early Mormons were among the many who also sought the healing powers of religion.

This legacy, in somewhat modified form, is still solidly in evidence in the twentieth-century church. While Mormons now more than ever seek out secular medicine when confronted by serious illnesses, they as well continue to turn in faith and confidence to some of the healing ordinances that proved so reassuring to their ancestors. For most Latter-day Saints, not even the miracle of modern medicine has greatly changed this perspective.

The nature of the secular help now sought in times of illness is itself a partial reflection of the nineteenth-century church. On the strength of early guidance that those with insufficient faith to be healed should eschew orthodox treatments in favor of herbal remedies, a significant segment of the LDS community continues disposed to seek out herbal and naturopathic cures. Twentieth-century church leaders oppose the perpetuation of this archaic facet of the Mormon tradition. Heirs to an undercurrent of pragmatism also evident from the earliest days, they with most Mormons seek out the best that modern medicine has to offer.

BY FAITH AND POWER

Among the signs of the Restoration anticipated by early Mormon primitivists were the charismatic gifts of the New Testament. Prominent among these was the gift of healing. Jesus had cured many and given to his twelve apostles the power "to heal all manner of sickness and all manner of disease" (Matthew 10:1, 8). Though the ancient Twelve were particularly identified with this power, it was to the elders that Christians of the primitive church turned in times of illness. In the familiar words of James 5:14–15, "Is any sick among you? let him call for the elders of the church; and let them pray over him, anointing him with oil in the name of the Lord: And the prayer of faith shall save the sick, and the Lord shall raise him up."

The *Book of Mormon* reported faith healing as well, for Christ's New World disciples like those in the Old "did heal the sick, and raise the dead, and cause the lame to walk, and the blind to receive their sight, and the deaf to hear" (Alma 16:5–11, 4 Nephi 5).

Expectedly, Joseph Smith's restoration also anticipated and experienced these healing gifts. Within days of the organization of the church, Smith healed an afflicted prospective convert, Newell Knight, by taking his hand and commanding that he be healed.[1] Just a few weeks later, the Prophet announced a revelation which in essence restated Mark 16:17–18 in cautioning expectant converts that miracles should not be demanded "except casting out devils, healing the sick, and against poisonous serpents, and against deadly poisons."[2]

By the end of the year, the faithful had revelatory promise that the time for bestowing New Testament gifts was almost at hand, when "I [God] will show miracles, signs, and wonders, unto all those who believe on my name. And whoso shall ask it in my name in faith, they shall cast out devils; they shall heal the sick; they shall cause the blind to receive their sight, and the deaf to hear, and the dumb to speak, and the lame to walk."[3] If converts would comply with a divine instruction to move from New York to Ohio (to escape local persecution), they would be "endowed with power from on high."[4]

A few weeks later, in Ohio, another revelation was received which became a cornerstone of Mormon belief and practice. Combining the therapeutic approach of James (5:13–14) and Mark (6:13) with the expected results of Matthew (11:5) and Luke (7:22), this statement instructed that

whosoever among you are sick, and have not faith to be healed, but believe, shall be nourished with all tenderness, with herbs and mild food, and that not by the hand of an enemy. And the elders of the church, two or more, shall be called, and shall pray for and lay their hands upon them in my name; and if they die they shall die unto me, and if they live they shall live unto me. . . . And again, it shall come to pass that he that hath faith to see shall see. He who hath faith to hear shall hear. The lame who have faith to leap shall leap. And they who have not faith to do these things, but believe in me, have power to become my sons; and inasmuch as they break not my laws thou shalt bear their infirmities.[5]

This encouraging message, now section 42 of the church's official *Doctrine and Covenants,* included provisions to accommodate all outcomes, including those in which physical ailments persisted. Either (1) the individual's faith was such that he was healed, (2) he remained ill but without jeopardizing his spiritual rewards or social standing, or (3) he died a "sweet death . . . appointed by the Lord."

Subsequent revelations regularly reaffirmed this basic message. A month later the Saints again were told that "to some it is given to have faith to be healed; and to others it is given to have faith to heal."[6] A new "high" priesthood was bestowed on selected elders in June 1831, further raising the expectation that this would usher in a new wealth of healing and other charismatic gifts. The next year, a revelation to "mine apostles, even God's high priests," again reaffirmed Mark 16:17–18 in describing the signs that would follow "them that believe": "In my name they shall cast out devils; in my name they shall heal the sick; in my name they shall open the eyes of the blind, and unstop the ears of the deaf; and the tongue of the dumb shall speak; and if any man shall administer poison unto them it shall not hurt them; and the poison of the serpent shall not have power to harm them."[7]

Early converts found much to confirm the presence within their community of the promised healing gifts. Newell Knight, within months of his own cure, was baptized, and as an ordained elder en route to Ohio he cured a woman's broken arm by "rebuk[ing] the pain with which she was suffering and command[ing] her to be made whole."[8] A few weeks later, a visitor to the Knights' new home in Ohio recovered from a "rheumatic arm" when Joseph Smith "commanded" her "to be whole."[9] The episode, triggered by the inquiry of some visitors about whether God had given "any power to man now on the earth to cure her," led to the conversion of several onlookers.

The early years in Ohio and Missouri (to which some Saints were sent beginning in the summer of 1831) were particularly marked by miraculous healings and the successful casting out of devils. Beginning in this period— but extending throughout the century—both Mormon diaries and periodicals abound with accounts of those who recovered after priesthood ministrations. Wilford Woodruff, early Mormon apostle and in 1890 church president, catalogued well over a thousand healing administrations which he performed during his lengthy career, noting that "many were healed by the power of God. Devils were Cast out, the Dumb spake, the Deaf heard, The blind saw, the lame walked The sick were raised up and in one instance the dead were raised in the Case of my own wife After the spirit left her body."[10]

Although a healing "ordinance" early became dominant in the Mormon community, involving the application of oil as prescribed in the New Testament, there were circumstances in which the laying on of hands alone seems to have remained relatively common. A particularly striking episode occurred during the summer of 1839, the first spent by the Mormons on the banks of the Mississippi, in what was to become the city of Nauvoo. As this marks what is still described as "the most massive charismatic healing of the modern Church,"[11] it is worth recounting in some detail. Many facets of the Mormon view of faith healing are well illustrated by events taking place during or following this event.

As described in a popular later account, Joseph Smith and many of his followers had fallen sick in their new refuge—in retrospect to what was undoubtedly one of two strains of malaria in the area.

> On the morning of the 22nd of July, 1839, [Joseph Smith] arose, reflecting upon the situation of the Saints of God in their persecutions and afflictions, and he called upon the Lord in prayer, and the power of God rested upon him mightily, and as Jesus healed all the sick around Him in His day, so Joseph, the Prophet of God, healed all around on this occasion. He healed all in his house and door-yard, then, in company with Sidney Rigdon and several of the Twelve, he went among the sick lying on the bank of the river and he commanded them in a loud voice, in the name of Jesus Christ, to come up and be made whole, and they were all healed. When he healed all that were sick on the east side of the river, they crossed the Mississippi river in a ferry-boat to the west side, to Montrose, where we were. The first house they went into was President Brigham Young's. He was sick on his bed at the time. The Prophet went into his house and healed him, and they all came out together. As they were passing by my door, Brother Joseph said: "Brother Woodruff, follow me." These were the only words spoken by any of the company from the time they left Brother Brigham's house till we crossed the public square, and entered Brother Fordham's house. Brother Fordham had been dying for an hour, and we expected each minute would be his last.
>
> I felt the power of God that was overwhelming His Prophet.
>
> When we entered the house, Brother Joseph walked up to Brother Fordham, and took him by the right hand; in his left hand he held his hat.
>
> He saw that Brother Fordham's eyes were glazed, and that he was speechless and unconscious.
>
> After taking hold of his hand, he looked down into the dying man's face and said: "Brother Fordham, do you not know me?" At first he made no

reply; but we could all see the effect of the Spirit of God resting upon him.

He again said: "Elijah, do you not know me?"

With a low whisper, Brother Fordham answered, "Yes!"

The Prophet then said, "Have you not faith to be healed?"

The answer, which was a little plainer than before, was: "I am afraid it is too late. If you had come sooner, I think I might have been."

He had the appearance of a man waking from sleep. It was the sleep of death.

Joseph then said: "Do you believe that Jesus is the Christ?"

"I do, Brother Joseph," was the response.

Then the Prophet of God spoke with a loud voice, as in the majesty of the Godhead: "Elijah, I command you, in the name of Jesus of Nazareth, to arise and be made whole!"

The words of the Prophet were not like the words of man, but like the voice of God. It seemed to me that the house shook from its foundation.

Elijah Fordham leaped from his bed like a man raised from the dead. A healthy color came to his face, and life was manifested in every act.

His feet were done up in Indian meal poultices. He kicked them off his feet, scattered the contents, and then called for his clothes, and put them on. He asked for a bowl of bread and milk, and ate it; then put on his hat and followed us into the street, to visit others who were sick. . . .

As soon as we left Brother Fordham's house, we went into the house of Joseph B. Noble, who was very low and dangerously sick. When we entered the house, Brother Joseph took him by the hand, and commanded him, in the name of Jesus Christ to arise and be made whole. He did arise and was immediately healed.

While this was going on, the wicked mob in the place, led by one Kilburn, had become alarmed, and followed us into Brother Noble's house.

Before they arrived there, Brother Joseph had called upon Brother Fordham to offer prayer.

While he was praying the mob entered, with all the evil spirits accompanying them.

As soon as they entered, Brother Fordham, who was praying, fainted and sank to the floor.

When Joseph saw the mob in the house, he arose and had the room cleared of both that class of men and their attendant devils. Then Brother Fordham immediately revived and finished his prayer.

This shows what power evil spirits have upon the tabernacles of men. The Saints are only saved from the power of the devil by the power of God.

This case of Brother Noble's was the last one of healing upon that day. It was the greatest day for the manifestation of the power of God through the gift of healing since the organization of the Church.

When we left Brother Noble, the Prophet Joseph went with those who accompanied him from the other side, to the banks of the river, to return home.

> While waiting for the ferry-boat, a man of the world, knowing of the miracles which had been performed, came to him and asked him if he would not go and heal two twin children of his, about five months old, who were both lying sick nigh unto death.
> They were some two miles from Montrose.
> The Prophet said he could not go; but, after pausing some time, he said he would send some one to heal them; and he turned to me and said: "You go with the man and heal his children."
> He took a red silk handkerchief out of his pocket and gave it to me, and told me to wipe their faces with the handkerchief when I administered to them, and they should be healed. He also said unto me: "As long as you will keep that handkerchief, it shall remain a league between you and me."
> I went with the man, and did as the Prophet commanded me, and the children were healed.
> I have possession of the handkerchief unto this day.[12]

This retrospective account, written by participant Woodruff and popularized in a series of books for young Mormons, is now included in the official history of the church.[13] Two aspects of the episode merit comment.

First, Smith accomplished these charismatic healings without any formal ritual or ordinance. Taking the afflicted "by the hand & in a loud voice [he] Command[ed] them in the name of Jesus Christ to arise from their beds & be made whole."[14] Although the twentieth-century church became concerned with the formalization of this and other ordinances, the earliest Mormons were not particularly constrained by form.

Second, the magic-like use of the handkerchief—presumably inspired by the example of Paul, who used handkerchiefs and aprons to accomplish healing (Acts 19:12)—was without precedent in the church to that point, and healing artifacts other than consecrated oil played a very limited role in the tradition thereafter. In later years Wilford Woodruff infrequently used this same handkerchief in blessing the sick;[15] and Heber C. Kimball, of the First Presidency, while in England occasionally blessed either his cane (made from the wood of a coffin in which Joseph Smith's body temporarily had been placed) or pocket handkerchief and sent one of these to those soliciting healing administrations to which he could not attend—"and they were healed by their faith in the priesthood of the God of Israel." The faithful English Saints were said also to have sought Kimball's cloak "and put it on the bed and often find immediate relief & recover."[16] At least one English patriarch later put his own walking stick to the same successful use as had Kimball.[17]

Notwithstanding the miraculous events of 22 July, the summer of 1839 was marked by high mortality and continual relapses among survivors—as would be expected in malarial infections. That the contemporaneous records indicate no disillusionment suggests that the Mormons, at least by this period, implicitly understood and accepted the limitations of the healing ordinance. The 1832 revelation on faith healing included ample provision for what might overwise have been disconfirming "failures." If the afflicted had not sufficient faith, or if death was "appointed by the Lord," even the power of the Twelve might prove insufficient. The Prophet warned his newly constituted quorum of twelve apostles in 1836, just prior to a promised new endowment of power to accompany completion of the Kirtland temple, that though much healing could be accomplished "through your instrumentality . . . you will not have power after the endowment to heal those that have not faith, nor to benefit them, for you might as well expect to benefit a devil in hell as such an one, who is possessed of his spirit and are willing to keep it for they are habitations for devils and only fit for his society."[18]

From at least the Ohio years it was acknowledged that even the faith of afflicted true believers could prove inadequate to the challenge. Apostle John Taylor noted that "the prayer of faith heals the sick and the Lord raises him up. They are not always healed but generally according to their faith."[19] He addressed this point again a few years later, at the close of yet another decimating summer, and wrote that "we believe that if we only had faith, 'all things are possible to them that believe.' . . . But if we have not faith to be healed, as many of us have not, then we think our course is clearly defined."[20] A contemporary historian, who had embraced then discarded Mormonism, put it more bluntly:

> The Mormons believe in, and constantly practice the laying on of hands and praying for the healing of the sick. . . . If they are healed they say it was because of their faith, as the Savior promised, 'According to thy faith be it unto thee; thy faith hath made thee whole,' etc. (Matt. 8:13, and 9:22). If partly healed, it is still according to their faith, as it was said of some in old times, 'And they began to amend from that very hour'; but if they are not healed, or benefitted at all, then it is for want of faith, as when the lunatic was brought to the disciples and they could not heal him because of their disbelief. (Matt. 17:20; 13:58.) But they think in this as in many other cases, practice makes perfect, and it is necessary to an increase in faith, confidence and the power of God.[21]

The record on this score was clear enough that church leaders advised members not to test manifestly inadequate faith through imprudent actions. In 1841, for example, immigrating English converts were told to avoid the Mississippi during the sickly summer season "till there is more faith in the

Church."[22] Similar advice was later given to those who would head West via the Missouri River, where cholera already had claimed over a hundred brethren. Unless the faith of Mormon travelers was exceptionally strong, they were "as liable as any other people to fall victims" and should find an alternative route.[23]

The assumption that deaths may have been appointed by the Lord has been addressed in Chapter 2. This notion was invoked frequently by parents seeking solace at the loss of a child. John Nuttall, for example, wrote in his diary of the death of a son years later, despite repeated administrations, including one from church president John Taylor, "The Lord seemed to want him."[24] More generally, apostle Woodruff no doubt spoke for many when he wrote in his diary, "Some are much tryed because all are not healed that they lay hands upon but I do not feel so. I had a Case during Conference concerning the case of Sister Baris. She was sick & I laid Hands upon her & blessed her with life & health & went to meeting. In an hour I had word that she was dead. It did not try me. The Lord saw fit to take her & all is right."[25]

There could be other impediments to a successful healing, as the relapse experience by Brother Fordham (quoted above) illustrated. It had been taught at least since the Ohio years that the healing gifts might become ineffective in the presence of skeptics. If necessary, elders were to use their inspired judgment in ordering skeptics away, which, though generating a critical response, was perfectly compatible with the core belief that it was inappropriate to exercise healing gifts in response to provocations. The Saints were taught that the Devil himself was behind taunts that they prove themselves, by cutting off an arm, for example, and then restoring it through priesthood power. In theory miracles were to follow belief, not generate it. In practice, of course, many early nonbelievers converted to the church after witnessing a Mormon healing.

Joseph also taught, echoing an early revelation,[26] that lack of faith on the part of the elder could be a problem. In the wake of the summer of 1839, apostle Parley P. Pratt recorded that Smith, "while in the Spirit, rebuked the Elders who would continue to lay hands on the sick from day to day without the power to heal them. Said he: 'It is time that such things ended. Let the Elders either obtain the power of God to heal the sick, or let them cease to minister the forms without the power.'"[27] In a less stressful spring two years later the Prophet put this more positively when he advised newly arrived English converts that all would not have the same gifts: "If a man has not faith enough to do one thing, he may have faith enough to do another; if he cannot remove a mountain, he may heal the sick."[28]

Relapses plaguing the Twelve themselves might have been more trouble-some. Even here there was a reasonable explanation. Apostles Brigham Young, Heber C. Kimball, John Taylor, and Wilford Woodruff, all partici-pants in the charismatic events of July 1839, were still seriously ill a month or more later when they set out on missions to England. As Woodruff viewed the relapses, however, "the enemy [that is, Satan] is striving to bind us down that we shall not go into the vineyard."[29] Through perseverance, however, he and his colleagues would—and did—prevail.

There were some in these early years whose failed expectations led to a loss of faith. For example, among the widely publicized charges of the "first Mormon apostate"—a minister originally converted by a charismatic heal-ing—was the claim that Joseph Smith failed to raise a child from the dead.[30] While this specific charge became popular in the press, it seems not to have been a major concern within the church.[31] One has the impression that the early elders performed their ordinances in faith and hoped things worked out. After the very earliest years few had expectations of universally success-ful results. Even what were reported as resurrections of the dead—resuscita-tions in the minutes immediately following apparent death—did not lead to overly optimistic expectations. As with those Saints who, during the very earliest months of the Mormon restoration, expected that by obeying the covenant they would never die, experience taught them "to the contrary."[32]

ANOINTING WITH OIL

While administrations could involve only the laying on of hands, with an associated healing blessing or "command," it was early the practice to follow the guidance of James 5 and Mark 6 and anoint the afflicted with oil. Exactly when this was introduced is unclear. The first known anointing occurred in November 1835, and perhaps spurred by the introduction of temple-related anointings the following year, it quickly became a common practice.[33] What-ever its date of origin, by the mid-1850s anointing had been identified as the appropriate response to illness, and not the laying on of hands alone. As a member of the First Presidency pointedly observed,

> People neglect to anoint with oil when they should and might use it. I have seen the Elders try to cast out devils, and to accomplish it they have fasted, and prayed, and laid on hands, and rebuked the devil, but he would not go out. I have then seen them bring consecrated oil, and anoint the person possessed of the devil, and the devil went out forthwith. That taught me a good lesson—that God Almighty, when He speaks, means what He says. . . Unless you anoint with oil, your prayers will not rise

higher than the fog, and you know that it seldom rises much higher than the tops of the mountains.[34]

When anointing for health was performed, olive oil was used, both in compliance with the biblical precedent and because it was the only oil in common use. While this was to become mandatory, initially there was some variation—as an early apostolic use of "oil of peppermint" attests. Before use the oil was consecrated through a simple prayer. Although consecrated oil later was made available as a service of Mormon temples, the fact that any elder has the authority to consecrate oil gradually led to this being done largely on an individual basis, or in a Sunday priesthood meeting.[35]

The healing ritual itself involved the administration of the oil and a "sealing" which ratified the ordinance. The latter took the form of a simple laying on of hands with an accompanying prayer very much akin to what occurred when the laying on of hands was used alone. The oil generally was anointed to the crown of the head of the sufferer, but at least as early as 1844 was applied elsewhere on the body or taken internally.[36] By this time a more extensive washing and anointing was part of the temple ceremony, including a symbolic anointing of various organs with a blessing of continued health. Temple-associated rituals therefore possibly provided further precedent for more extensive applications in the healing ordinance.

Oil that had been consecrated was early understood to have a therapeutic or medicinal role as well as a purely ritualistic one. This unquestionably encouraged the practice of anointing both the head *and* the area where it would do the most good. From the 1840s to the early twentieth century, private diaries and published accounts detail innumerable therapeutic applications, to burns and sore eyes, under bandages on wounds, and over aches and pains. Abnormal swellings, from goiter to lifelong malformations, typically were anointed directly; and for internal problems, such as bowel disease, the oil was taken by mouth.[37]

The anointings could be quite extensive and, as in the nineteenth-century temple ordinance, involve the copious application of oil. Confronted by a case of serious skeletal deformities, one administrator applied oil simultaneously to head, back, ribs, and chest. Another local leader recorded the beneficial effects of first bathing "with whiskey," then anointing "all over with consecrated oil."[38] Brigham Young himself reported feeling "much Better" after an anointing "from the Crown of his head to the Soles of his feet."[39] Alternatively, in systemic or more generalized conditions, oil could be administered by mouth. It was also given orally when emotional problems were prominent. In one case, a woman ranting "out of her mind" responded to applications to both head and throat.[40]

A confirmatory view of the medicinal merits of olive oil was held by mid- to late-nineteenth-century American physicians, a point noted with satisfaction in church periodicals.[41] Eventually LDS physicians themselves addressed the therapeutic question through the pages of the *Salt Lake City Sanitarian*. "The Lord in His divine laws and regulations exhibits 'in all His ways' an exalted degree of the 'eternal fitness of all things,'" these faithful physicians wrote, "And in the selection of olive oil for the 'anointing of the sick' He has not deviated from the divine rule."[42] They unhesitatingly recommended olive oil—consecrated or otherwise—both topically and internally. Believing that the oil was absorbed through the skin, they argued that it nourished at the same time it reduced fever, and they specifically commended its "profuse" usage for skin conditions, for wasting diseases such as consumption and typhoid, and for eruptive fevers like measles, scarlet fever, and smallpox. They also found it useful for constipation, burns, joint and muscle pain, pneumonia, and poisoning. Depending on the circumstances, the doctors suggested that it be applied locally, administered as a bath or an enema, or taken by mouth in "large draughts."[43]

With emerging public health awareness, pioneer sanitarians had one pointed suggestion. The "cheaper grade [of olive oil] so extensively purchased [in Utah] is adulterated with pernicious oils and fats that render it absolutely unfit for anointing the sick or giving internally." It was "miserable stuff, possibly a good deal of Chicago lard . . . or something worse." More prudence was clearly indicated in the purchase of oil. Some also suggested— presumably on therapeutic grounds—that the recently popularized cottonseed oil would serve as well "if not better" than olive oil.[44] Though perhaps sensitized to the adulteration issue by the doctors' comments, church leaders declined to abandon traditional usage. Subsequent official guidelines consistently have advised that "pure olive oil" be used exclusively in administering to the sick.

The turn of the century brought a revision in church thinking on the role of consecrated oil in illness. In the wake of the revolution in scientific medicine, the medicinal-like usage of consecrated oil was discountenanced in favor of a much more narrowly conceived role in a ritual that itself became much more institutionalized at this same time. By 1903 there was counsel against using consecrated oil internally.[45] However, in specifying that the crown of the head was the appropriate site for ordinary administrations, it also was reaffirmed that there were "occasions of disease or accident when it is desirable that other parts of the body be anointed."[46] (The latter practice was probably sustained to some extent by health-related temple rituals discussed below. As in the case of anointings, these rituals were reconsidered about this time, and some discontinued.) Over the next two decades the usage of oil became even more circumscribed. A transition can be seen during which limited topical use of oil was endorsed where some plausible medicinal value could still be assumed, for example, as an adjunct when massaging a young child. As late as 1914 a Relief Society health lesson suggested "cotton dipped in warm consecrated oil" be used to relieve earaches.[47]

By the 1920s, the therapeutic topical use of consecrated oil seems no longer to have been sanctioned. Remnants of this long-engrained tradition continued, of course, but in a more sub-rosa setting. In 1928, for example, a woman suffering from a breast lump unresponsive to previous administrations was advised to anoint it "every day with olive oil" but to "tell no one."[48] Over a decade later, in 1939, the church still felt the need officially to instruct priesthood holders that "giving consecrated oil internally is not a part of the administration and should not be done" and the following year to remind local leaders "that it is the prayer of faith that saves the sick, and the Lord who raises them up, not the oil, though we are commanded to anoint with oil, in the name of the Lord. Consecrated oil should not be used indiscriminately or comingled with other ointments."[49]

Given the assumed medicinal qualities of consecrated oil, it is not surprising that whatever the site of anointing, early sufferers often received multiple applications. Joseph Smith advised his followers that when the elders did not prevail, if the family "should get power by fasting & prayer & anointing with oil & *continue so to do*[,] their sick shall be healed" (emphasis added).[50] Throughout the nineteenth century, therefore, serious or prolonged illnesses called forth multiple anointings—on a daily, hourly, or even minute-by-minute basis.[51] Brigham Young affords a well-known example, as he was administered to repeatedly throughout his week-long final illness. As late as the turn of the century, church periodicals carried numerous accounts of such persistent efforts, including administrations daily over a period of several weeks, of the consumption of a bottle of consecrated oil "every twenty-four hours," and of anointings repeated a number of times in succession.[52] In one illustrative account, a "little Mormon girl" wrote that she had been sick for four months, "but papa has taken to administering to me every night, and I am almost well."[53]

The rationale for the repetitions seems to have varied. Even when a cure was not effected, there appears often to have been temporary improvement following an anointing, which clearly would encourage repeat administrations. A continued illness might suggest a need for greater faith, perhaps requiring more fasting and prayer, or the need to summon a person of greater stature—such as an apostle—to repeat the ordinance. Early in the century, there also were a number of occasions when it was believed that a banished devil was repeatedly returning to the body of the afflicted, who thus required continual priesthood intervention.

Unquestionably a major function of repeated administrations was to reflect continued concern on the part of those in attendance, and to assure that everything possible was being done to stay the course of disease. This was especially so in those too frequent cases that followed an unrelenting, terminal course. As one faithful father wrote in his diary, in the midst of what proved to be a fatal illness in his young daughter: "Felt calm. I have done all that lay in my power. Had the Elders administer to her; had her prayed for in the temple and the Doctor [h]as done what he thought best for her, yet she keeps sinking in a dull stupor."[54]

At about the same time church leaders moved to circumscribe the site of anointings, they also began to discourage repeated applications. In 1903 church president Joseph F. Smith wrote that "care should be taken to avoid unwarranted repetitions. When an administration is made, and when the blessing pronounced upon the afflicted one has been received, the ordinance should not be repeated."[55] Smith's counsel was quoted in subsequent priesthood instructions, which labeled the previous practice "vain repetitions"— an allusion to a *Book of Mormon* prophet's warning that "when ye pray, use not vain repetitions, as the heathen, for they think that they shall be heard for their much speaking." (3 Nephi 13:7) This has remained the authoritative view of the church ever since. The guidance currently given is that when asked to administer "several times" the priesthood holder "usually does not need to anoint with oil after the first time, but he may give a blessing by the laying on of hands and the authority of the priesthood."[56] While church periodicals continued for some time to carry accounts of successes following what could have qualified as "unwarranted repetitions," church members eventually discontinued routine repeated administrations to their sick. Members continue to pray repeatedly for the recovery of loved ones, and successive major crises in a serious illness may lead to more than one anointing, but more typically the ordinance is performed only once.

OTHER HEALING ORDINANCES

Anointing with oil followed by laying on of hands was the most widespread nineteenth-century ritual for administering to the sick and is the only one currently in use. Through the nineteenth century, however, other ordinances of healing developed as offshoots of the church's doctrinal and ritualistic evolution.

Following the advent of the Mormon temple, a new source of help for the afflicted became available. Late in 1841 the Twelve sent out a general "epistle," aimed among other things at generating support for the Nauvoo temple then under construction. The temple baptismal font was about to be completed and was described as the place "where the saints may enter . . . for their dead relations [that is, perform the ordinance of baptism for the dead, introduced the previous year] . . . ; [and] a place, over which the heavenly messengers may watch and trouble the waters as in the days of old, so that when the sick are put therein they shall be made whole."[57] The reference was to John 5:2–4 and the pool of Bethesda at Jerusalem, near which "lay a great multitude of impotent folk, of blind, halt, withered, waiting for the moving of the water. For an angel went down at a certain season into the pool, and troubled the water; whosoever then first after the troubling of the water stepped in was made whole of whatsoever disease he had."

Just a few weeks later, at the dedication of the font, Joseph Smith advised brother Samuel Rolfe that his infected hand would heal if he washed it in the font.[58] The offending lesion cleared in a week—not in the several months doctors had predicted—and soon many others were being baptized for their health. Within weeks another letter from the Twelve reported that "one of those privileges which is particularly attracting the notice of the Saints at the present moment, is baptism for the dead, in the font . . . by which the sick have been made whole."[59]

Although it was first specified that baptisms for health had to be performed in the temple, this requirement soon was set aside.[60] When there was a temple font available, it was especially sought out, but rivers, streams, and lakes were all put to use. As with ritual anointing, baptisms for health were repeated several times when necessary for the same illness, on the same or consecutive days. In one of the most heroic such efforts, one early Saint cut into a frozen river on seven consecutive mornings to rebaptize a friend for his health.[61] (In this instance Elisha's advice to a leper, in 2 Kings 5:10, to wash seven times in the Jordan, provided some precedent.)

To judge from contemporary accounts, there ofttimes were significant albeit sometimes temporary improvements in those baptized.[62] This occasionally had been the case even before this ordinance was introduced, at the time of an individual's baptism into the church.[63] While this suggests a possible antecedent it seems more likely that, as with many aspects of the Restoration, the notion emerged directly from the scriptural precedent believed present in John (and possibly 2 Kings). If a co-antecedent is present, more likely it relates to the efficacy of cool-water immersion in reducing fever and otherwise relieving many symptoms, a therapeutic insight just then giving rise to a national hydrotherapy movement. As early as 1834 Mormons suffering from cholera found relief from their purging, vomiting, and cramping in a cooling local stream.[64]

Baptism for health in the temple font was well established by the time the pioneers left for Utah, but for years it was of necessity performed outside the temple (as there were no temples from 1846 to 1877). When temples were finally reestablished in the Great Basin baptism for health was soon prominent among their activities. In at least one temple, Tuesdays were set aside for those seeking a renewal of health. And many came, among them church leaders and their families.[65]

The temple early offered yet another option to those suffering physical ailments. The practice of washing and anointing as part of temple rituals begun in Kirtland and formalized as the introductory or initiatory portion of the Nauvoo temple ritual, was also used in conjunction with administrations for health. By the Nauvoo period the liturgy associated with washing (performed in a large tub) and anointing echoed the language of Proverbs (3:8) as well as a latter-day revelation on health (*D&C* 89:18) in blessing initiates with "health to [the] navel and marrow to [the] bones." This portion of the temple ritual soon took on a life of its own as yet another healing rite. Because this washing and anointing was in fact the introductory portion of the temple ordinance, it generally was performed in the temple, often in later years on the same days on which baptisms for health were performed. In essence this was simply a more elaborate version of the common practice of anointing for health, with the added appeal of association with sacred space and liturgy.[66]

Baptisms and temple anointing for health both remained popular throughout the nineteenth century. Once again, however, by the century's end questions about the propriety of such practices began to be raised. In 1889, for example, apostle Matthew Cowley published a healing account which stated that "baptism was for the remission of sins, rather than the healing of physical disease." (It being early in the transformation in church thinking, in this case—which involved possession by evil spirits—oil was applied to the head and administered by mouth.[67]) This notwithstanding, baptisms for health continued to be officially sanctioned and remained popular for yet another decade.[68]

During the church presidency of Joseph F. Smith (1901–18) a near-consensus was reached to discontinue all *re*baptisms other than those performed in vicarious ordinances for the dead.[69] In spite of this, some hierarchical support remained, and the practice continued, albeit with reduced frequency. The formal end seems to have come in 1922 when the First Presidency under Smith's successor, Heber J. Grant, issued instructions to both temple workers and those who continued to come seeking help that "baptism for health is not part of our temple work, and . . . [is] a departure as well from the provision instituted of the Lord for the care and healing of the sick of His church." The practice was to stop.[70]

Washing and anointing specifically for the restoration of health also lost church sanction during these years, especially when performed in the temple. While this reduced the frequency with which members sought healing rituals in the temple, a dwindling number of washings and anointings of women by women continued to be performed in outside settings, especially in conjunction with childbirth. Notwithstanding their concurrent efforts to refocus church healing practice, in 1914 the First Presidency reaffirmed the propriety of this latter practice, which they termed "in no sense a temple ordinance."[71] During this time, however, the role of Mormon women in healing rituals also was being circumscribed, and it was only a matter of time before this vestige of a once common temple ritual came to an end. The last washings and anointings for health apparently were performed in the 1940s, about the time when all healing ordinances by women were discontinued. (A health-related blessing remains in the intitiatory portion of the traditional temple endowment, but as an integral part of the ritual regardless of the health status of the recipient rather than an ordinance focused on the ill. In practice, *re*baptism is now exclusively a vicarious ordinance for a deceased ancestor.)

ADMINISTRATIONS BY WOMEN

As noted previously, the gift of healing was early held by revelatory instruction to be the province of the priesthood. It was therefore to the elders that the sick initially turned, and soon to the high or Melchizedek priesthood—among which the elders were shortly to be counted. Current policy states that authority to administer to the sick is a special privilege of those holding this priesthood. Nonetheless, the New Testament promise that *all* who believed, "whether male or female," could have the faith to heal the sick opened the door to female participation in earlier times.[72] From at least the Ohio years Mormon women blessed sick members of their own families, and in Nauvoo the practice remained relatively common. When complaints and criticism arose, Joseph Smith gave a qualified endorsement to the healing efforts of his female disciples. Feeling that "there could be no devil in it, if God gave His sanction by healing; [and] that there could be no more sin in any female laying hands on the sick then in wetting the face with water," he advised that "if the sisters should have the faith to heal, let all hold their tongues, and let everything roll on."[73]

Extant accounts suggest that women initially may not have anointed with oil when they blessed the sick. In 1842, however, Joseph Smith apparently instructed the recently organized women's Relief Society "respecting the propriety of females administering to the sick by the prayer of faith, the laying on of hands, or the anointing of oil."[74] He also indicated that things would be clearer when the Nauvoo temple was completed.

A few weeks later the Prophet privately introduced to selected priesthood leaders the expanded ritual later performed in the temple, which in part involves an extensive washing and anointing. A year later some wives were allowed to participate in this ritual for the first time, and as this washing and anointing involved unclad initiates, the ordinance in the case of women was always performed by women.

The involvement of women in the administration of sacred temple practices served to reinforce the propriety of women exercising the healing gift. Soon they were performing washing and anointing (often the latter alone) outside the temple as well as within, frequently in anticipation of childbirth.[75] Further reinforcing these developments was the decision of church leaders to "set apart" several community midwives by a formal priesthood ordinance.

As washings and anointings by women became firmly entrenched in Utah, questions of propriety periodically were raised. Church leaders always reaffirmed the legitimacy of these activities, with reference to the same New Testament precedent invoked by Joseph Smith. The First Presidency, for instance, advised in 1880 that "it is the privilege of all faithful women and lay members of the church, who believe in Christ, to administer to all the sick or afflicted in their respective families, either by the laying on of hands, or by the anointing with oil in the name of the Lord."[76] Several women became well-known for their healing gifts, and wives often joined their husbands in administering to children; it was considered acceptable for a child or youth to join in as well.[77]

While reaffirming the right of women—and children—to participate in healing ordinances, church leaders generally distinguished between this practice and the healing ordinance of the priesthood. Women washed and anointed "not as members of the priesthood, but as members of the Church, exercising faith for, and asking blessings of the Lord upon, their sisters, just as they, and every member of the Church, might do in behalf of the members of their families."[78]

Late-nineteenth-century concerns over the role and authority of the priesthood focused further attention on distinctions between the healing efforts of men and women. It was reiterated that the temple ordinance of washing and anointing, the priesthood anointing for healing purposes, and the other washings and anointings for health (performed by women) were distinctly different practices and that the last of these was "not, strictly speaking, an ordinance."[79] Traditional guidance that women should "rebuke disease in the name of Jesus," and not by "authority of the priesthood," was amended with the commendation that women omit altogether the term *rebuke* when administering to the sick—because of its connotation of priesthood power.[80] This was followed by further guidance that women not "seal" their anointings but rather "confirm" them. The former, once again, was held to imply priesthood power.

Initially, administrations by women per se were not in question. An 1894 editorial even termed "densely ignorant" an elder who had condemned a woman for self-administering consecrated oil (to her throat) because of his belief that such oil was appropriately used "only in the hands of the Priesthood." Indeed, a "theology" lesson for young women at this time advised self-administration of oil as an initial response to illness, "and if you still feel sick ask your mother or your father to administer to you. Try that; then if that fails, and they wish to call in Elders, let them do so, and thus exhaust the ordinances of the priesthood. . . ."[81]

Less than a decade later, however, another editorial explained that "an ordinary anointing of the head, according to the established ordinances of the Church . . . should be done by one holding the Priesthood, not by a sister when an Elder is present." To do otherwise would be "clearly out of order."[82] Moreover, should it be desirable to anoint "other parts of the body" of an afflicted sister, "it would be obviously improper for any but a sister to attend to such an anointing, but when this had been done, it is quite consistent for the Elders to anoint the head in the usual form, and then to seal the anointing."[83] A joint effort was also endorsed by church president Joseph F. Smith when he wrote that a wife "with perfect propriety" could join with her husband "or with any other officer holding the Melchizedek Priesthood" in laying hands on the sick.[84]

A subtle but continued shift in emphasis was evident several years later when the First Presidency again reaffirmed the "privilege" of women to anoint the sick but added that it should "always be remembered that the command of the Lord is to call in the elders to administer to the sick, and when they can be called in, they should be asked to anoint the sick or seal the anointing."[85] This point was made more emphatically in an address by Charles Penrose of the First Presidency in General Conference in 1921. There were occasions "when perhaps it would be wise for a woman to lay her hands upon a child, or upon one another sometimes," he said, "that is all right, so far as it goes. But when women go around and declare that they have been set apart to administer to the sick and take the place that is given to the elders . . . by revelation, that is an assumption of authority that is contrary to scripture." When people were sick they should "call for the elders of the Church and they shall pray over and officially lay hands on them." This message was officially reinforced the following year when the First Presidency reaffirmed its view that the healing efforts of women were based on prayer rather than priesthood-like authority and advised the relief societies to stop setting women apart to anoint the sick.[86]

Administrations by women dwindled in frequency for the next two decades. In 1939 an influential priesthood manual limited its remarks on "the use of oil by women" to the brief quotation in which Joseph Smith observed that there was no more harm in it "than in wetting the face with water; it is no sin for anybody to administer that has faith, or if the sick have faith to be healed by their administration."[87] By this time, however, those women most associated with personal healing gifts were gone, and in practice ordinances under the hands of the priesthood had become the order of the day.

What has been labeled "the official death knell" of this spiritual gift came in 1946 when an apostle instructed the women's auxiliary leadership that "while the authorities of the Church have ruled that it is permissible, under certain conditions and with the approval of the priesthood, for sisters to wash and anoint other sisters, yet they feel that it is far better for us to follow the plan the Lord has given us and send for the Elders of the Church to come and administer to the sick and afflicted."[88] Although on one later occasion it was reaffirmed that a woman could join her husband in laying hands on the sick when another priesthood holder was not available (but that the husband also could proceed alone), the church now views the healing ritual as solely the domain of the priesthood. Mormon women pray for the recovery of loved ones, but for at least twenty years there has been no official provision for them to assist in administrations even in their own family. Currently official guidance specifies:

> Normally, two Melchizedek Priesthood holders administer to the sick.
> A father who holds the Melchizedek Priesthood should administer to sick

members of his family. He may ask another Melchizedek Priesthood
bearer to assist.

If no one is available to help, a Melchizedek Priesthood holder has full
authority to both anoint and seal the anointing. If he has no oil, he may
give a blessing by the authority of the priesthood.[89]

Notwithstanding the clarity of the church guidance, increased sensitivity
to women's issues in recent years has led to greater interest in this subject
in some Mormon circles. While much of this attention has been more theoretical than applied, privately Mormon women again occasionally administer
to their own children (apparently without an anointing) or participate in a
priesthood anointing performed by their husband. As yet there has been no
explicit formal response to this still very limited activity.

In the context of this new interest, it has been suggested by some that
the twentieth-century withdrawal of the "healing gift" from women was motivated by male/patriarchal concerns. It seems more likely that the immediate
goal was—as church leaders said—to assert more fully the institution of the
priesthood per se. Among many other changes the early twentieth century
also saw priesthood prerogatives asserted as never before. New responsibilities were assigned to priesthood quorums, while presiding priesthood coun-
cils took firm control of all facets of church organization, including women's
auxiliaries formerly allowed near autonomy. It was in this context that one
finds the message that however laudable the expression of faith by those
women who administered to the sick, their actions fell short of the exercise
of priesthood power through a divinely instituted healing ordinance.

Concurrent with the guidance on administrations by women, the church
also sought actively to put an end to the healing efforts of others whose
personal power or influence as healers seemed to overshadow the role of
the institution of their priesthood office. This specifically included certain
"brethren strongly gifted with the power of healing [who] have visited far
and near amongst the Saints (to the neglect sometimes of other duties), until
it has almost become a business with them." Their visits had "assumed
somewhat the character of those of a physician, and the people have come
to regard the power so manifested as though coming from the man, and not
that he was simply an instrument in the hands of God of bringing blessings
to their house." This view, warned church president Joseph F. Smith in
1902, "is exceedingly unfortunate when indulged in, and is apt to result in
the displeasure of the Lord." The practice was contrary to the "recognized
order and discipline of the Church" and "should therefore be discountenanced and discouraged."[90] In future years Smith's counsel was repeated
verbatim in guidebooks for priesthood holders, to the degree that one vis-

iting high priest refused to administer to a sick child because he "was outside his own ward." Clarification quickly followed that an "Elder's opportunity for doing a purely good deed should [not]be confined to a ward or any other limit, and when he went into a house and the head of that house made such a request of him it was clearly not only his privilege or right but his duty to comply."[91]

In essence, then, administrations by Mormon women were in part a casuality of a conscious decision to emphasize the institutional rather than charismatic aspects of religious healing. This decision, in conjunction with the concurrent movement—in the wake of a growing respect for scientific medicine—to limit authorized healing ordinances to a single, simple ritual almost guaranteed that women would no longer be involved.

HERBS AND MILD FOOD

The pivotal 1832 revelation that elders be called to "pray for and lay their hands upon" the sick also required that those who "have not the faith to be healed, but believe shall be nourished with all tenderness, with herbs and mild food, and that not by the hand of an enemy."[92] The endorsement of herbal remedies was reaffirmed the following year in another revelation on health which commended "all wholesome herbs" and recommended "tobacco . . . for bruises and all sick cattle, to be used with judgment and skill."[93] Collectively, this divine counsel heavily influenced LDS medical beliefs for years. Even today a legacy remains evident in the practices of a significant segment of Mormon society.

Given the extraordinary level of disease in Mormon (and other nineteenth-century American) communities—and their shortfalls in faith—there was ample opportunity to inculcate the merits of the herbal approach. The guidance of the *Doctrine and Covenants* allowed this to be accomplished generally without apology. Apostle Taylor early explained that "inasmuch as all have not faith, those that are strong ought not to condemn the weak, inasmuch as they make a judicious means of those things which the Lord, in his mercy, has been pleased to provide, and appoint for the infirmities and diseases of human nature."[94] Joseph Smith was even more succinct in advising his disciples that "when they were sick, and had called for the Elders to pray for them, and they were not healed, to use herbs and mild food."[95] Moreover, if their faith was inadequate, they should not hesitate to send for help and get "some little remedy" in the "first stages."[96]

That there were some who dissented from this view is suggested by Taylor's comments above, but in such cases Smith moved swiftly to correct their point of view. Lyman Wight, selected as one of Smith's first Twelve, once espoused another view. He was convinced and openly taught that "the Church ought to live by faith" and therefore that "medicine administered to the sick is of the Devil." His understanding was rebuffed in a church court where the Prophet informed him that it was "not of God" to condemn the use of "roots and herbs" and "wholesome vegitables [*sic*]" in caring for the sick. Such condemnation was itself "of Satan."[97]

Mormonism's endorsement of herbalism was not without some qualifications. If there was "danger, or wrong, in the administration of herbs, it is from their being in the hands of unskillful men, and particularly in the hands of an enemy." "Quacks" abounded in their community, and "nostrums of all kinds have been administered by injudicious hands, producing the most deleterious effects." The Saints should be careful to seek care only from those who were "acquainted with the physiology of the human system, and the nature and medicinal properties of herbs" as well as "the nature and effects of disease."[98]

The greater problem was not with botanic doctors but rather with their orthodox counterparts. "What greater sign of death, and loss of faith, can be supposed," noted a Nauvoo resident, writing in the church's periodical *Times and Seasons*, "than to see a physician's horse hitched before a sick one's door?" Such clearly was contrary to the divine will.

> If, in any age, when the church of God had power and authority on the earth, a command had been received that the doctors had power over diseases, and they shall heal the sick, then the trade might have flourished under a sacred sanction; and the world could have branded Jeremiah as a false prophet for saying, "Thus saith the Lord: cursed be the man that trusteth in man, and maketh flesh his arm. . . ." No doubt but cases may occur, where medical operations may be requisite; but generally speaking, "herbs and mild food," with good nursing, [are] better for the patient's person and pocket, than all the nostrums of materia medica.[99]

Nonbotanic physicians want "to kill or cure you to get your money," Joseph Smith once announced, and will give calomel—the highly toxic orthodox panacea of the day—"to cure a sliver in the big toes; and they do not stop to know whether the stomach is empty or not; and calomel on an empty stomach will kill the patient."[100] So far as Brigham Young was concerned, "a worse set of ignoramuses do not walk the earth." They were no more than "learned fools"; "I could put all the real knowledge they possess in a nut shell and put it in my vest pocket, and then I would have to hunt for it to find it."[101]

There was one consistent exception to the condemnation of conventional, "regular" medicine. Like their contemporaries, the Mormons always considered "medical operations" a special case. It was appropriate to turn to orthodox specialists to have bones set, limbs amputated, or teeth extracted.[102] As Brigham Young once explained, this was because anatomy and surgery were "mechanical" skills (that is their remedies were self-apparent) and did not require the "revelation" or "intuitive inspiration" necessary for the proper selection of medicines taken internally.[103]

Early critics were quick to attribute Mormonism's proherbal stance to the influence of botanic physician Frederick G. Williams, who joined the church shortly before the revelation on the subject, and in whose home Joseph Smith briefly lived. While Williams unquestionably impressed the Prophet, who soon made him a member of the church's First Presidency, Mormonism's herbal roots run much deeper.

As with many aspects of the Restoration, converts found ample confirmation of most of their medical beliefs in the works they accepted as scripture. There were dozens of references to the use of herbs in the Bible, including reassuring passages in Ezekiel (envisoning a medicinal tree in the new Jerusalem) and 2 Kings (in which Isaiah heals with a dressing of figs).[104] A *Book of Mormon* prophet as well had noted "the excellent qualities of the many plants and roots which God had prepared to remove the cause of diseases" (Alma 46:40).

Beyond this, there was the immediate context from which Mormonism emerged. The 1820s and 1830s could well be considered both the apex of the age of "heroic medicine"—in which regular physicians confidently "puked, purged, blistered and bled" those who sought their aid with a formidable array of potentially lethal "remedies"; and the nadir in public opinion regarding the medical profession—as large segments of the population abandoned orthodox medicine to embrace the more benign herbal remedies of homegrown practitioners. In his youth Joseph lost a beloved older brother when a lump of "heroically" prescribed calomel lodged in his bowel; and his sister and mother recovered from grave illnesses only when the family turned away from the treatment of orthodox physicians to the prayer of faith.[105] Even a brilliant surgical intervention by the distinguished and orthodox Dr. Nathan Smith which saved the young Joseph both his leg and ultimately his life was remembered negatively by the Smiths—because of the initial and orthodox recommendation of amputation for what in retrospect was a typhoid infection in his leg.[106]

As with the vast majority of converts, Joseph Smith and his family found divine confirmation of their personal beliefs in the 1832 revelation endorsing the use of herbs, but they first accepted the virtues of botanic medicine before, not after, their conversion to Mormonism. The Smiths, like the others, readily turned for care to the many botanic practitioners who joined the church. Prominent among these were men like Frederick G. Williams, mentioned above, Thomas B. Marsh, who became the senior apostle in Smith's Quorum of Twelve, and Willard Richards, who was for years a member of the First Presidency. They, like Richards's brothers, Phineas and Levi (characterized by Joseph Smith as "the best physician I have ever been acquainted with")[107] were all of the school of Samuel Thomson, a popular evangelist of anti-orthodox herbal medicine whose influence preceded the Mormons into virtually every area they entered. Thomson's remedies appear regularly in both Mormon diaries and sermons, and he allegedly once was described by the Prophet to be "as much inspired to bring forth his principle of practice according to the dignity and importance of it as he [Smith] was to introduce the gospel." Herbal "principles" were thus to be viewed "as an appendix to the gospel, as a temporal salvation."[108]

Although this characterization of Thomson, coming many years later from an enthusiastic botanic practitioner, is in some regards suspect, it is clear from the totality of the early Mormon experience that it approximates the Prophet's views. It is more likely that Smith, like most other Jacksonians, would have viewed Thomson as one among several who were on the right track. Other widely respected botanic authorities to whom they no doubt also turned were John Wesley and Wooster Beach, both of whose best-selling self-help books were then readily available—the latter directly from the bookstore run by the Prophet's brother—and largely consistent with the Mormon point of view.[109]

Several more concrete steps were taken which supplemented the words of general counsel. Mormon botanic practitioners were "set apart" by the laying on of hands both in Illinois and pioneer Utah, and predominantly botanic boards of health were organized in Nauvoo and Salt Lake City. Friendly botanic societies were organized in the Great Basin to facilitate the dissemination of botanic wisdom into more remote Mormon communities. Through these societies, prophesied Willard Richards of the First Presidency, principles eventually would be published "to the world [which] would never die out or cease until [they] had revolutionized the earth."[110] At the least, these zealous practitioners were confident that "our exertions . . . will shake the faith of many in the propriety of swallowing, as they have long done with implicit confidence, the most deleterious drugs . . . believing in the goodness of the creator that He has placed in most lands medicinal plants for the cure of all diseases incident to that climate, and especially so in relation to that in which we live."[111]

Isolated in their Western settlements, the Mormons could not only assure the availability of appropriate care but also bar that which was unacceptable. On the heels of an episode in which Mormon volunteers during the Mexican War were forced to take calomel for their illnesses—contrary to leadership instructions to rely on faith and herbs "and let the surgeon's medicine alone"—an explicit territorial law was passed on the subject. This barred the dispensing of most orthodox medical remedies ("deadly poisons") "without first explaining fully, definitely, critically, simply, and unequivocally [to the patient and his friends] . . . in plain, simple, English language, the . . . design of said poison . . . and procuring . . . unequivocal approval, approbation and consent." Convicted offenders were subject to a $1,000 fine or not less than a year at hard labor.[112] This was informed consent with teeth, one of the earliest such statutes in the country. Its function, however, seems more symbolic than practical. The self-taught herbalists to whom the faithful usually turned for help, especially in the outlying communities, would never have considered such remedies in the first place.

SCIENTIFIC MEDICINE

The last third of the nineteenth century saw dramatic shifts in the way Mormons and most others viewed health and disease. The germ theory and the development of rigorous criteria for proving therapeutic effectiveness eventually transformed thinking everywhere. Many cherished remedies were discredited and fell into disuse. Considering their isolation and doctrinal commitment to herbalism, some within the Mormon community remained surprisingly current with these developments. A number of factors were responsible, several still operating today.

To some extent Mormon thinking was pushed or pulled ahead by developments outside the LDS community, in Utah and elsewhere. In the decades after the Mormon exodus, medical practice in America moved increasingly away from both heroic and herbal ideology. This shift was reflected in the attitudes of the non-Mormon regular physicians who settled in Salt Lake City primarily to treat overlanders enroute to California. While most of these physicians were only temporary residents, a few stayed longer and exerted lasting local influence. Notable among these was Dr. Washington F. Anderson, who came in 1857 and within a few years was named surgeon to the Nauvoo Legion (Utah's territorial militia). Well-liked by Brigham Young,

Anderson became "dean of medicine" to the intermountain West, a highly respected consultant, and a pathbreaker in modern surgery in the territory.

In the 1860s the Civil War and the transcontinental railroad brought another major influx of non-Mormon physicians. Still others came as surgeons assigned to the federal troops stationed in the territory. As early as 1870 the Utah governor (a non-Mormon appointee) moved against the antiorthodox "informed consent" legislation passed twenty years earlier. Concurrent with these developments a mining boom sprang up, sustained largely by non-Mormon workers (Brigham Young having discouraged participation). Health problems, especially lead poisoning, led to a joint effort between miners and Episcopal and Catholic churchmen to establish the first regular general hospitals in Salt Lake City. St. Mark's Hospital opened in 1872 and Holy Cross Hospital in 1875. Both were staffed by recently arrived non-Mormon physicians.

There also were a few well-trained regular physicians among the Mormon converts. Initially they were discouraged from going into full-time practice. As Brigham advised one prospective immigrant, there were doctors in the territory "who find considerable employment, yet it is no uncommon thing to see them at work in the canyons getting out wood, plowing, sowing, or harvesting their crops, which, I think betokens a healthy state."[113] The church itself gave a number of orthodox physicians nonmedical assignments, including work as clerks or general advisors to church leaders, or sent them on nonmedical missions. Nonetheless several Mormon physicians played an important medical role in their community and, with their non-Mormon colleagues, were not infrequently consulted in serious cases.

In addition to the growing reputation of these physicians—even within the LDS community—there was another impetus toward further concessions to regular medicine. Orthodox practice was always most acceptable in the purely "mechanical" cases requiring the services of a surgeon or dentist. Childbirth, with its risks of "mechanical" problems, was thus an area in which regular practitioners were sometimes summoned. The subject was a delicate one, as many church leaders felt it inappropriate to have a male physician treat women, during pregnancy or otherwise. The church's *Deseret News* in an article also reprinted in the *Millennial Star* once warned that "a woman who employed a male doctor to wait upon her in illness was possessed of an adulterous spirit, and the doctor who delights in nursing women, instead of advising them how to wait on themselves and each other, is possessed of the same spirit."[114] The message was not fully heeded, however, for two decades later Brigham Young again warned of "a growing evil in our midst": the time was rapidly approaching when "not a woman in all

Israel will dare to have a baby unless she can have a doctor by her."[115] With only two or three women physicians among the Mormon immigrants, the implications were clear.

In this overall setting Young concluded it was time to send some second-generation Mormons back East to be trained in medicine. Not coincidentally the first of these—a son of his former counselor and Thomsonian practitioner, Willard Richards—went in 1869, the year which marked the opening of the transcontinental railroad. And among the earliest to go were a number of women, with the hope that they would return and train nurses and midwives. Soon there was a small but steady stream of Mormons heading East to study in the nation's leading medical schools.

These developments seem not to have posed any doctrinal crisis within the church. Despite their historic commitment to herbalism, many Mormons were quite open to emerging secular insights. Among those who went East for medical training, two in fact were the wives and one the son of church leaders (General Authorities). At least six other wives or children of deceased or future Authorities were also among those early trained. Dr. Seymour Young was himself inducted into the church leadership in 1882, just eight years after returning from his training.

This willingness to shift perspective was in keeping with an underlying Mormon pragmatism evident almost from the first. Wilford Woodruff, for example, was one of many in Nauvoo who, still afflicted with malaria following a faith healing—and despite three botanic emetics and fifteen minutes of steaming—found relief without erosion of faith when he took the "highly recommended" quinine-containing "Sapington's Anti fever pills." "[B]lessed be the Lord," he wrote in his diary, "they have entirely broaken [sic] the ague entirely to all appearance."[116] Brigham Young once made the broader point effectively when he advised his followers:

> If we are sick and ask the Lord to heal us, and to do all for us that is necessary to be done, according to my understanding of the Gospel and salvation, I might as well ask the Lord to cause my wheat and corn to grow without my plowing the ground and casting in the seed. It appears consistent to me to apply every remedy that comes within the range of my knowledge, and to ask my Father in Heaven, in the name of Jesus Christ, to sanctify that application to the healing of my body.[117]

The pragmatic Young entrusted his own care to his nephew Seymour, when he returned from medical training and became city physician. And with Brigham's concurrence, Dr. Young sought help from his non-Mormon colleagues during Brigham's final illness a few years later.

When Brigham Young finally decided in the late 1860s to seek out some of the insights of secular medicine, his timing could not have been better. The first of the LDS students began their training just as the new scientific medicine was beginning to unfold. As a consequence they and their successors were able to offer those who were interested a distinctly modern medical view. On their return they participated in the fledgling local medical society, staffed the first "Mormon" hospital when it opened in 1882, and began classes and training programs for mothers, nurses, and midwives. Later they also published a short-lived community-oriented monthly medical journal, the *Salt Lake City Sanitarian*, devoted to the latest in preventive and curative medicine.

The church's Relief Society sponsored the (Mormon) Deseret Hospital, which opened in 1882, and actively recruited candidates (three per community) for early nurse and midwife training programs. In 1898 a formal Relief Society Nurse Training School for practical nurses was instituted, and with the opening of a modern LDS hospital seven years later a separate registered nurse program also was begun. For years the First Presidency solicited participants for the church-sponsored practical nursing programs and further showed support by "setting apart" (that is, administering blessings to) graduates. Through this effort hundreds of LDS nurses were trained. Eventually the church discontinued its school, in the 1920s, relying thereafter on the LDS hospital-based program. It in turn eventually was absorbed, in 1952, into a newly formed Brigham Young University School of Nursing, which continues to offer degrees in the nursing field.[118] Beginning in the 1890s, the Relief Society and other church auxiliaries also carried regular medical advice columns in their official periodicals. Almost always reflecting the latest medical thinking, these articles in essence sought to make all Mormon mothers capable of functioning as reasonably sophisticated home nurses. Although the subject now is less extensively treated than earlier in the century, home health care remains an integral part of the church curriculum for Mormon women.

An even more tangible indication of the growing commitment to modern medicine can be seen in the advent of the LDS hospital system. While church leaders chose not to intercede when financial problems closed the Relief Society's Deseret Hospital in 1892, they willingly provided funds in 1902 to allow completion of a greatly expanded new facility. The original impetus for this project came from a Mormon dentist who bequeathed $50,000 toward construction of a modern hospital. The balance of the $175,000 needed for the project was provided by the church. Modeled after America's leading hospitals, the Dr. W. H. Groves Latter-day Saint Hospital at its opening in 1905 was described as "one of the best equipped hospitals in the West." Among its state-of-the-art amenities were an X-ray machine, "automatic elevators," electric lights, telephones in each room, and individual "call-buttons" for every patient bed.[119]

The opening of LDS Hospital was accompanied by editorial commentary which made clear to all "that 'Mormon' enterprise is abreast of the times and the L.D.S. are ready to avail themselves of scientific knowledge and progress, and are not slow to move with the movement of modern thought and learning."[120] Eventually the church hospital system would total fifteen hospitals, with over two thousand inpatient beds. With the growth of this system, members turned increasingly to hospital care for serious problems. In the 1930s, a final milestone was reached when a church-supported statewide movement to reduce Utah's disproportionately high infant mortality rate resulted for the first time in the majority of births being hospital-based. (By 1960, 99 percent of the deliveries in Utah took place in hospitals, and infant mortality among the Mormons—as noted in Chapter 3—had fallen well below the national average.[121]

In this increasingly orthodox medical setting Mormons have received entirely conventional medical care—without church condemnation—from an increasingly male-dominated medical profession. The number of registered midwives and the proportion of women doctors declined significantly in Utah during the early twentieth century, and any concern about the gender of physicians passed into history. A 1980 study of the attitudes of Mormons on this question started tellingly with the assumption that because of their "patriarchal" environment Mormons would be inclined to view women physicians in a *negative* light. The results showed that indeed they did (65 percent of respondents having an unfavorable view of women doctors), but no more so than non-Mormons in the survey area (64 percent having an unfavorable view).[122] As in nearly all other areas of modern medicine, Mormon opinion on the subject had become largely undistinguishable from that of the surrounding community.

There were several additional early-twentieth-century developments. One of these was an unmistakably heightened emphasis on the importance of seeking out competent care. For example, in language reminiscent of that given sixty years before, church president Joseph F. Smith wrote in 1902 that when personal faith could not effect a cure, "let a reputable and faithful physician be consulted. By all means, let the quack, the traveling fakir, the cure-all nostrum and the indiscriminate dosing with patent medicine be abolished like so much trash."[123]

Other changes included replacement in 1912 of the common sacramental cup in weekly congregational services with "hygienic" individualized cups, and the barring of those with "skin diseases" from participation in temple rituals. This latter prohibition probably derived from the continued use of a tub in the washing phase of the ceremonies. Later, tub washings were discarded in favor of an entirely symbolic administration, and the "skin"-related prohibition was dropped. It also was decided about this time that sacred temple-related undergarments, which faithful Mormons were expected to wear continually, could be set aside when medically necessary, and that those with serious diseases (for example, diabetes) should forgo the monthly fast expected of faithful members. While perhaps unremarkable in and of themselves, collectively these modest changes in policy underscore a major change in attitude, and especially so against a nineteenth-century backdrop in which those afflicted with rashes sought out the temple for a curative baptism, while all wore their garments in part as a shield against death and disease.

The transition to an almost unrestrained embrace of modern medicine was not totally uneventful. An herbalist tradition was still solidly entrenched throughout the Mormon West in 1900, and particularly so in rural Utah. Although Mormons were committed to "continuing revelation"—and thereby to potential revisions in official counsel—a deeply held belief in scriptural near-infallibility made it difficult for many to set aside the explicit divine endorsement associated with herbal remedies. Unsophisticated in evaluating the merits of various therapies, they also found continuing anecdotal evidence of the apparent value of cherished treatments. Many steadfast adherents to this legacy continue to this day to seek out "naturopathic" cures for their ailments. Most conspicuous among this group are those collectively termed Mormon "Fundamentalists." Though excommunicated from the main body of the church (primarily because they continued to practice polygamy after its official abandonment by the church in 1890 and 1904), Fundamentalists teach that the church itself fell into apostasy when it abandoned divinely mandated polygamy, and they hold to many since-discarded beliefs and practices common to the pioneer years. Among these is a near-exclusive reliance on herbalists and midwives.

This tendency to herbalism is not limited to the Mormon fringe, however. Many mainstream members, especially in the Mormon heartland, still turn regularly to various herbs, though generally not to the exclusion of conventional modern medicine. A recent survey in LDS congregations in Utah and California found that half those surveyed used herbal medicines, with 20 percent doing so frequently (four or five herbs *daily*). Similarly proherbalist books aimed at LDS audiences—and drawing heavily on authoritative early guidance—remain popular within the Mormon community.[124]

Periodically, especially in recent years, the church responds publicly to this persisting tradition. A 1977 *Church News* editorial, for example, disavowed church endorsement of the herbalist fad then current and sternly warned members "with serious illnesses . . . [to] consult competent physicians, licensed under the laws of the land to practice medicine." Similarly a 1981 priesthood *Bulletin* advised that "Expectant mothers need to get the best prenatal and delivery care available from medically and legally qualified practitioners." Several specific cautions were given:

> 1. Any person practicing medical care should have the legal sanction of the authorized government agency.
> 2. Births and deaths of newborns must be registered with the authorized government agency.
> 3. Methods and locations of prenatal care and delivery are a matter of personal choice, not a matter of Church doctrine.
> 4. Pregnant women should include in their diet nutritious foods such as milk, fruit, vegetables, grains, and moderate amounts of meat."[125]

Official guidance to local leaders on "medical and health practices," which until 1989 indicated that the church "discourages" the use of questionable practices, is now quite emphatic:

> Members should not use medical or health practices that are ethically or legally questionable. Local leaders should advise members who have health problems to consult competent professional practitioners who are licensed in the countries where they practice. Bishops may not use fast offerings [charity] funds to pay for unproven medical care without First Presidency approval in each case.[126]

Despite this near-century-long perspective, the categorical nature of the nineteenth-century guidance does pose a dilemma for many, including some in high office within the church. Literal-minded believers can find no easy way to reject early instruction in the medical arena while continuing to accept as the word of God intertwined nonmedical guidance. The solution for many has been to view the discovery of more effective medical remedies as itself inspired (in the sense that Mormonism believes that scientific advancement in general is a form of revelation). Within the LDS medical community, apologists generally note that modern medicines often emerged from botanical sources and thus argue that the early inspiration has not been so much rescinded as transformed. It also is noted that whatever the intrinsic merits of early herbalism, at least it discouraged members from seeking out the more dangerous orthodox practices of the day.

HEALING TRANSFORMED

A potentially greater challenge than the abandonment of herbalism was the reconciliation necessary in the area of faith healing. As one participant later recalled, when word got around that "the President of the Church and the chief officers . . . had regularly attended physicians whose services were actually called into use even when the sickness was not serious, it was something of a shock."[127] In fact, many in the church leadership were themselves concerned that a growing reliance on medical practitioners could seriously undermine individual faith; they repeatedly warned that members should remember first the healing powers of priesthood blessings. An 1893 editorial on the subject by George Q. Cannon of the First Presidency spelled out the issue quite clearly:

> Children who are taught by their parents to desire the laying on of hands by the Elders when they are sick, receive astonishing benefits therefrom, and their faith becomes exceedingly strong. But, if instead of teaching them that the Lord has placed the ordinance of laying on of hands for the healing of the sick in His Church, a doctor is immediately sent for when anything ails them, they gain confidence in the doctor and his prescriptions and lose faith in the ordinance. How long would it take, if this tendency were allowed to grow among the Latter-day Saints, before faith in the ordinance of laying on of hands would die out? . . . There is great need of stirring up the Latter-day Saints upon this point. Faith should be encouraged. The people should be taught that great and mighty works can be accomplished by the exercise of faith. The sick have been healed, devils have been cast out, the blind have been restored to sight, the deaf have been made to hear, lameness has been cured, and even the dead have been raised to life, by the exercise of faith. And this too, in our day and in our Church, by the administration of God's servants in the way appointed. All these things can again be done, under the blessing of the Lord, where faith exists. It is this faith that we should seek to preserve and to promote in the breasts of our children and of all mankind.[128]

Cannon's editorial proved prophetic. Despite the attempted retrenchment, a new perspective was dawning. Members increasingly turned to secular medicine in times of need, and Brigham Young's pragmatic philosophy on the futility of praying for the growth of unplanted corn came to dominate church counsel on health matters. Soon medical self-help articles in official church publications pointedly warned members that when potentially serious problems were present to send immediately for a good physician. The new perspective was succinctly summed up by the influential apostle James Talmage when he wrote in 1921, "we must do all we can, and then ask the Lord to do the rest, such as we cannot do. Hence we hold the medical and surgical profession in high regard. . . . When we have done all we can then the Divine Power will be directly applicable and operative."[129] Even more direct was a 1932 priesthood manual which, having quoted Brigham Young on the question, asked class members to "consider the uselessness of asking the Lord to do something which we can do ourselves."[130]

Concurrent with these developments came the clarifications discussed above concerning the specific definition of an appropriate healing ordinance and the elimination of all medicinal or therapeutic overtones in the administration of oil. The relegation of anointing to a purely symbolic role thus must be understood in the context of this major transformation in LDS thinking on medical practice.

A subtle illustration of the emerging new perspective is seen in the turn-of-the-century discussion—in the context of the rigorous quarantines then being enforced—of the propriety of administering to those with highly contagious diseases. At specific issue was the propriety of the bishop or other priesthood holders breaking the quarantine in order to administer to the afflicted person. Ultimately this subject was addressed editorially, again by the influential George Q. Cannon, who concluded:

> But if one have such faith as this, having no fear for himself, let him at least be warned against exposing others to such plagues as have been named. He ought to complain of no proper regulation adopted as a precaution for the safety of the neighbors and the community, submitting if need be to restraint of liberty to come and go at will, and manifesting thus a consistent interest not alone in the sick but in the well also.[131]

The endpoint in this progression in thinking is well illustrated by the instructions issued to all members three decades later on "The Healing of the Sick." After first recounting "a few don'ts"—don't run into contagion, overeat, use stimulants, or neglect personal sanitation and hygiene—members were advised that should they still become sick they should try a "practical common sense" remedy but not delay too long before seeking competent medical care. "Early in our troubles," the message continued, "we should send for the elders of the Church" and "have faith in the Priesthood." "But with all your faith, we cannot expect to stop the course of nature, and oppose the will of Him who knows what is best for us. . . . Let us be reasonable and practical in all these things, remembering that the blessings of the Lord are predicated only upon our obedience to law, and that the laws of nature will always operate unless set aside by superior law, and that the intervention of our Heavenly Father cannot be invoked with success, except by those who have faith in him."[132]

Without formally coming to grips with the question, the twentieth-century church in essence has acknowledged that despite the myriad faith healings of the past, modern medicine now affords a more secure first line of defense against serious disease. With this development Mormonism would seem to have have lost what once was perceived as a divine therapeutic. In fact this has not really proved to be the case. While not viewing consecrated oil and priesthood administration in entirely the same light as their forebears, modern Mormons still find in this tradition an emotional resource similar to that available in an earlier time.

A continued role for faith healing has been assured by both the prominence it initially held within Mormonism and the practical attention it continued to receive as the church increasingly embraced modern medicine. Late-nineteenth-century Mormon physicians administered both modern medications and priesthood anointings to their patients, and a goal of the first Mormon hospital (1882) was to afford a setting in which both approaches to healing could coexist sympathetically. Church-sponsored hospitals ever since have made ample provisions for an unembarrassed priesthood role. Although the church in recent years has divested itself of its hospital holdings (for reasons discussed in Chapter 7, "On Caring," and not because of any lessening of commitment to modern health care), hospitals in Mormon communities continue to experience and respect the regular visits of Mormon elders to attend to Mormon patients. In virtually any area in which a Mormon congregation is located, local priesthood leaders accept responsibility for providing blessings in area hospitals to which any member has been admitted.

Home-based anointings also have received continued emphasis, just as has the importance of seeking out competent physicians. Instruction in the consecration of oil and the blessing of the sick remains an important part of the priesthood instruction received by all male members, and anointings within the family still abound in the Mormon community. Where a priesthood holder is not available within the family, this responsibility is explicitly assigned to the priesthood-bearing "home teachers" who regularly visit all members. In this way, anointings still continue to fill the caring role so effectively served in the past.

Beyond these practical steps, some theoretical doctrinal readjustment accompanied the healing ordinance into the twentieth century. Nineteenth-century church leaders had characterized the healing power in almost exclusively supernatural terms. While individual faith, of both patient and healer, always was deemed important, the healing itself was believed to require the direct intervention of God—who could choose to act (but generally didn't) despite a lack of faith or worthiness in one of the participants. (Thus even animals were administered to, albeit infrequently, with some expectation of success.) Moreover, the only "legitimate" instruments for invoking such power were believed entrusted to the restored church, and specifically to the Mormon priesthood. All healings outside the church, however well-intended, were believed dependent to some extent on the power of the devil. These included both the healings claimed by "false religion" and the more secular successes then reported by mesmerism.[133]

Toward the close of the century, the emergence of both modern hypnotism and Christian Science "mind-curers" and an increasingly "scientific" view within the church led to some modification in this understanding. Eventually it was concluded that such cures when accomplished outside the church usually were achieved "upon natural principles" and that even among the faithful the dependence of healing on personal faith could be understood in similar terms. In the latter circumstances, however, priesthood administrations potentially offered much more, not only because of association with revealed religion but because God's power extended to conditions well beyond the "functional" (nonorganic) disorders believed most often responsive to non-Mormon practitioners. Although not so often discussed in recent years, this seems to remain the general understanding within the church.[134]

Eventually even hypnotism as a medical adjunct has become acceptable within the church. Though hypnotism has long been free of the satanic associations attached to mesmerism, recreational participation in hypnotism continues to be condemned because of the power it allegedly places in the hands of the hypnotist. Hypnosis "under competent, professional supervision for the treatment of disease," however, is now deemed a "wholly medical question."[135]

In actual practice, present-day Mormons are not encouraged to "test" the extent of the healing gift within the church. As a 1977 editorial advised, Mormon "belief in the divine power of healing should in no way preclude seeking competent medical assistance." Even when priesthood administrations are sought in serious cases, there generally is implicit acknowledgment within the sealing prayer itself of dependence on the unprecedented powers of modern medicine. Additionally, a subtle shift in emphasis has seen many twentieth-century healing failures (with unfulfilled promises of recovery) explained as what might be termed "wishful" thinking on the part of those performing the ordinances, that is, as reflecting more a lack of inspiration than a lack of faith. Indeed, early in the century elders were advised that they "should not pronounce life and health merely because [they had] been called to perform a holy ordinance" but rather only when they feel "divinely inspired" to do so.[136]

Typically healing blessings now invoke divine guidance for the attending physicians into whose care the case is entrusted. Should dramatic results follow, as occasionally still is the case, these are viewed as joint victories. Perhaps a precarious case has been stabilized through priesthood intervention, until the stricken person can reach the hospital; or a case termed uncertain or doubtful by attending physicians has ended happily. In such instances, "the hand of the Lord" inevitably is seen in the outcome—just as it was in analogous cases 150 years before.[137]

If any controversy remains in this arena, it is in the role of Mormon physicians in the anointing ritual. In some Mormon communities, LDS physicians are requested, or make themselves available, to administer priesthood blessings to their patients—as their predecessors did a century ago. Though not often discussed publicly, this practice is problematic on several counts. As one LDS physician has observed, it is "difficult to promise healing in a blessing when knowing the medical aspects of the case, such healing did not seem possible."[138] The dilemma is particularly perplexing, for if the physician demurs and the patient fails to recover, the outcome is sometimes attributed to a lack of faith (rather than skill) on the part of the physician. On balance, and judging from informal conversations, most LDS physicians apparently decline to participate in the priesthood blessings of their own patients; others no doubt choose the words of their blessing carefully.

On the other hand, some physicians who are willing to perform such administrations have been viewed by their colleagues with skepticism. At issue is the underlying motivation, detractors believing it to be the demonstration of religious commitment (at the possible expense of a meaningful evaluation of medical qualifications) or avoidance of criticism should an untoward outcome result. While there is probably some basis for these concerns, there also are many faithful and well-meaning physicians who correctly see their participation in both aspects of the healing process as entirely compatible with a long-established tradition within Mormonism. So far as the church leadership is concerned, no particular guidance has been issued on the question; it remains like many other aspects of modern medicine a matter of individual conscience.

A related concern is the perceived willingness of some LDS physicians to depict successful but ostensibly unexpected recoveries in miraculous terms—with the unspoken benefit that association with such divine intervention might have for the physicians involved. Put off by the "deific certitude of some doctors who do this," critics note that this only leads to a net devaluation of the medical profession at large, as a message of medical ignorance or ineptitude becomes implicit in the public retellings of the faith-promoting episode.[139]

A Mormon humorist recently summarized the present standing of "blessing" for health in the modern church by defining it as "the ordinance of anointing and laying on hands to heal the sick; most commonly done to those not sick enough to need a doctor or so sick the doctors have given up hope."[140] While overstating the case, there is enough truth in this to make many Mormons smile. On the other hand, a resource believed effective under those circumstances is surely still to be valued.

Mormonism's embrace of modern medicine has proven enduring. Mormons seek out medical careers in ever-increasing numbers, with thousands now holding medical degrees. LDS physicians have achieved many individual successes, several having acceded to the presidency or chairmanship of major professional societies. Within the church the standing of physicians remains equally strong. Many are called to positions of ecclesiastical leadership, as mission or stake (diocese) presidents. In 1984 cardiovascular surgeon Russell M. Nelson was called to be one of the church's presiding Quorum of Twelve Apostles, the first physician to be so honored. (Nelson was, in fact, the first physician to be called into the ranks of the General Authorities since Seymour Young was selected as a somewhat lower ranking "authority" 102 years before.)

To some extent, the further advance of medicine simplified things for the church. Greater knowledge of epidemiology and the relative disappearance of serious contagious diseases, for example, led public health authorities to abandon the extreme forms of quarantine practiced in the first half of the century, thereby rendering moot some of George Q. Cannon's concerns. Modern medicine also limited substantially the therapeutic indications for agents proscribed by the Mormon health code. Medicinal alcohol, for example, is now limited largely to its use as a solvent in cold remedies, and caffeine to analgesic mixtures. The seeming inconsistency long present in which church leaders endorsed the medicinal role of alcohol, coffee, or tea while condemning their social use is thus now avoided.[141]

One of the last subjects of disagreement between the church and modern medicine was that of organ transplantation. For reasons never publicly explained, members who had been endowed in the temple were advised for a decade or more around 1960 not to will their organs for medical use. Implicit was a ban on living donations as well. One can surmise that this related to a persisting notion about the literalness of the resurrection. There also may have been some initial concern about preserving the sanctity of the physical body. Whatever the case the counsel ultimately was discarded. The donation of organs more recently has been described as an act of "selfless love," and notable transplant successes among members are publicized in church periodicals. Officially the church now simply advises.

> Whether an individual chooses to will his own bodily organs or authorizes the transplant of organs from a deceased family member is a decision for the individual or the deceased member's family.
> The decision to receive a donated organ should be made with competent medical counsel and confirmed through prayer.[142]

(Transfusions, it should be noted, seem always to have been viewed as a "wholly medical question."[143] While this might have been a precedent for other organs, traditional Mormon belief holds that there is no blood in the resurrected body, rather that "spirit" will course through the immortal veins.)

All other medical issues of concern to the church, save one, have now been resolved. Of the issues that persisted into this century, the controversy surrounding immunization, discussed in Chapter 3, ended long ago; the medical use of hypnotism and organ transplantation, both discussed above, have achieved more recent approval. Only the field of sexual and reproductive medicine remains in some regards controversial within the church; this will be discussed in Chapter 6.

Though it is probable that church periodicals will never again achieve the concentration of tutorial and otherwise supportive articles found in the first third of the century, there is no indication that there ever will be a significant slackening in Mormonism's underlying commitment to the best in modern medicine. The increasingly heroic "state-of-the-art" medicine espoused and practiced throughout this century will surely continue to be judged not so much by a doctrinal yardstick as by what Apostle James Talmage once labeled the "intelligent exercise of common sense."[144]

The most widely publicized recent advance, of course, was the landmark 1982 implantation of an artificial heart. Significantly for present purposes, both surgeon William DeVries and patient Barney Clark were Mormons. Among the questions addressed in the ethical postmortem of this pathbreaking case was the role of Mormon values. Unlike what might have been the case a century before, there was manifestly no concern with the propriety of heroic intervention, much less concern whether this was orthodox medical care. Rather, one commentator listed the relevant "basic principles of Mormonism" as "its pioneering, innovating history and perspective; its sense of manifest destiny; the at-once secular and spiritual importance it attaches to health and education; its conception of the human body as a tabernacle; the practical and this-worldly, but transcendental significance it accords to personal and collective improvement, accomplishment, mastery, and progress, through human effort, animated by rationality, knowledge, and intelligence." The Mormon respondent, then a vice president at the University of Utah, correctly chose to play down the distinctiveness of such qualities. "Mormon culture is uniquely American," he said. "While it may be more vigorously expressed in 1983 in the Mormon land than in Marin County, it is American!"[145] With regard to most aspects of medical practice, Mormons are indeed no longer a "peculiar people."

·5·

On Madness

The Mormon response to "madness" was shaped initially, as was its view on other forms of illness, by contemporary conventional wisdom and by an understanding of sacred text. In this Latter-day Saints differed very little from other restorationists who saw demons behind bizarre or dramatic manifestations of mental illness, while responding to more commonplace occurrences in entirely naturalistic ways. The modern church still applies scripture to the field of mental health, but the interest now is primarily the identification of divine psychotherapeutic insights. Though superseded, the early perspective is not altogether gone from Mormon thinking.

EVIL SPIRITS

From the outset Mormons accepted fully the reality of devils and demonic possession. The New Testament linked the gift of healing with the power to cast out the devil and his minions and offered multiple accounts of both.[1] Similar evidence was found in the *Book of Mormon,* which described a Satan recognizable to students of the New Testament, albeit in a largely Old Testament context.[2] (Early Saints, like other restorationists, assumed that this insight—along with the New Testament view of life hereafter—had been lost through error from the Old Testament record.) Moreover, the power to cast out devils was promised to faithful Mormon converts in at least five later-day revelations.[3]

What has been labeled the "first miracle" in the church occurred when Joseph Smith exercised this gift. Newell Whitney, an early convert, was "suffering very much in his mind, and his body acted upon in a very strange manner; his visage and limbs distorted and twisted in every shape and appearance possible to imagine, and finally he was caught up off the floor of the apartment and tossed about most fearfully." The Prophet took Whitney by the hand and "rebuked the devil," and immediately the victim "spoke out and said that he saw the devil leave him and vanish from his sight."[4]

This was only the first of dozens of similar experiences, many published in the official journals of the church. Particularly well known is an illustrative episode involving Apostle Parley P. Pratt. As a missionary he encountered a young woman who had been "taken down very suddenly . . . with a strange affliction":

> She would be prostrated by some power invisible to those about her, and, in an agony of distress indescribable, she would be drawn and twisted in every limb and joint, and would almost, in fact, be pulled out of joint. Sometimes, when thrown on to the bed, and while four or five stout men were endeavoring to hold her, she would be so drawn out of shape as to only touch the bed with her heels and the back parts of her head. She would be bruised, cramped and pinched, while she would groan, scream, froth at the mouth, etc. She often cried out that she could see two devils in human form, who were thus operating upon her, and that she could hear them talk. . . . She would have one of these spells once in about twenty-four hours, and when one of these spells were over she would lie in bed so lame, and bruised, and sore, and helpless that she could not rise alone, or even sit up, for some weeks. All this time she had to have watchers both night and day, and sometimes four or five at a time. . . .[5]

Eventually Pratt summarized what he viewed as the most common manifestations of demonic possession in his doctrinally influential *Key to the Science of Theology* (1855). According to Pratt, evil spirits on entering human bodies could "distract [those they possessed], throw them into fits, cast them into the water, into the fire, etc. They will trouble them with dreams, nightmare, hysterics, fever, etc. They will also deform them in body and in features, by convulsions, cramps, contortions, etc., and will sometimes compel them to utter blasphemies, horrible curses, and even words of other languages."[6]

To judge from published LDS sources, Pratt could have added that violent behavior or contortions were nearly always seen, that the victims typically were adolescents or young adults, especially young women, and that the evil spirit on occasion even volunteered its name, which—as in the prototypical New Testament accounts—could be "Legion" (Mark 5:9). The most common variant of this experience occurred when the victim was an elder attacked in the course of his duties. In this case there usually was only a feeling of suffocation or strangulation or an inability to speak. Joseph Smith experienced such symptoms just before his First Vision, and similar symptoms almost invariably were reported when an elder fell victim while attempting to cast out a devil.

When someone was possessed by an evil spirit, the indicated response was to summon an elder to "rebuke" the spirit "in the name of Jesus Christ." *Rebuke* inevitably was the operative term, derived from Matthew (17:18) where Christ "rebuked the devil" in a "lunatick." While this rebuke often was without benefit of consecrated oil, it was preferable (and more reliable) if there was an anointing. When used, oil typically was applied to the head, but could be applied to the throat or given internally.[7] The mere sight of consecrated oil was said to agitate and repel some evil spirits, and on one occasion simply pouring it on the floor banished poltergeist-like activity from a house. (This was a particularly edifying episode, as a Catholic priest had failed previously to exorcise the offending spirits by sprinkling "holy water" on the same floor.[8])

Almost all published accounts were priesthood successes, though often there were relapses enroute to eventual victory. Repeated repossessions could lead to confrontations lasting hours, perhaps a day or more, and sometimes involved more than one victim. Such was the case in an 1844 episode in which an evil spirit alternately possessed two sisters for a period of thirty-six hours, while young Mormon missionaries did their best to deal with the situation. The symptoms varied from "a trance, motionless, and apparently without breathing," to singing, speaking in tongues, or talking about the priesthood, to choking up, "ceasing to breathe until they were black in the face. . . . Sometimes they would froth at the mouth and act like they were in a fit. If standing they would fall and act like they were struggling for life with some unseen power."[9] In this encounter cure finally came when an attending elder commanded the offending spirit to return to the home of a neighbor (who was bitterly opposed to the Mormon gospel), whose daughter had been similarly afflicted since childhood.

A particularly striking account was published in 1847 in the church's *Millennial Star*.[10] It detailed the day-and-a-half effort of "some evil spirits (devils)" to prevent the ordination of a man to the office of priest. All together thirty separate priesthood administrations were required in this case, either to the principal victim or to a faithful onlooker set upon when the planned ordination was finally accomplished. By the conclusion of this ordeal, 319 devils—by actual count of the attending elders—had been cast out, in groups ranging from 3 to 27. Despite what might have been seen as a series of relapses (or treatment failures)—and an associated two-hour incarceration by local police "for having a devil" and "for casting him out, and thus causing a disturbance"—this was a faith-promoting experience for those involved.

Seeing themselves as repeatedly successful in a confrontation of cosmic magnitude, the attending elders turned after each successful administration to a growing crowd of onlookers to bear testimony of the divinity of their work. Moreover, among the vanquished devils were some who identified themselves as presidents of "seventy" in Hell, a faith-confirming revelation of the efforts of the Adversary to duplicate the divinely revealed structure of the church (there being a comparable entity within the Mormon hierarchy).

Relapses, and especially those that ultimately failed to respond to further ministrations, nonetheless could be a troublesome problem. Explanations varied considerably. Perhaps the most commonly invoked was that many evil spirits were involved, some of which were yet to be confronted. Alternatively, as with healings in conventional illnesses, relapses were attributed to lack of faith, failure to anoint with oil, or to the disbelief of onlookers. It was also possible that something in the victim's personal life, a "hidden vice," was a factor. In 1879, for example, Andrew Jenson was asked to administer to a man who "for some time had been tormented by an evil power." Jenson rebuked the evil spirit, only to have the man begin "to rave like a maniac, making hideous expressions of the face while his limbs were twisted in a fearful manner." Jenson and his colleagues eventually prevailed, but the man relapsed two days later only to respond once again to administration. Not until this pattern of relapses continued into the future, wrote Jensen, was it learned "that he led an unclean life and was guilty of self-abuse and thus had become a fit subject for the devil to torture":

> We decided that we would not administer to him again until he repented
> of his sins. This experience with evil spirits taught me this lesson, that it
> is not a desirable task to attack the devil on his own ground, or endeavor
> to drive him away from places where he has a right to be. This man had
> made himself liable to the attacks from this evil source because of his
> unholy practices.[11]

When faced with recurring relapses, the elders had few available options. Beyond repeated administrations, additional fasting and prayer might be indicated, especially if the spirits involved were believed of the type alluded to in Matthew (17:21) and Mark (9:29) "that came out only through fasting and prayer." One resourceful group of elders, confronting an intractable case and "knowing the devil is not over fond of music," "commenced to sing 'Hail to the Prophet' [a favorite Mormon hymn], and then attended again to the ordinance," whereupon the victim "was restored to her right mind, and has continued so."[12]

A briefly troublesome variant of the "possession" theme was the "display of the power of God" manifest within the church itself. During some Mormon meetings in Ohio members "would seem to swoon away, and make unseemly gestures, and be drawn or disfigured in their countenances. Others would fall into ecstacies, and be drawn into contortions, cramps, fits, etc."[13] Often those so affected spoke "in tongues," an unintelligible "language" which usually was "interpreted" by another member of the congregation. Joseph Smith, responding to these meeting-associated "spirits and manifestations"—during which members claimed to receive instruction from God—announced a revelation which warned, "that which doth not edify is not of God, and is darkness."[14] He addressed the point in a general meeting, labeling the questionable behavior "the spirit of the Devil." When a man spoke by the Spirit of God, he said, "even should he be excited, it does not cause him to do anything ridiculous or unseemly."[15]

Following the official disapprobation, this early adjunct to worship soon stopped. A transition can be seen at an important conference soon after at which the high priesthood was first bestowed. In conjunction with ordination to this new priesthood, the previous "manifestations" again took place, involving several people and continuing "all day and the greater part of the night."[16] Notably, however, on this occasion priesthood ministrations were credited with ending the episodes. Such intervention and the negative social overtones of the condemned behavior brought it to an end. With the exception of speaking in tongues, which still was viewed as an authentic "gift of the spirit" and continued to a lessening degree throughout the century, demonstrative "manifestations of the spirit" faded from the Mormon scene. In later years infrequent similar cases were viewed as an attempt by the devil to stop, for example, a planned priesthood ordination and were dealt with accordingly. In one instance in which this was not felt to be the case, a brother carried away in a "Methodist spasm" was simply called to account for his behavior before a church court.[17]

Though demonic possession usually was manifest through a constellation of what now might be termed hysterical symptoms, other behavior also was considered of potentially demonic origin. Joseph Hunting, for example, a homicidal "maniac" whose family joined the church in Kirtland, was said to be possessed by spirits. For years he had been chained in a barn, clothed in a "long, strong linen frock reaching from his neck to his feet," which, whatever his initial status, must surely have left him insane.[18] The severity and persistence of Hunting's condition was particularly troublesome to his would-be benefactors. Initially, his case was believed recalcitrant because he was possessed by spirits that came out only through fasting and prayer. (The requisite prayers, it might be noted, were performed kneeling in his presence, but judiciously "beyond the length of his chain.") While Hunting eventually responded to these efforts, and an anointing, he later had increasingly violent relapses. The problem was traced to his mother's periodic failure to comply with the church's health guidelines. Whenever she returned to the use of tea and tobacco, the devil was somehow able to reassert power over her son.[19]

Even the delirium of febrile or grave illness was attributed occasionally to evil spirits. A person also might simultaneously be afflicted both by spirits and by a conventional "burning fever on the brain." In one such case those in attendance "lade hands upon her & commanded the devil to Depart, & the fever to Stand rebuked in the name of Jesus Christ & it was done though not without a great Struggle & we left her ca[lm] in her mind & principly delivered of her pain."[20] An analogous circumstance occurred when a child recovered from scarlet fever through priesthood administration and "good nursing" but within a few days developed "dropsy" (a complication related to inflammation of the kidney). Despite a physician's efforts, this progressed to "spasms" in which the child's "eyes rolled back in his head, [and] his muscles began to twitch," symptoms which were perceived "by the Spirit of God" to be due to an evil spirit. Elders administered to the child, "rebuking the evil spirit," and "he rapidly recovered his health and strength."[21]

The publication or republication in official church periodicals of accounts of evil spirits throughout the nineteenth century attests fully to the strength of this Mormon belief. Indeed, *new* episodes were reported every decade well into the twentieth century. As late as 1926 the returning president of a regional proselyting mission testified to the church's annual General Conference of his successful healing of a missionary possessed by Satan himself.[22]

By the end of the nineteenth century, however, and amidst the church's beginning embrace of scientific medicine, there were signs of discomfiture about the imputed role of evil spirits. Church apologist Charles Penrose was mildly defensive when he wrote in 1898:

> Christ did not say that palsy, epilepsy, deafness, insanity and other diseases were always "caused by devils." It does not follow, because certain notions were commonly entertained in the days of Jesus Christ, that he also believed them. But that he and his apostles recognized the existence and power of evil spirits is certainly true, and the testimony of the New Testament writers goes to show that those spirits were rebuked and cast out of people by Christ and his disciples on numerous occasions. . . . The evidence is just as direct and complete and conclusive that devils some-

times cause disease, and sometimes possess the bodies of men, as that disease exists and afflicts the bodies of men. Individuals have been afflicted by the presence within them of a power which causes agony unspeakable, and endows with unnatural strength the unfortunate victim so that a dozen strong men cannot hold one ordinarily weak person. Under this influence sometimes such persons have not only rent their clothing, but torn their bodies with a violence horrifying to behold, and at the rebuke of a servant of God in the name of Jesus Christ, the influence causing these disorders has instantaneously departed, leaving the patient in his right mind and healed of his infirmities.[23]

The words of Penrose notwithstanding, the turn-of-the-century church continued its increasing embrace of the tenets of scientific medicine, among which were more conventional "psychological" explanations for mental illness. This trend was facilitated by the efforts of church leaders to end a growing belief in some Salt Lake City wards that certain chronically ill members of their congregations had been "bewitched" by other members of the ward. President Joseph F. Smith's editorial condemnation of this belief had potentially broader implications:

The danger and power for evil in witchcraft is not so much in the witchcraft itself as in the foolish credulence that superstitious people give to the claims made in its behalf. It is outrageous to believe that the devil can hurt or injure an innocent man or woman, especially if they are members of the Church of Christ—without that man or woman has faith that he or she can be harmed by such an influence and by such means. If they entertain such an idea, then, they are liable to succumb to their own superstitions. There is no power in witchcraft itself only as it is believed in and accepted.[24]

Later LDS discussions of mental health simply abandoned reference to demonic etiologies. And, as noted in Chapter 4, on healing, the cures of those with "functional" or non-organic disorders—especially at the hands of Christian Scientists and hypnotists—came to be attributed to entirely naturalistic mental or psychological factors. Despite the mission president's conference testimony in 1926, affirming satanic possession, just four years later a comprehensive church-sponsored health manual was comfortable passing by the issue with the observation that "a great deal of superstition still persists regarding the causes of insanity. For instance, there is the 'demoniacal' theory that the insane person is 'possessed of devils,' a view which scientists consider untenable."[25]

PHYSICAL AND MORAL CAUSES

The Mormons, in fact, never had assumed that all bizarre behavior originated with devils. The delirium of grave illnesses typically was noted in terms that presupposed only disease-related physical origins. Asahel Woodruff's death of "congestive fever of the brain," for example, was described as "sick 10 days & deprived of his reason 4 days before his death" with no indication whatever of associated demonic possession.[26] Similarly, head injuries—such as that inflicted by a mob on early Mormon leader Sidney Rigdon—were believed to account for much aberrant or irresponsible behavior, especially soon after the injury.[27]

More broadly, the Mormons shared with their nineteenth-century contemporaries a belief that there were numerous, as then termed, physical and moral causes of mental illness. Intemperate, immoral, or undisciplined habits, and hereditary factors were widely believed to underlie most mental (and some physical) disorders. This conventional nineteenth-century perspective could not have been better tailored to Mormon beliefs and values, either in the specific behaviors condemned or commended, or in the implicit assumptions about personal accountability. Toward century's end such "moral" explanations for madness readily filled the void left by declining emphasis on demonic possession. Unlike other aspects of medicine, this required no transformation in LDS understanding but only a wider application of already accepted principles.

The church periodical *Improvement Era* carried an instructive turn-of-the-century discussion of the causes of insanity which succinctly summarized nineteenth-century thinking on the subject. Based on twenty-six years (1885–1910) of admissions to the Utah State Mental Hospital, this analysis found that most cases resulted from one of five broad etiologic factors: mental habits, sexual immorality, the use of alcohol and other poisons, physical diseases, and heredity.[28]

"Mental habits" were said to be "the most important cause of some forms of insanity." Shock, grief, fear, anxiety, disappointment, shame, "brooding over slights," and religious and political excitement could all result in "mental derangement." Asylum admissions clearly bore this out: "worry" and "trouble" alone accounted for 11 percent (167) of the admitted cases. "Religion" contributed another 3 percent (47). These categories, plus others such as "disappointment in love," domestic trouble, fright, overwork, and "reading novels" accounted for nearly a fourth of all cases.

LDS discourse and writing regularly echoed this general understanding, often citing national or international authorities (one implicating failure to curb tempers as a contributor to insanity in women).[29] Spiritualism was a special case, being seen also as an effort by the devil to counterfeit and undermine revealed true religion. Even before disaffected Mormons founded a small spiritualist movement in Utah, church leaders had responded to spiritualism with harsh condemnation. Among the cited risks, recalled later church president Heber J. Grant, were "apostasy, insanity, suicide and death."[30] (For years church leaders believed spiritualists actually communicated with—and were deceived by—evil spirits, so the risk was felt to go beyond mental stress to the possibility of being "overcome" by satanic influences and destroyed.)[31]

Syphilis and masturbation accounted for almost all admissions to the Utah State Mental Hospital attributed to "sex immorality." The former, allegedly a leading cause of insanity nationally, was less a problem in Utah, accounting for only 3 percent (39) of admitted cases. Masturbation, however, was said to account for over 7 percent (102) of admissions over the twenty-six years reviewed, and in the 1880s, ranked first among all causes.[32] At that time it received high-level attention within the church, with Apostle Erastus Snow explicitly warning the brethren that "the baneful effects of the sin of Masturbation or self abuse" included "chronic and life long debility, insanity and even Madnes, terminating in [untimely] death."[33]

Cases believed resulting from "alcohol and other poisons" (the latter, mostly lead poisoning) accounted for just over 6 percent (89) of the admissions in temperate Utah—well under the estimated national experience which was said to range from 10 to 30 percent. Nonetheless the danger posed by stimulants—especially alcohol and tobacco—was the major insanity-related theme in nineteenth-century LDS discourse, an emphasis that only increased with time.

A number of "physical ailments" also were implicated as contributing to or directly causing mental breakdowns. These included typhoid fever, influenza, diphtheria, tuberculosis, heart disease, and epilepsy. The last of these was a significant cause of admissions to the Utah mental hospital and alone was blamed for 133 admissions—nearly 10 percent of the total.

The exact relationship of heredity to insanity was held to be uncertain, but evidence was cited that one-fourth to one-half of cases elsewhere in the country had a "history of insanity" in the family. Given sensitivities over polygamy, and the lineage consciousness of the Mormons, it was considered "very significant to note . . . that in the case of Utah, as far as it is ascertainable, only 218 out of 1450 cases, about one-sixth, have a history of heredity." (The implications of contemporary views in this area are discussed more fully in Chapter 6.)

ASYLUM IN THE WEST

When demonic possession was not the problem (or when priesthood administration did not succeed) nineteenth-century Mormonism responded to mental illness much as did society at large—with custodial care, generally provided by the family. In early Mormon Utah, when there was no family, the court appointed someone to the task. In this instance the appointee was selected on the basis of submitted bids (this being a paid service). Because of the potential for abuse, the legislature eventually passed a statute (in 1879) making it a misdemeanor to be neglectful of or "unnecessarily harsh, cruel or unkind . . . towards any idiot, lunatic or insane person."[34]

Continued growth of the territorial population, through both Mormon and "Gentile" immigration, soon led the Mormon city council of Salt Lake City to provide institutional public care for the small but increasing number of indigent mentally ill. The Salt Lake City Insane Asylum and Hospital was opened in 1869, a year also marked by the arrival of the transcontinental railroad and the departure of the first Mormon "called" to attend an orthodox Eastern medical school. Significantly the asylum opened three years before the first general hospital in the territory.

The goal of the Salt Lake City Insane Asylum was to protect both those admitted and the community at large; the approach remained basically custodial. It was located well away from the city, near where medically suspect immigrant groups were examined and quarantined, and the first superintendent was a former sheriff who soon requested that "strong cells be erected . . . for turbulent insane persons." The resident population varied from 10 to 15.[35]

A few years later the city gave control of the asylum to Seymour Young, nephew of Brigham, and the second Mormon sent East for medical education. Dr. Young returned from his training in 1875 to be named city physician, and the following year he asked to take over the asylum as a private venture. His offer was accepted, on the condition that he care for the inmates "properly at the rate of 85 cents per day averaging the whole lot." Medical credentials may not have played an essential role, as the terms specified that "if we should need his services as Doctor, that we will so notify him, and tell him what we want."[36]

During the nine years Young and his wife ran the asylum, it was variously characterized as "clean and well provided with clothing and bedding . . . [and of] healthy appearance" and as "one of the vilest institutions of the kind. . . ." Not long before his hospital closed (in conjunction with the opening of a territorial asylum), Dr. Young was called to the hierarchy of the church. In later years, in addition to his ecclesiastical and medical activities he wrote a number of health-related articles for official church periodicals. Some related to mental health issues and generally showed him to be current with recent developments in the field.[37]

The Utah Territorial Insane Asylum was authorized by the heavily Mormon territorial legislature in 1880, a year after the Salt Lake Asylum was sold outright to Seymour Young. It was the legislators' intent that the territorial facility be modern in every regard. Joseph M. Benedict, a prominent non-Mormon physician who had practiced in the Utah community for over a decade, was retained as an adviser and as such visited leading institutions in the East before making his recommendations. When the Territorial Asylum opened in July 1885, it was heralded as incorporating "all the improvements, conveniences and appointments of a modern asylum."[38]

The first appointed superintendent, Walter R. Pike, was probably the most qualified person in the territory. A young associate of Benedict who apparently also was consulted in the planning phase, Pike had lived in Utah since 1864 when he arrived from England with immigrant Mormon converts. He was one of the several Utahns who had gone East for medical education in the 1870s, and during an internship he had specialized in insanity and nervous diseases.[39] He served as superintendent for a decade, until 1896, when he was succeeded by Milton Hardy, a Mormon physician who once was his assistant at the hospital.

From 1885 to the present, this asylum—now called the Utah State Hospital—has been the main inpatient facility for the insane in Utah. While Mormons early showed their commitment to the institutional approach to care, through their instrumentality in founding and staffing both the asylum and its governing boards, they viewed inpatient care as primarily in the secular rather than ecclesiastical arena. The only formal LDS ties to the institution were in the provision of religious and other compassionate service to those confined in its wards. One interesting informal connection existed for a time: among the many patient work projects undertaken early in the twentieth century was the manufacture or mending of thousands of the ritually significant garments worn in the Mormon community.

The twentieth-century history of the state mental hospital is only of indirect relevance to Mormon attitudes, though it is perhaps important to recall that the hospital represents a psychiatric reference point for the Mormon-dominated state. Overall, the institution has a story typical of state asylums throughout the country. From the start it was headed by physicians, though until 1933 none were trained psychiatrists. It adopted "modern" diagnostic categories in conformity to the National System of Statistics of Mental Diseases in 1918, finally discarding "moral" etiologies from its annual reports.

The patient load grew from 51 in 1885 to over 300 by the turn of the century and further doubled in the next fifteen years. By the 1950s inpatients exceeded 1,300, but thereafter the advent of psychotherapeutic medications, the community health movement, and psychiatric wards in private hospitals drove the census down to only about 300 patients.[40] There were problems with space and staffing for most of these years, and periodic community outcries over "conditions" at the hospital. At one point in the 1920s the LDS women's Relief Society was particularly active in an effort to upgrade the hospital. As elsewhere, the adequacy of state funding seems always to have been in dispute.

From the earliest decades the expressed goal of the hospital has been to return the patient to a "normal condition" that harmonized "physical, spiritual and mental activities."[41] Especially in the early years, expectations for "cure" swung cyclically between excessive pessimism and excessive optimism. The actual care received has reflected national trends, with treatment initially ranging from work projects (to occupy the patient's time and provide some revenue) to restraint in a Utica crib (an adult-sized baby crib with a lid). Over time work projects eventually matured into more sophisticated occupational and recreational therapy. Utica cribs and related restraining devices—such as "tranquilizing chairs," Oregon boots (an eighteen-pound anklet), and straitjackets—periodically were "abolished" or reinstated until modern pharmacologic tranquilizers became available in the mid-fifties. Hyrotherapy was introduced in 1917 ("acknowledged by all authorities to be most efficacious"), followed by insulin shock therapy in 1937, and finally in 1946 by electroshock therapy. While transorbital lobotomies were not performed in the hospital, some 500 of these procedures were performed during the 1940s elsewhere in the state.[42] With the 1950s, of course, came psychopharmacology, which has dominated treatment of the seriously ill ever since.

In short, for one hundred years the Mormons have had available in their heartland a conventional mental hospital, with all that might imply about community attitudes and values. While data specifically on Mormon utilization of the hospital is not available, the steady growth in the number of admitted state residents strongly suggests a degree of acceptance among the

Mormon majority. The fact that for its first half-century admission rates were well below national averages led some LDS observers to conclude that there was less insanity in Utah (and less among the Mormons). A more informed analysis suggests that while demonstrably utilizing the state hospital, Utahns in fact were somewhat less accepting of institutional solutions than the norm elsewhere—and that insufficient staffing and facilities also played a role.[43]

The church never issued concrete guidance on the difficult choices inherent in the decision to institutionalize a family member. It is clear from the earliest decades, however, that even when the affected individual was himself one of the leading brethren, the state hospital was occasionally deemed the appropriate recourse. On the unhappy related question of placing a mentally handicapped child in a special institution, LDS parents presently are advised to rear handicapped children in their home "whenever that is a reasonable option" but to "consider the interests of each family member in deciding the best course of action." Recognizing that families simply may not be able to provide the care the child needs, members are counseled that they "should not feel guilty about placing your child where he can receive proper care."[44]

MENTAL HYGIENE, HEALTH, AND HANDICAP

With the turn of the century, and the church's growing commitment to scientific medicine, LDS attitudes toward mental health issues aligned almost completely with national thinking. Initially, the dominant perspective—both within the church and without—was a close variant on the preventive "hygiene" message then dominating other aspects of medical care. Well-being, be it physical or mental, was largely a matter of informed self-discipline and inheritance. The keys to "mental" hygiene, according to LDS periodicals, were attitude, activity, and diet. Hygienic thoughts ("as a matter of health, not considered in the light of religion or morality") should be good and pure. Anxiety and worry, on the other hand, were particularly harmful and to be avoided, along with "overconscientiousness" and "fear." Work or study should be of moderate intensity, and reading, neither "desultory" nor excessively stimulating. Special heed was to be paid to sleep, exercise, bowel control, and breathing habits. A number of "nerve foods" were particularly encouraged, including whole wheat and vegetables. Alcohol, coffee, and tea, of course, were to be avoided, as were other nerve "poisons" such as sugar and, especially, patent medicines containing narcotics and bromides.[45]

The rise early in the twentieth century of both "dynamic psychology" and the "mental health" movement soon were reflected in the evolving Mormon point of view. As the emphasis began to shift to external determinants of emotional development and such things as parental attitudes and early environment, church-sponsored instruction dealt more and more with issues of childhood. By the mid-twenties the Relief Society decided to adopt for its year-long text a popular, entirely secular work on *The Challenge of Childhood* by non-Mormon Dr. Ira Wile of the National Commission on Mental Hygiene.

This milestone decision was followed over the next decade by a number of related articles and lessons. By the late 1930s, nearly a generation of Mormons had been exposed to matter-of-fact discussions of psychoses and "psycho-neuroses," the role of the unconscious, and the contribution of Freud. Among many other concepts, hysterical fits, phobias, paranoia, morbid guilt, hypochondria, and depression had been covered at least briefly in formal church adult instructional programs.

Though official recognition of the legitimacy and importance of mental health issues continues to the present, the subject never again enjoyed quite the prominence it achieved during those years. Nor has the officially sponsored discussion been so accepting of (or dependent upon) the conventional scientific wisdom of the day. Typically, in the decades that immediately followed, LDS commentary became much more general and emphasized broad gospel precepts such as the role of love in emotional well-being and the importance of parental obligation.

A particular focus of early and continuing attention was the status of the mentally handicapped. Utah, as elsewhere, for years treated those who were severely retarded in much the same manner as it did the insane (and epileptic). Not until 1909 did the state mental hospital take steps to house these conditions separately, and even then the effort proved insufficient.

The LDS Relief Society devoted much attention to the subject in the 1920s. A number of weekly lessons were prepared on the causes of retardation (noting especially the locally important role of iodine deficiency); the nature and interpretation of intelligence tests; and the social circumstances of noninstitutionalized retarded individuals (males disproportionately were said to be delinquents, and females sexually promiscuous). Eventually LDS women joined a campaign with others to establish a training school for "mental defectives," which led to the opening in 1931 of the Utah State Training School. (By this time Utah was one of only three states without such a facility.)

Almost concurrently Utah responded to a related movement to allow sterilization of certain institutionalized individuals. Supported by both mental health and eugenics enthusiasts, this national effort led to legislation in most states. The discussion in Utah began with a 1912 request from the state hospital for legislation on the subject. Though none was forthcoming, occasional sterilizations ("for the prevention of vicious practices") began a few years later. Ultimately legislation was enacted in 1925 and as amended slightly in 1929 remains in effect to the present. It authorizes sterilization under specified circumstances of a person who "is habitually sexually criminal, or is insane, mentally deficient, epileptic, or is afflicted with degenerate sexual tendencies, and . . . unlikely to perform properly the functions of parenthood." By 1930 seventy-nine "eugenic sterilizations" had been performed under this law (of nearly 11,000 such procedures nationally).[46]

While the church did not take an active stand on the issue, there is little reason to believe that even privately it harbored ethical reservations. Years before, a leading Mormon had suggested in a still influential doctrinal treatise that "the idiot, the confirmed, irreclaimable drunkard, the man of hereditary disease, or of vicious habits" should not be allowed to marry.[47] Moreover, the legislature passing the statute remained heavily Mormon. In reviewing the subject in 1930, however, a church manual took an ambivalent stand on the actual practice, especially since as then performed it could involve asexualization (castration) as a precondition to discharge from an institution. The manual finally concluded that such sterilizations did have a place, "especially in the case of certain feebleminded females of child-bearing age who may be released to the community, even under supervision."[48]

In retrospect, the role of these sterilizations in Utah was very limited, as few were performed after 1930. The church nonetheless continues to the present to endorse in principle this course of action. The current official LDS guidance approves as an exception to a general rejection of sterilization the situation in which "a person is born with defects or has suffered severe trauma that renders him mentally incompetent and not responsible for his actions."[49]

Considered at another level the ecclesiastical status within Mormonism of those who are mentally handicapped always has been clear. The notion implicit in LDS scripture that "accountability" was a prerequisite to baptism (or any other personal ordinance) was early understood to apply not just to young children but to any who were mentally incapable of accepting responsibility for their own actions. Thus there has been no requirement of baptism or any other formal ordinance for those who are either severely retarded or insane. Mormonism teaches that the former, at least, are destined for the celestial kingdom (and full faculties). Autistic children are viewed similarly.

Decisions about extent of accountability of the mentally handicapped are left to local priesthood leaders. The only concrete instruction ever published on the question came very recently, as part of a lengthy *Guidebook for Parents and Guardians of Handicapped Children* (1986). It advised:

> To be eligible for baptism, a child must be at least eight years of age and mentally capable of being held accountable. If there is any question, the child's mental ability may be determined by professional testing. A mental age of eight years means that the child's performance on the test is equal to that of an average eight-year-old. . . .
> Local priesthood authorities should seek the Spirit in deciding whether or not to approve baptism. Generally, baptism should not be administered when the individual does not understand the significance of the covenant; the ordinance would be a meaningless ritual. . . .[50]

Decisions regarding other ordinances, such as conferral of the priesthood (which now typically takes place at age twelve), also are left to the discretion of local leaders. No mental age or ability levels have been set other than for baptism. "Appropriate" accountability and worthiness are the only suggested standards.

The above quoted *Guidebook* is part of a concerted effort in recent years to assist ward leaders as they reassure, counsel, and accommodate handicapped members of their congregations and their families. It makes clear that although we do not have "complete answers" to the difficult question about why God permits his "spirit children" to be housed in "defective, malfunctioning tabernacles," there is comfort in knowing all are born "according to the plan prescribed by our Heavenly Father."

> Some believe that God permits handicaps to test the nonhandicapped and to give them opportunity to lose themselves in Christlike service. Whatever God's exact intent, the presence of the handicapped brings an opportunity for others to serve, to become less selfish, and to develop godlike attributes.[51]

REENTER THE DEVIL

Although to a significant degree repressed by modern Mormons, belief in demonic possession has never been vanquished altogether from LDS thinking. In fact, the writings of conservative church leaders to the present day reaffirm this as a very real possibility. Apostle Joseph Fielding Smith, the most influential "scriptorian" of the mid-twentieth-century church, for example, acknowledged in 1954 that humankind had at times erroneously ascribed "diseases of the mind as well as of the organs" to evil spirits, but he added:

> The fact remains however, that the cases of spirit-possession as recorded in the New Testament, are true. It is also true that under some conditions Satan has bound the bodies of individuals by his power. This is not only true of such conditions in the days of our Savior and his apostles, but we have the evidence of such being true in this dispensation in which we now live. . . . There are scores of cases, fully attested in our own day of demon influence and possession. Cases which were not caused by derangement of the mind, but by actual overpowering of the individual and taking possession of his body.[52]

While there are no published surveys on the subject, one suspects that church leaders and most members remain open on this issue. Many believe that while demonic possession was over-"diagnosed" in the past, genuine cases probably existed. Even among Mormons trained in the field of psychology and psychiatry, there is a notable reluctance to reject categorically a demonic explanation for at least some of the historical episodes they readily acknowledge as having hysteric or other psychiatrically well-known qualities. Even now one hears, albeit infrequently, of instances in which a local leader has concluded that a member is possessed or otherwise harassed by an evil spirit, and rebukes it through priesthood administration. (Much more typically, disturbed individuals are considered to have emotional problems and referred to various professional therapists.)

A revealing indicator of the persistence of early beliefs was reported in a recent issue of the *AMCAP Journal* published by the Association of Mormon Counsels and Psychotherapists. In early 1984 a licensed certified social worker and family therapist who is a professor of clinical social work at Brigham Young University reported his "confrontation and rejection of an evil spirit in a therapy session." The case involved a thirty-five-year-old woman diagnosed by the therapist as having a multiple ego state (that is, multiple personality) disorder, who had failed to respond to several traditional psychotherapeutic approaches.

During a session in which the patient was under hypnosis, the therapist reported,

> the suspicion that I was dealing with an evil spirit grew in my mind. . . . I asked the Loser [the name assigned to the ego-state then manifest in the patient] if he was Lucifer. He responded, "No, but I am close to him!" With this information, I confronted the *Loser*, telling him that he was to terminate his control over Paula [the patient]. His response, in a sneering,

disdainful voice, was to the effect that, "How do you think you are going to accomplish that?"

At this moment (and not until then) I realized that this evil spirit (for such was its reality to me) must be dealt with on the basis of spiritual power. Extending my arm and pointing my finger toward him, I commanded, "IN THE NAME OF JESUS CHRIST AND BY THE POWER OF THE HOLY MELCHIZIDEK PRIESTHOOD WHICH I HOLD, I COMMAND YOU TO GO!"

I felt something akin to an electric charge coursing through my shoulders, up my neck, and down my arms and hands. Paula's arms and hands shook. Her entire body stiffened and trembled.

The patient's trembling soon stopped, and after this session she showed great improvement. In retrospect she recalled one earlier experience "which was like someone else entering her body (not sexually) and which caused her to be flung from the bed on which she had been lying."[53]

On the basis of this experience the therapist, who reported he "had never before directly confronted an 'evil spirit,'" concluded that it was probable that no one was "exempt from the possibility of demonic influence." A later postscript to this episode added that after several weeks of "marked improvement" the patient suddenly relapsed. As explained in the *AMCAP Newsletter:*

Realizing that all the client's ego states had been identified, [the therapist] approached her about the possibility of there being another evil spirit. They agreed that he should attempt to likewise rebuke it.

[The therapist] placed his client into a hypnotic state and called upon any other evil spirits to identify themselves. One came forth saying that there were five of them. He commanded them to depart. His client later recalled that upon hearing his words of rebuke she saw five ethereal entities leave her body. [The therapist] reported that again his client demonstrated remarkable improvement in her behavior.[54]

When the case was subsequently presented to the annual AMCAP convention, discussion reportedly centered not on the authenticity of the event but rather on whether the "victim" herself somehow was to be blamed. In briefly summarizing this the AMCAP reporter proposed that a "more charitable and accurate" understanding would be "to view these attacks much as we view rape or other violent physical assault—on a case by case basis." It also was noted that "it is important to demonstrate a degree of sophistication when dealing with the subject of possession and evil spirits.

Don't believe everything you hear, but strive to be able to discern—possession can only be discerned by the spirit."[55]

GOSPEL-BASED PSYCHOTHERAPY

For years Mormon accommodations in the mental health field required only modest adjustments. The eclipse of moral etiologies early this century initially was followed by an emphasis on mental hygiene, which included values and principles with which Mormons were quite comfortable. But further evolution to a nonjudgmental, value-neutral view of behaviors still condemned by the church was not so readily accommodated. "An individual may go to a psychiatrist," one popular mid-twentieth-century doctrinal compendium observed,

> for treatment of a serious guilt complex and consequent mental disorder arising out of some form of sex immorality—masturbation, for instance. It is not uncommon for some psychiatrists in such situations to persuade the patient that masturbation itself is not an evil; that his trouble arises from the false teachings of the Church that such a practice is unclean; and that, therefore, by discarding the teaching of the Church, the guilt complex will cease and mental stability return. In this way iniquity is condoned, and many people are kept from complying with the law whereby they could become clean and spotless before the Lord—in the process of which they would also gain the mental and spiritual peace that overcomes mental disorders.[56]

Ecclesiastical concerns over this issue and even more alarming reports that psychiatrists encouraged extramarital sexual encounters as a way station to emotional well-being led to more than one pointed conversation between church leaders and LDS practitioners. The intensity of feeling was well indicated in the compendium quoted above by its doctrine cross-reference of "psychiatry" to "Church of the Devil."

The subject, however, was not viewed in the simple terms this suggests. There also was, about this time, growing awareness and concern over an unexpected level of serious mental health problems among the rapidly expanding missionary force.[57] Moreover, psychiatry already had achieved sufficient institutional acceptance that treatment could be supported out of church welfare funds, just like other forms of medical care. And, also in the 1950s, a decision had been made to open a modest psychiatric section at the church's flagship LDS hospital in Salt Lake City. Unfortunately, given the tenor of the times, when the new LDS hospital program opened, it soon added what later was characterized as a secularly oriented, "call-it-as-it-is" adolescent treatment program, embarrassing both hospital and church. The psychiatric spaces soon were lost to a hospital renovation project which stretched from the few months originally projected to several years. Ultimately the department did reopen, shorn of the flamboyant elements of the original program.[58] Eventually an inpatient psychiatric unit also was opened, in 1972, in the church's Primary Children's Hospital. There remained considerable ill ease over a perceived outside pressure to "secularize" mental health care for young people by hiring non-LDS psychiatrists. Partially in response to such concerns the church-owned hospitals did not accept federal construction funds, hoping to avoid federal intervention in hospital operations.

Tension over mental health issues gave rise to several developments. First, church leaders became more direct and more concrete in their guidance on some subjects. Second, a number of LDS professionals joined together to create a "forum for counselors and psychotherapists whose common bond is membership in and adherence to the principles and standards of the church." And, third, a concerted effort was made to construct what came to be termed a "gospel-based psychotherapy."

The first of these responses encompassed both a strong reaffirmation of the primacy of priesthood-based personal counseling and the identification of a number of doctrinal absolutes that had to be accommodated in any ecclesiastically acceptable understanding of mental health issues. The priesthood counseling mandate was built on a revelatory "gift of discernment" promised to Mormon bishops in 1831 (*D&C* 46:27, 28). As senior apostle—and later church president—Spencer W. Kimball explained to a group of LDS psychologists and psychiatrists in 1963,

> A Bishop is ordained with an everlasting endowment. He is set apart as Bishop of a ward [congregation] to provide its leadership. He becomes the spiritual adviser, inspirer, counselor, discipliner. He becomes by ordination and setting apart the father of his people and should know them individually by name and nature and weakness and strength. He should foresee and forestall possible problems and if some develop, be able and ready to help in their solution. His ward family should be his enlarged family and receive general interest as his own flesh and blood.[59]

Direct counsel from Apostle Kimball continues to be incorporated into instructions for bishops on counseling and interviewing:

> Some church leaders sometimes find situations when the trained psychiatrist is called in for assistance, and several doctors in that field have

responded most generously. Numerous times the Church has been urged by certain of its members to train bishops in these special fields to make them efficient in handling of the social problems confronting them, but this has not been done, the feeling being that if the bishop is in tune, he may get his help from above.[60]

At present the official policy guidance issued by the church on "Counseling" states:

Church members who have problems or questions that trouble them should make a diligent effort themselves, including earnest prayer, to find solutions and answers. If they need help, they are to consult freely with their bishops or branch presidents and receive from them the assistance they need. If members call, visit, or write to Church headquarters about intimate personal matters, they deprive themselves of a great blessing.

The Church organization makes a bishop or branch president, who is a spiritual adviser and temporal counsel, accessible to every member. He knows his members intimately and understands the circumstances that cause their problems. These local leaders are, by reason of their ordination or setting apart, entitled to a heavy endowment of the discernment and inspiration necessary to advise those who seek help. If a bishop or branch president needs assistance, he may go to his stake [diocese] president, who may, in turn, seek counsel from his Regional Representative [ecclesiastically responsible for several stakes].[61]

With regard to the relevant doctrinal absolutes, while not systematically set forth, a number of points have been made in both official and informal settings. The latter principally are through invited addresses to annual meetings—now spanning two decades—of LDS counselors and psychotherapists. As recently summarized, counsel in this setting has emphasized three broad messages. First, psychotherapists are advised that to be successful in their field, they themselves must live by and be actively involved in the Mormon gospel (and put LDS gospel values and inspiration through the Holy Ghost above professional dicta). Second, they should bring their clients to repentance (thus implying, in many cases, an ultimate goal of sending those who have sinned to their bishop where guilt and repentance can be worked through). And, third, they should help their clients acquire traditional values.[62] Implicit in the foregoing counsel, of course, is an emphasis on sin, guilt, repentance, and righteous living as key factors in mental health, and thereby, the treatment of mental illness.

More formal commentary, such as that issued by the First Presidency, has been infrequent and much more narrowly focused. The Presidency, for example, in 1972, issued a statement of "Caution Against Unsound Studies Dealing with the Human Personality," which advised:

> Church members should be cautioned against becoming involved in
> unsound studies or systems dealing with the complexities of the human
> personality which are not based on any controlling or demonstrable prin-
> ciple. Our knowledge that man had a premortal existence which influences
> personality and which is beyond the reach of scientific research demon-
> strates the need for great caution in these matters.[63]

In the wake of the "sexual revolution" of the sixties and early seventies,
there were frequent warnings on sexual immorality (discussed more fully in
Chapter 6, on sexuality), which for the first time included homosexuality in
the public discussion. Such issues, of course, involved questions of guilt and
the fundamental attitudes of those involved. Church leaders, in clear response to therapists who held a contrary view, emphatically condemned
homosexual activity as a grave "sin" which should and could be overcome
through repentance and adherence to gospel principles (that is, it was neither inborn nor "incurable"). The doctrinal implication for mental health
professionals was that this behavior must be viewed as acquired (that is,
learned). Here again the church confronted cases in which the "partner in
sin [was] a psychiatrist, a medical man, a psychologist . . . [who] teaches
that these immoralities are harmless." The leadership response: "he is either
deceived or a vicious deceiver. Shun him."[64]

Official church guidance on issues relating to drugs and alcohol also had
implications for the mental health field. A lengthy guide for those dealing
with alcoholism, for example, clearly presupposed that the first drink (rather
than first intoxication) set the alcoholic on his unfortunate course. This view,
representative of the thinking of many professionals in the field, of course
also derived from twentieth-century LDS attitudes toward the Word of Wisdom.[65] Another official statement responded to the popular practice of using
reformed offenders in awareness programs. In a "Caution Concerning People
Who Have Had Special Social Or Emotional Problems," the First Presidency warned:

> Discretion is urged regarding the widespread use of people who have
> or have had special social or emotional problems. While reformed drug
> addicts, ex-convicts, and others are interesting and often effective in testi-
> fying about the unpleasantness of sin, when such speakers are used too
> widely, it can appear to be giving great attention to the sin rather than
> the process of repentance.
> At the same time, for these people to return completely to full fellow-
> ship, they must be given the opportunity to mingle with ward members
> without stigma or undue attention. To advertise them based on their past
> behavior is not in keeping with the Savior's mercy and forgiveness. Bishops
> are responsible for clearing all firesides [informal talks] held within the

ward. Certainly, bishops will want to use only those who have unquestionable backgrounds to teach the youth of the Church. We do not want to place those who have had unfortunate transgressions in their lives on pedestals before our young people.[66]

In general, LDS practitioners have been receptive to—and have often welcomed—leadership counsel in the mental health field, for both the insight and the institutional legitimacy they bring to their profession. As early as 1960 LDS members of the American Personnel and Guidance Association (APGA) considered creating a forum in which they could discuss issues involving the maintenance of both professional and gospel standards. This led, beginning in 1964, to an annual LDS adjunct meeting at the time of the APGA convention. A decade later the LDS adjunct to the APGA, with a quadrupled membership now totalling 400, was transformed into the Association of Mormon Counselors and Psychotherapists (AMCAP), a more diversified organization including other "helping professionals" such as psychologists, psychiatrists, and social workers. The *AMCAP Journal* (eventually a quarterly) was inaugurated, and annual conventions scheduled to coincide with the church's fall General Conference.[67]

The stated goal of AMCAP was "to promote fellowship, foster communication, enhance personal and professional development, and promote a forum for counselors and psychotherapists whose common bond is membership in and adherence to the principles and standards of the Church of Jesus Christ of Latter-day Saints, both in their personal lives and professional practice." A corollary goal was to "provide leadership in stemming the tide of materialism, amorality, and immorality that threatens to engulf professional organizations and society at large."[68]

Over the years AMCAP, as reflected in its published articles and conferences, has supported the legitimacy of integrating religion with therapy. Guided (with copious citations) by the words of both sacred text and "living prophets," authors have striven to uncover a "revealed approach to counseling." Counselors at Brigham Young University (one of only six schools nationally to offer a doctorate in "marriage and family counseling") also responded to leadership counsel. Among other steps, a Board of Review for Psychotherapeutic Techniques was organized in 1975 "to recommend policies governing the use of sensitive treatment techniques" at BYU. This group identified eight therapies which they felt to be doctrinally questionable, including sensitivity training (which some church leaders had openly condemned), hypnosis, and what has been summarized as "the therapeutic use of confession, sex, and self-disclosure."[69]

Efforts to identify and develop a "gospel-based therapy" accelerated with the creation in 1976—in response to specific leadership prompting—of an Institute for Studies in Values and Human Behavior at Brigham Young University. The first director, psychologist Allen Bergin, explained that "too many LDS behavioral scientists do not harmonize their professional concepts with their religious stands," and that the institute's "first project [would] be to state as clearly as possible to the behavioral scientists . . . that Jesus Christ teaches in principles of behavior." "What we can do is receive inspiration in our research and then seek reviews by the authorities [of the church] for their interpretations, disapproval, or whatever, if doctrinal questions are raised by it." A co-worker further explained, "our basic theme is that truth lies with the scriptures and prophets, not with secular data or debate."[70]

The following year, in a university-wide address on the subject, psychologist Bergin identified seven foundational givens that shaped this effort:

(1) [P]ersonality, personal identity, is the ultimate reality in the universe. There is nothing more powerful, nothing higher than personhood or intelligent identity. God is a glorified, exalted person. . . . [T]he most serious inadequacy of the behavioral and social sciences [is the lack of an] adequate or comprehensive . . . theory [referring] to him. . . . They proceed as though God is not relevant to an understanding of human behavior.

(2) Nowhere in the professional literature—experimental, social, or clinical—do we find an adequate account of the nature of man and his relationship to God. . . . None are in harmony with the revealed picture that shows the personhood of men and women to be akin to the personhood of God. . . . [And that m]an's soul, consisting of body and spirit, is essentially good and "theotropic," growing toward the bodily and spiritual image of God unless he yields himself to the influence of evil. . . .

(3) The most vital and intimate facts about human nature are unseen and are discernible only by spiritual means; therefore, the secular, physicalistic rules of observation that currently govern the behavioral sciences must, of necessity, lead to obscure or misleading viewpoints when applied to human conduct. . . .

(4) The alienation of behavioral science from the spiritual realities has caused serious problems of both substance and form in the professions. A most important consequence has been a widespread denial of the free agency of man. . . .

(5) It is timely for us to consciously originate a new system of thought and inquiry, or more correctly, to reenthrone the ancient modes of revelation. As we do this, new techniques of research and practice will come into being. This amounts to integrating the empirical and rational with the religious approach to inquiry. . . . Since that which is spiritual is that which is most real, we need to pursue it by making a methodological break

with traditional scientific thought that is as dramatic as the break science made with medieval thought. . . .

(6) [S]piritual methods of inquiry and change can add significantly to our professional practice if they are used wisely and appropriately. . . . [These, when appropriate, could include prayer with the client, the use of parables in counseling to link "our procedures to the Lord's way," and "appropriately delegated" priesthood administration.]

(7) [T]he BYU and Church scholarly community have a special role to play in achieving all that I referred to. The great universities of the world were established on a religious foundation but most have betrayed their foundations. It is therefore necessary for us to revive our fields by bringing the [Mormon] restoration to them. . . .[71]

Several important additional points were made by Bergin in this address. As a "first principle of the new abnormal psychology," he proposed that "emotional disturbances arise when gospel laws are violated." The nature of emotional problems is thus "basically spiritual":

The therapist recognizes that his role as a practitioner of a gospel psychology is different from the traditional one, because healing, when it does take place, is a blessing from God obtained through personal discipline and good works. The therapist role is therefore one of helping the agent to partake of the principles and ordinances of the gospel; it is they which will heal the person when his soul understands and assents to them. This means that the therapeutic process can only be as good as the person who is conducting it. Professional role-playing cannot cover the spiritual deficiences of the therapist. In gospel therapy, personality is higher than technique.[72]

Bergin's "second principle of the new abnormal psychology" was that "all of the pathologies, defenses, and deceptions mentioned earlier begin with the undermining, distortion or destruction of [the] basic loving relationship." The "core of therapy," Bergin explained,

is an inspired replication of the loving relationship we experienced originally in heaven and which is offered to us again in mortality largely through the example of Jesus Christ and the influence of the Holy Ghost. . . .

The repairing of one's capacity for love, constructive work, and accurate self-perception is established not just by the therapist's offering of a healthy loving relationship, as is assumed in some therapies, but by using that love to open the person to the love of the Father and the Son and to the witness of the Holy Ghost. Through the renewal of these important ties to one's premortal relationships with God, the roots of deep, permanent change are established. . . .

. . . it is through the atonement of Christ and by putting Him at the center of our lives that real healing occurs.[73]

In the more reassuring context reflected in Bergin's remarks, the church approved during the early 1970s a previously rejected proposal to expand its social services resources, particularly outside Salt Lake City, to include more professional counseling on personal, marital, and family problems. Historically the church's social services department existed to provide licensed services—foster care, adoption, and the Indian Placement Program—which usually could not be provided legally by ecclesiastical leaders.[74] While the new service, like the old, was intended as a resource to priesthood leaders, it soon acquired its own heavy load of counseling. In general these church-employed counselors, like their colleagues at Brigham Young University, have been more disposed to seek gospel-based (that is, pastoral) solutions than their noninstitutional LDS colleagues, who often have been viewed as "too secular in their approach." In turn, those not church-employed have wondered if "LDS Social Services practitioners are competent or adequate in their professional training" (they are often trained to the master's level or less).[75] Thus, despite general movement in the mental health field, sources of strain remained.

SIGNS OF SYNTHESIS

The last decade or so has seen further apparent lessening in the centrifugal forces that previously surrounded issues of mental health in the church. Evolving views and subtle shifts in perspective seem to herald a beginning synthesis. The quest for a gospel-based therapy has lost much of its urgency, and church-originated referrals increasingly are to secular (albeit preferably LDS) specialists. A number of church-sponsored publications have been issued for local leaders and members reminiscent in their depth and openness to publications last seen some fifty years ago. These include *Resource Manual for Helping Families with Alcohol Problems* (1984), *Guidebook for Parents and Guardians of Handicapped Children* (1986), and *Identification and Prevention of Suicidal Behavior* (1974).

With evidence that a "gospel-based psychotherapy" was elusive in actual practice, the Brigham Young University Institute that had been created to give it birth and form was dissolved (after some five years of work). Psychologist Bergin explained, "the plan itself was unrealistic. In perspective, it is clear that the results sought could not be obtained in a few months or a few years, or with limited budgets. These hopes are unlikely to be realized in less than a generation." More broadly, he continued, it was assumed that a revolution was required in order to overturn existing approaches. I now think this was an incorrect premise. I was unnecessarily harsh in my criticism of deficiencies in the field. While I still think it is important to establish legitimacy for spiritual perspectives in the professional arena, it isn't necessary to dismiss other viewpoints as having little value.

I have returned to my previous view that many approaches contain considerable truth; and that the approach of the future will be an eclectic one that embraces many secular discoveries as well as valid spiritually oriented developments. . . .[76]

The tangible legacy of BYU's Institute for Studies in Values and Human Behavior was one book, privately published, on human intimacy;[77] some work influential within the church on homosexuality (and its treatment) as learned behavior; and a number of addresses and publications in national forums—both conventions and journals—advocating the legitimate role of spiritual and moral values in the therapeutic arena. Perhaps more so than the others, this latter point remains one of general interest and agreement among LDS professionals in the mental health field. Religious beliefs and church activity play such a central role in the lives of most Mormons that they almost of necessity must be accommodated both diagnostically and in otherwise basically "secular" therapeutic interventions.

Professional counseling continues to be offered by church Social Services, albeit with an increased emphasis on the qualifications and in-service training of the staff. Periodically this resource is redirected more exclusively into a consultation and evaluation service for priesthood leaders, and since 1984 members seeking help from LDS Social Services have been charged $25 per hour for assessment and therapy. Increasingly, members with significant problems are referred to local community resources, preferably Mormon, who have been identified by Social Services as both qualified and responsive to LDS values and beliefs. A small but growing number of LDS psychiatrists (of which there probably are less than 50 churchwide) are forthrightly involved in this member-counseling effort, and typically—as in the past—handle the most serious cases.

Despite ill ease with the profession, the church leadership never fully withdrew support for psychiatric care. This reflected their growing recognition of the severity of some forms of mental illness, the influence of a handful of respected practitioners, and the advent of an effective psychopharmacology which only physicians (usually psychiatrists) could dispense. A recent article on mental health in the church's *Ensign* magazine underscores this point. This brief but unusually sophisticated discussion was designed to help lay Mormons recognize and deal with several major categories of mental illness, including anxiety disorders, severe depression, and schizophrenia. And in it, the author emphasized repeatedly the essential role of medication—and competent professional care—in any successful treatment plan. As was the case a half-century before, the article provided readers with the addresses of reputable secular sources for additional information and support.[78]

Psychoactive medications seem never to have been particularly controversial within the church. From the outset Joseph Smith was comfortable with biblical (Proverbs 31:6) and nineteenth-century thinking which commended "wine unto those that be of heavy hearts" and endorsed "strong drink to him that is ready to perish." LDS physicians continued to quote and follow this advice until the therapeutic efficacy of alcohol came into question in the early twentieth century. This legacy and the general Mormon acceptance of modern medicine facilitated acceptance of modern psychopharmacology when it was introduced in the 1950s. If ever there was hesitancy on this subject, it came at the latter period, at a time when Utah legislators also were apprehensive about other intrusive new treatment modalities—such as electroshock and lobotomy. The concerns led the Mormon-dominated legislature to block a bill supporting community mental health centers until a clause was added barring therapists working under its provisions from changing the patient's belief in God.[79] Given this caveat and the assumption that an individual is in the hands of a professional qualified to prescribe medications, there have been no expressed leadership objections to the judicious use of tranquilizers, antidepressants, antipsychotics, or related drugs. Overall a generally secular course continues evident in the practice of most LDS psychiatrists. Although sensitive to Mormon values, the latter seem likely to understand pathology in basically nongospel terms and to seek at least partially psychopharmacologic solutions for many of their patients.

A good illustration of developments in LDS thinking can be seen in commentary on the subject of suicide. As noted in Chapter 2, an official LDS response to this subject was first issued a century ago. At that early date, it was recognized that some suicide victims were "mentally deranged" and thereby in Mormon theology not accountable for their actions. The issue was believed complex, however, because of the notion at the time that much if not most mental derangement derived from ecclesiastically condemned behaviors like intemperance and sexual immorality. This point was underscored by the First Presidency in 1886 and emphasized regularly thereafter. A stereotypical portrayal of the problem came in 1892 in a serialized short story entitled "Which Path" in which a fine young man, having foolishly joined his unworthy friends in the use of coffee, progressed over several installments to cigarettes, alcohol and inebriation, and finally to sexual immorality. Despondency followed, and the final chapter saw him "put a revolver to his temple."[80] The implication was clear: some allowance might be made for the final act of an unbalanced mind, but the individual remained accountable for having brought himself to that state.

Over the years factors leading to suicide were mentioned in LDS writings, most believed in some way to contribute to mental instability or depression. All were drawn from conventional secular thinking, which eventually moved away from frankly "moral" (or immoral) etiologies. Heredity and home environment came to be cited as common contributing factors, and church periodicals therefore discussed the proper preparation of children for life's "disappointments." In general, however, the feeling was that such contributing factors still did not absolve suicide victims from responsibility for their actions. Instead of confronting life's "trials and difficulties," they had "cowardly shun[ned] them by self-murder" and thereby succumbed to the spirit of the devil.[81]

As recently as 1958 an unofficial compendium of Mormon beliefs remained quite harsh on the subject, asserting that

> suicide is murder, pure and simple, and murderers are damned. There is no more justification for self-murder than for the wilful destruction of another. There is a common and supposedly compassionate tendency on the part of many to reason that all who commit suicide must be mentally unbalanced and that therefore they are not accountable for their crimes. . . . But the great probability is that nearly all self-murderers— though they may be depressed and mentally ill—do in fact know right from wrong, the same as most killers do.[82]

By 1966, however, in a remarkable transition, the second edition of this influential work took a much more restrained tone:

> No man has the right to run away from [the physical, spiritual, and mental tests of man's "probationary" mortal state], no matter how severe they may be, by taking his own life. Obviously persons subject to great stresses may lose control of themselves and become mentally clouded to the point that they are no longer accountable for their acts. Such are not to be condemned for taking their own lives. It should also be remembered that judgment is the Lord's; he knows the thoughts, intents, and abilities of men; and he in his infinite wisdom will make all things right in due course.[83]

This summary (by Apostle Bruce R. McConkie) was incorporated into 1974 guidance on the identification and prevention of suicidal behavior prepared by the church's social services department to assist local leaders and others in spotting and avoiding this tragedy. The guidance contained in this still-current resource is notable for its reliance on mental health professionals as a first-line resource when suicide threatens. Local leaders are advised to "be sensitive to suicidal clues" and to seek qualified professional help in further identifying and responding to any acute problem. Only "after the crisis period has passed" does the valued support from home teachers (assigned visitors from the local congregation) and others in the church come into play "in helping the individual learn to deal with personal problems in an effective way."[84]

In 1989 the church issued through the *General Handbook of Instructions* its first formal policy guidance on suicide since the First Presidency's statement of 1886. This succinctly summarized the present LDS point of view:

> A person who takes his own life may not be responsible for his acts. Only God can judge such a matter.
>
> A person who has considered suicide seriously or has attempted suicide should be counseled by his bishop and may be encouraged to seek professional help.
>
> Bishops should counsel and compassionately console the family members of a person who has committed suicide. The family, in consultation with the bishop, determines the place and nature of a funeral service for a person who has died under such circumstances. Church facilities may be used without restriction.[85]

Given the overall record to date, it seems likely that LDS attitudes toward mental illness will follow the same course as have attitudes toward other forms of disease. Brigham Young once exempted orthopedics and dentistry from his general condemnation of orthodox medical practice because they both involved self-apparent mechanical skills and therefore required no inspiration. Science eventually rendered most of medicine equally "obvious" (or at least conclusively validated many of its remedies), and church leaders soon embraced the full range of scientific medicine. The history of psychiatry affords a reasonable parallel to this story. Recent decades have seen the development of a demonstrably effective psychopharmacology, and increasing evidence of a biochemical basis for such "mental" conditions as schizophrenia, manic-depressive and panic disorders, and Alzheimer's disease. These developments would seem to offer the church a familiar path, which almost surely it will follow to the end point previously attained in all other aspects of modern medicine.

·6·

On Sexuality and Birth

A diversity of medical themes relate to issues of birth and sexuality in the LDS culture, as elsewhere. There is a certain logic to bringing these themes together in a single chapter, despite the resulting juxtaposition of such apparently disparate subjects as abortion, dance, and sex-change surgery. The procreative process is so central to Mormonism's cosmic view that at one time or another developments in every issue here addressed have been measured in terms of their impact on or implications for LDS thought in this area. In this context, the present chapter traces—in approximately the order they became of concern to the modern church—LDS perspectives on sexuality and sex education, birth control, abortion, sterilization, infertility, homosexuality, and sex-change surgery. As with nearly all other LDS teachings, those related to birth and sexuality can be understood only in the context of a considerble historical legacy, elements of which remain in evidence today in various segments of Mormon society. The subjects of masturbation and dance, discussed in a brief digression, offer prototypes of broader developments in this general field. Taken in its totality, the record that unfolds in this chapter is without parallel in the window it offers on the evolution of authoritative guidance within the LDS church.

SEXUALITY AND SEX EDUCATION

Joseph Smith provided the doctrinal underpinnings for an almost unique view of sexuality; and Mormons very early accepted a remarkably exalted view of the place of reproductive sex in the grand eternal scheme. The *Book of Mormon* affirmed that Adam's Fall "was the cause of all mankind becoming carnal, sensual, [and] devilish" (Mosiah 16:3), but it implicitly rejected any notion that sexual relations were involved in an "original sin." As recounted in Mormon text, Adam and Eve were instructed from the very outset to "have seed." Fulfillment of this divine command depended on the commission of a (nonsexual) transgression which brought with it both mortality and fertility. The Mormons thus viewed the Fall as having been—in the words of a recent church leader—"in the right direction," or as the *Book of Mormon* expressed it: "Adam fell that men might be; and men are, that they might have joy."[1] There was no obligatory depravity associated with mortality, and certainly none in the sexual relationship. Rather the Fall ushered in an exposure to evil influences that could lead to sin and thus begin the "test" the premortal spirits of mankind willingly accepted before coming to earth.

The early Mormon view went far beyond a simple rejection of a devilish origin of sex. Like "knowledge of good and evil," reproductive sexuality itself was soon held to be an attribute of deity. Indeed, with the development of their anthropomorphic view of God, Mormons quickly came to take quite literally Paul's proclamation (Acts 17:28) that mankind was the "offspring" of God. A parallel latter-day revelation spoke of mankind as the "begotten sons and daughters" of God,[2] and early commentators clearly assumed both that God was anatomically in the image of man ("possessing every organ, limb, and physical part that man possesses") and that reproduction in his world was probably accomplished in essentially the same manner as on earth (that is, our "embryo spirits" had been "begotten of a Father, and born of a Mother in Heaven").[3]

Following the introduction of LDS temple rites and covenants, the faithful looked forward to a continuation of their own reproductive powers throughout the eternities, a privilege which they believed would set them apart from all who failed to attain the most exalted degree of the celestial kingdom.[4] While initially a prerequisite to such exaltation was a willingness to enter into plural marriages, polygamy was viewed as both a test and an opportunity, for it was held that the more extensive one's progeny, the greater the eternal reward.

Despite its explicitly exalted status, the sexual relationship per se was rarely discussed in print. The Apostles Orson and Parley Pratt were among very few to touch on the subject in a published source. Orson, writing in the *Seer* (1853), explained that "God is the Author of sexual or conjugal love, the same as He is of all other kinds of pure love. . . . God has ordained that pure and virtuous love should be incorporated with sexual love; that, by the combination of the two, permanent union in the marriage covenant may be formed, and the species multiplied in righteousness."[5] Brother Parley, in his more influential *Key to the Science of Theology* (1855), carried a less explicit but similarly positive message:

> The object of the union of the sexes is the propagation of their species, or
> procreation; also for mutual affection, and the cultivation of those eternal

principles of never ending charity and benevolence, which are inspired by
the Eternal Spirit; also for mutual comfort and assistance in this world of
toil and sorrow, and for mutual duties toward their offspring.[6]

Our "natural affections," Parley wrote elsewhere, were not "carnal, sensual,
and devilish" attributes, as some taught, which "therefore ought to be re-
sisted, subdued, or overcome as so many evils which prevent our perfection,
or progress in the spiritual life"; rather, "so far from this being the case, our
natural affections are planted in us by the Spirit of God, for a wise purpose,
and they are the very mainsprings of life and happiness—they are the cement of all virtuous and heavenly society—they are the essence of charity,
or love; and therefore never fail, but endure forever."[7]

Counsel given orally or in less public settings was grounded more firmly
in nineteenth-century understanding but was still implicitly positive. The
"lower passions" were placed in men and women "for a wise purpose," Apostle George Q. Cannon once explained in the tabernacle, but unfortunately,
when constrained by the rules of monogamous society, there was great potential for evil and injury. Men were known to outnumber women in most
societies, he said, and their "procreative powers" remained functional well
past the age at which those in women ceased. Moreover, many women were
"sent to the grave prematurely through the evils they have to endure from
their husbands during pregnancy and lactation," and "irremediable injury" is
often sustained by their children through the same process. In non-Mormon
society the alternatives were equally evil: practicing "that which is vile and
low," submitting to "a system of repression," or having recourse to "illegal
connection with women." The Lord's solution to this problem was, of course,
the "principle of plurality" (though Cannon was quick to add that "the mere
increase of faculties to gratify the lower passions" was not sufficient induce-
ment to accept the "grave" responsibilities associated with this system).[8]

Brigham Young, speaking on a related concern, advised his colleagues to
follow the counsel of Leviticus (12:1–5) and avoid sexual relations for forty
days following the birth of a boy and for seventy days following the birth of
a girl. He also suggested that the healthiest children would result if parents
abstained "till seven days after the cessation of the menstrual discharge." So
far as "sexual connection during pregnancy," however, Young thought "just
as they pleased about that, they could suit themselves."[9] Apostle Erastus
Snow amplified this latter advice years later when he recommended that
intercourse be continued during pregnancy "where it was right and consistent that they might not entail on their offspring unholy desires and appe-
tites." A balance was essential, as the husband could visit "disease and
suffering on his Posterity thru not governing himself during the times when

his wife was bearing children or nursing them." Moreover, the men themselves risked "premature decay and early death by the too frequent use of
sexual intercourse."[10] (All of this was, of course, reflective of a pre-Mendelian
misconception about inheritance, discussed below. This concern with "lost
manhood" was a particular obsession with nineteenth-century American
males and spawned many profitable patent medicines. Included among these
were Mormon Elders' Wafers, Brigham Young Tablets, and Mormon Bishop
Pills—each allegedly containing the secret to the manifest staying power of
Mormonism's pioneer patriarchs!)[11]

It was, of course, the sexual aspects of polygamy that attracted the most
attention nationally, and Mormonism, as is well known, was early identified
in the popular mind with an aberrant, highly sensual view of sexual relationships. With word of polygamous marriages spreading throughout America,
a stereotype soon emerged of licentious Mormon harems and lascivious
temple rites. Allusions to the attitudes of Mormon men and the status of
Mormon women found their way into the humor of Mark Twain, the mysteries of Sherlock Holmes, and even presidential inaugural and State of the
Union addresses. Dozens of novels and exposés appeared, each shocking—
and fascinating—their Victorian readership with accounts of Mormonism's
"chiefly licentious" "system of masked sensuality."[12]

In this broad context whatever promise Joseph Smith's early vision held
for the public espousal of a uniquely affirmative philosophy of sex was largely
extinguished. Sensitized by the unrelenting attacks on their sexual mores,
Mormon leaders themselves dwelt almost exclusively in published sermons
and writings on a theme of sexual immorality as a sign of the depravity of
the world. Given the full sweep of Mormon teachings, this was an easy step.

In practice, as Lawrence Foster has noted in his study *Religion and Sexuality,* nineteenth-century Mormonism was "even harsher in [its] condemnation
of unauthorized sexual liaisons than was the larger society."[13] Within a year
of the organization of the church, revelation had identified adultery as among
the most serious of all sins and specified that unrepentant (or second-time)
sexual offenders were to be "cast out" of the church.[14] Soon sexual sin came
to be labeled "second only to murder" (Alma 39:5). Even Mormon plural
marriage has been labeled "Puritan polygamy," and at least from the Nauvoo
period devout Mormons pledged marital fidelity as part of their suspect
temple rites.

Given the tenor of the times, few contemporary observers were aware of,
much less sensitive to, this basically conservative Mormon stance. In addition to the threat polygamy was believed to pose to monogamous domestic-
ity—then held to be the keystone of a stable society—graphic depiction of

the "organized indulgence" of the Mormons is said also to have offered some vicarious outlet for a broader society ostensibly committed to an almost ascetic self-restraint.[15] And, in fairness, Mormon sexual unorthodoxy extended further than a simple polygyny. Though eventually discarded, and generally unknown even at the time, a limited form of polyandry also had been introduced, under narrowly defined conditions. Moreover, it was not infrequent for sisters, or even mother and daughter, to be married to the same man (the daughter being from an earlier marriage). There was open anticipation that, because the spirits of all were literally brothers and sisters in the family of God, ultimately marriages would be possible between this-worldly brothers and sisters as well.[16]

Beyond counterattacking their critics, Mormon leaders focused increasingly on and acted against sexual offenses within the faith. The eternal consequences of sexual sin were repeatedly called to the attention of church youth. Activities such as certain dances believed conducive to sexual abandon were formally and repeatedly condemned, and serialized accounts of the fall—and even suicide—of youth who had strayed were published in official young people's magazines. An adulterous affair involving an elder came to require excommunication "regardless of his repentance,"[17] and even continued sexual relations with a spouse cut off for adultery was deemed potential grounds for church court action.

The impact of contemporary scientific and societal notions on Mormon thinking is demonstrable throughout the last century, but it is particularly in evidence from about 1890 on. In part through the influence of LDS physicians, and especially LDS women physicians, science-based sex education became a major focus of attention within the church. For nearly fifty years thereafter, until the late 1930s, this was one of many recurring medical themes in the church's education program. Initially the paramount goal was the physiological protection of the female reproductive system. In courses, public lectures, and articles in church periodicals, LDS mothers and daughters were warned of the hazards of inappropriate dress (said to place too much pressure on the reproductive organs or expose them unduly to the elements), excessive study (said to draw necessary blood away from these organs and lead to uterine underdevelopment), and unduly exciting food or activity (said to cause premature—or delayed—reproductive maturation). Another, lesser concern was premarital kissing, which for a time could be condemned both as morally inappropriate and unhygienic (and "a pestilent practice").[18]

In general, discussions in church periodicals were remarkably forthright and on occasion carried detailed anatomical illustrations. References to specious physiological and hygienic risks eventually were supplanted by information on the real dangers of sexually transmitted infections. The approach remained candid and open, even including detailed statistics on disease incidence.[19]

The late 1920s and most of the 1930s saw a more explicit "sex education" in church lessons to a degree not matched before or since. As one invited speaker explained to a general conference of the Relief Society, adults needed to realize that "you and I have been brought up in a generation where we just could not talk about sex. Not so our youngsters. They are talking and thinking about sex as frankly as anything else, and so far as I can discover, as wholesomely."[20] Official manuals advised members to purchase secular works on the subject—specific titles were suggested—and that the expression of sexual interests "should be guided and directed, not inhibited." An apogee (in the Mormon context) was reached in lessons which warned against creating emotional problems in adolescent children by an "unintelligent" overresponse to the discvoery that they practiced masturbation.[21]

There were other signs of liberalization. Restrictions on certain dances were lifted. The recommended dating age dropped from seventeen or eighteen to sixteen. Mandatory excommunication for adultery was replaced by a case-by-case approach, and especially when young unmarried couples were involved a forgiving attitude adopted. Churchwide, excommunications fell to very low levels.[22]

For reasons not altogether clear, this rather open attitude was succeeded by a somewhat different stance toward midcentury. "Sex education" as a term largely disappeared, and discussions of the subject were limited increasingly to a reaffirmation of the church chastity standard. A recently published content analysis of Mormon literature found this general trend to have intensified even further through the sixties and seventies, with stronger and more explicit guidance being issued. Unlike a half-century before, this was not associated with any endorsement of public sector programs. Efforts of such groups as SIECUS (Sex Information and Education Council of the United States) to make information available through schools and other public programs now were condemned—on the grounds that their programs were value-neutral—and members advised against involvement.[23]

The "sexual revolution" experienced in the U.S. in recent years unquestionably sparked some of the attention given this subject by church leaders. Their expressed concerns were also backed up with action. While in principle sex-related offenses were evaluated on a case-by-case basis, members guilty of extramarital affairs—especially after participating in the temple endowment—were almost routinely excommunicated or disfellowshipped.

By 1970 excommunications, perhaps half for "adultery and fornication," had risen to ten times the rates experienced a half-century before, and subsequently the rate again tripled.[24] Though to some extent these figures reflected a new notion that such action was not so much punitive as an opportunity for true repentance, it is clear that the influence of an increasingly permissive society was also at work. Penitent excommunicants may be reinstated after a year and have their temple entitlements restored, but since the mid-1970s those whose adultery has led to divorce have not been allowed to be sealed (that is, to obtain a temple marriage) to the third party in the relationship unless specifically authorized by the First Presidency.[25]

A major revision in church policy on formal disciplinary action was introduced in 1989 which should dramatically reduce the number of excommunications for sexual as well as other offenses in favor of less severe and less publicized disciplinary actions. This reflects not so much a lessening of concern about sexual sin as the pragmatic judgment that harsh public actions have been relatively unsuccessful in returning offenders to full participation.

There always has been greater leniency for youthful, unmarried offenders. However, since abortion has been grounds for court action, the church has expected that out-of-wedlock pregnancies will be carried to delivery. Although in theory marriage is the optimal solution, there is no ecclesiastical objection under these circumstances to putting the child up for adoption. Indeed, a major function of LDS Social Services is the arrangement of temporary homes for unwed mothers and the provision of adoption services for those who choose not to keep the baby.

Within the past decade there has been increased breadth in church-sponsored discussions of sex-related matters. In the mid-1970s several articles were carried in a church periodical on "family life education,"[26] and more recently manuals again have begun to touch on the subject, albeit lightly. Faced also with the inclusion of sex education programs in a growing number of public school curricula, the church has prepared *A Parent's Guide* to assist parents in teaching related moral values and responsibilities. In this the First Presidency has charged parents

> to ensure that the instruction given their children [in school] is consistent with appropriate moral and ethical values. With encouragement from parents and other citizens, many schools that are currently offering sex education can be persuaded to include instruction on the importance of chastity, marriage at the appropriate time, the role of parents in prescribing moral standards for family members, and the moral and ethical responsibilities of family members to one another.[27]

The Mormon emphasis on the chastity issue has met with some measurable success among its youth. When sociologists survey the attitudes and practices of LDS college students, they have found them consistently more conservative than non-Mormons on sex-related subjects. Even comparing only regular church attenders, one representative survey in 1972 found Mormons twice as likely to believe that sex outside marriage was immoral than did non-Mormons, while actual nonmarital sexual involvement was only one-tenth as frequent. Serial studies spanning the sexual revolution of the sixties did show some erosion in adherence to church standards, but overall church leaders could feel their efforts highly successful.[28]

The sexual revolution, of course, didn't really end in the sixties, and little has been published examining the staying power of the LDS record more recently. One still preliminary study suggests that the erosion of standards previously noted may have accelerated substantially in the 1980s. Although Mormon respondents remain significantly more likely than most others to restrict sexual activity to marriage, it is clear that upholding the church's position on chastity will remain a major leadership challenge for a long time to come.[29]

SCIENCE, SOCIOLOGY, MASTURBATION, AND DANCE

As noted, the progress of science has had an impact on LDS views on sex and sexuality just as it has on healing practices and other aspects of the Mormon record. Coitus, conception, pregnancy, and lactation were all to some degree misunderstood by nineteenth-century church leaders—and the rest of American society—and greater understanding in these areas has either forced, or been accompanied by, significant changes in Mormon teachings. Particularly striking examples are found in the views of church leaders on prenatal influences and the hazards of masturbation.

In the decades preceding the discoveries of Mendelian genetics, it generally was believed that attitudes and habits at the time of conception, as well as the experiences of the pregnant or lactating mother, greatly influenced the development of her child. Physical as well as emotional attributes (even physical scars) could be shaped by the most transient exposures on the part of a pregnant mother. Allusions to this can be found in Mormon discourse for most of the last century. Apostle Orson Pratt early warned that "the state of the parents' mind at the time of conception, and the state of the mother's mind during her pregnancy, will be constitutionally impressed upon the offspring." Brigham Young as well later warned that the mother who "stimulate[s] her system with tobacco, tea, coffee, or liquor, or suffer[s] herself to hanker after such things at certain times, . . . lays the foundation for the destruction of her offspring."[30]

The implications of this perspective could be profound, as was made clear in an article on "Pre-natal Influences" published late in the century in the Mormon *Juvenile Instructor:*

> These thoughts suggest one important point for the consideration of our law-makers. The crippled, the deformed, the victims of sin, accident, war or unfortunate pre-natal influences should not be allowed to parade themselves on our streets or in public places. This is one of the most effective methods of propagating these evils. The time will come—it ought to be now—when all these classes, including drunkards, will be cared for at the public expense, where everything necessary for their comfort, their instruction, their health, and, so far as possible, their cure will be provided, but when they will not be permitted to perpetuate in others the afflictions they suffer by making public spectacles of themselves.[31]

Ironically, to a number of outside observers the Mormons themselves afforded the best case study of this process at work. The "gross" and "sensual" nature of polygamy, beyond being socially offensive, was widely believed to insure the eventual emergence of a "new race" which would manifest the degenerate characteristics of similarly debased society. Indeed reports reprinted throughout the United States, and in England, from medical correspondents visiting Utah confirmed that by 1860 this development was already evident: "the yellow, cadaverous visage; the greenish-colored eyes; the thick, protuberant lips; the low forehead; the light, yellowish hair; and the lank, angular person, constitute an appearance so characteristic of the new race, the production of polygamy, as to distinguish them at a glance."[32]

The Mormons differed from their contemporaries only in where they discovered such evidence of moral depravity. In their eyes, the *good* health of Mormon children was a natural consequence of parental compliance with God's decrees, the "physiologic side of the question" being "one, if not the strongest, source of argument in favor" of the practice of polygamy. It was rather in the "generally sickly and shortlived" children of New England that Mormon leaders found clear indicators of parental vice.[33]

With the progress of scientific understanding, such notions were abandoned. Early-twentieth-century non-Mormon commentators no longer found evidence of "added congenital ills" among the Saints, and one observer even accepted the notion that in Utah the children of polygamous families were *healthier* than those from nonpolygamous backgrounds because "plural families were restricted by the Church authority to a select class of the population," which "would explain the average superiority of the polygamous families."[34]

Within the church such arguments also disappeared, without apology or explanation. New light simply brought new understanding. In a sense the part of the legacy which was intended to promote "moral" behavior did survive. The argument was simply sustained by somewhat different facts, such as the physical risks to the unborn of sexually transmitted disease or, most recently, of the maternal consumption of alcohol and tobacco. Ironically, recent medical research once again has implicated inheritance (albeit by an entirely different mechanism) in the development of many psychiatric disorders. The church per se has not taken note of this, though several LDS writers have wondered about its implication for the LDS notion of free agency, or free will.

The history of Mormon guidance on masturbation ("self-abuse") is another illustrative example. Initially Mormon leaders accepted the popular notion that this led to genital atrophy and a variety of other physical ailments and could even result in insanity or death. Mormon brethren received explicit apostolic warning of the "chronic and life long debility, insanity and even Madnes" which followed this practice. Such was popular confidence in the latter association that otherwise unexplained psychiatric admissions late in the century frequently led to speculation that the "secret sin" must have been involved. And the scientific record bore this out: among the "presumed causes" for admission to the Utah Territorial Insane Asylum, masturbation initially exceeded any other cause, and over the first twenty-six years of its operation, from 1885 to 1910, was alone said to be responsible for 7 percent of all admissions.[35]

The twentieth century brought a different understanding, both nationally and to the Mormons. Eventually an official instructional manual for adult Mormons on a variety of health issues spoke forthrightly of "the pernicious fallacy that insanity is the result of excessive masturbation. The facts do not support any such view, and if they did, the attempt to control self-abuse— injurious as it is—by capitalizing the child's fear of insanity, would still be morally reprehensible and mentally unhygienic."[36]

Continued development of psychiatric thinking eventually led to the entirely nonjudgmental view of what was still viewed by the church as sexual sin, so there has been a parting of the ways. As noted above in the discussion of madness (Chapter 5), an influential mid-twentieth-century compendium of church doctrine emphatically condemned psychiatrists who persuade guilt-ridden patients "that masturbation itself is not an evil; that [their] trouble arises from the false teachings of the Church that such a practice is unclean; and that, therefore, by discarding the teaching of the Church. the guilt complex will cease and mental stability return."[37]

This remains the general perspective within the church. When addressing the subject of masturbation, Mormon professionals generally condemn it on moral grounds—as a "misuse" of a divine function—but sometimes argue that though not a health risk per se, it may be associated with an unhealthy escapism, or other psychological problems, beyond the anxiety and guilt it unquestionably also generates in a Mormon context.[38] Official counseling guidance to local leaders on the subject of masturbation (which, notably, is incorporated into general instructions on dealing with homosexuality) recently has shifted away from a predominantly physical, "hands off" orientation (for example, advice to take short baths, wear restricting nightwear, get a snack) to an approach designed to preclude unacceptable behavior through a generally more "wholesome" life-style (for example, reading books, beginning a fitness program).[39] All this notwithstanding, the subject remains an awkward one within the church, perhaps as much now as ever.

Just as the progress of science has influenced Mormon belief, changes in societal values eventually affect church thinking as well. This is perhaps nowhere more in evidence than in matters relating to sexuality. A prototype is found in the history of church teachings on dance, an activity long believed by church leaders to be fraught with serious moral risk.

The initial Mormon response to dance was briefly negative. One group of Kirtland saints was disfellowshipped "for uniting with the world in a dance."[40] By the Nauvoo years, however, dancing had become an accepted and popular form of recreation, which grew during the difficult years following the Mormon exodus virtually "to the point of being a type of sacrament."[41] When converts were called to colonize a new area, at least one fiddler was included. Even without a musician, the sound of a lone whistler might be enough accompaniment for a dance. And this was exuberant dancing, as one observer noted, and "none of your minuets or other mortuary processions of gentiles in etiquette, tight shoes, and pinching gloves, but the spirited and scientific displays of our venerated and merry grandparents, who were not above following the fiddle to the Fox-chase Inn, or Gardens of Gray's Ferry, French fours, Copenhagen jigs, Virginia reels, and the like forgotten figures executed with the spirit of people too happy to be slow, or bashful, or constrained."[42]

In actual fact these happy pioneers were constrained, and continued so for over fifty years, because Mormon leaders shared with many others grave concerns about the "round dances" then gaining popularity throughout the country. Unlike traditional American dances, these involved a "close embrace," and Brigham Young was "opposed to them, from beginning to end, from top to bottom." They were "first commenced in and still continue as brothel-house dances," he said, and they were not for the Saints. Round dances, which included waltz, polka, and schottische (a polka-like English dance), therefore were banned.[43]

Despite repeated editorial warnings that excesses in this "class" of dance were "destructive to health and comfort" and risked a "girl's ruin," some bishops eventually bowed to the persisting entreaties of Mormon youth and allowed two or three waltzes at a dance, and perhaps an extra "waltz quadrille" (which had an innocuous title and began innocently enough—but ended with couples waltzing around the square). Following Brigham Young's death the Quorum of the Twelve finally issued a circular letter ratifying this concession but recommending that there not be more than "one or two [round dances] permitted in an evening." These guidelines were reiterated to a new generation a decade later.[44]

Just before the turn of the century a modest additional concession was made, as new official guidance authorized two waltzes per person per evening, thus allowing more than two waltzes to be played to accommodate all potential dancers.[45] Some wards then issued rationlike waltz tickets to monitor this entitlement, which young devotees parleyed into a much fuller evening of dance by surreptitiously collecting tickets from cooperative friends.

Through these years, church periodicals continually warned of the risks being taken in this "dance of death." As the nineteenth century came to a close, the antiwaltz campaign was stepped up for what proved to be a last-ditch effort. In keeping with the relative candor of the day, the counsel was reasonably explicit. As a member of the First Presidency warned, while there may be no impropriety in a "husband and a wife, a brother and a sister, or two young ladies" dancing a round dance (beyond the bad example), "when persons of both sexes dance promiscuously . . . evil is likely to result."[46] Perhaps most arresting was the account carried in the church's *Young Women's Journal* of one who failed to heed counsel. "Julia" wrote to the "Confidential Talks With Girls" column about a friend who recently had been married "not in the temple . . . but at home in disgrace and sorrow." Like other young women in her ward, she had not felt an evening complete without a waltz with "A_____." One thing apparently led to another, and a precipitous marriage followed. In hindsight it was clear: "if I had never waltzed with him, I never, of necessity should have become his wife." Such was "the testimony of my unfortunate friend," concluded a sobered Julia, "which if it benefits no one else, has decided me never to waltz again."[47]

Notwithstanding the fate of Julia's friend, and a half-century of consistent leadership counsel, the twentieth century brought a new perspective. Following a decade of relative silence, the church in 1910 quietly withdrew its objection to the waltz (and two-step), and three years later also approved the polka and schottische.[48] Soon handbooks for youth leaders began to encourage the waltz, even providing specific instructions for novice dancers. Within a decade it had become for all practical purposes the official church dance.[49]

Significantly these developments were accompanied by continued formal warnings on the dangers of dance. The focus, however, had shifted. Ragtime was sweeping the nation, with its "exaggerated movement of the shoulders and hips." Compared to the Texas Tommy, Bunny Hug, Grizzly Bear, and Turkey Trot, the waltz apparently seemed reasonably harmless. In this context the First Presidency—two years after the waltz was approved—advised local leaders to prohibit "dances that require or permit the close embrace and suggestive movements."[50] By 1913 one youth leader could unblushingly lament the passing of the old days when "our fathers and mothers . . . took eager part in the waltz, polka and schottische."[51]

The official church view of dancing thus responded to an evolving societal standard by itself moving, eventually, in the same direction as society at large. In many ways this is a prototype, albeit perhaps somewhat more dramatic, of other shifts in the Mormon point of view. This is especially so in areas that are deemed related in some way to issues of sexuality, as the waltz—and, in turn, dancing to ragtime, jazz, jitterbug, bop, and twist— once was. As will be seen, this evolutionary development is an ongoing— if sometimes uncomfortable—process and not, as many have assumed, a characteristic of only the formative early years of Mormonism. Attitudes toward dance, music, and a variety of other subjects continue to follow a predictable course.

Recent years have seen dance fads come and go with such speed that it has been difficult if not impossible to formulate any authoritative response before a suspect style is out of vogue, but the topic also is no longer viewed with the same level of concern. Presently youth leaders are advised that "a dance should not be suggestive or sensual in any way, and that it should not be a grotesque contortion of the body. However, it cannot be said that one dance is banned and another is not."[52]

The point to be drawn from this brief review is not so much that LDS "standards" erode over time in the face of evolving societal influences but rather that underlying concerns tend to be reflected in practical guidance which itself may progress over time. Throughout the present history, church leaders sought to protect church youth from a society viewed as abandoning eternally significant moral values. In theory, promulgated restraints both limited undesirable social contacts (for example, at offending dance halls) and discouraged the casual physical intimacy seemingly embodied in suspect dances. Although the absolute guidance changed over the years, the perspective relative to standards has changed much more slowly. As a result Mormon youth generally remain on the conservative side of societal trends, where church leaders hope they will be least vulnerable to the most morally destructive influences.

MARITAL SEXUALITY AND BIRTH CONTROL

In 1976, BYU professor of family relations Kenneth L. Cannon published an essay entitled, "Needed: An LDS Philosophy of Sex." Cannon was concerned that so far as this subject was concerned church leaders appeared to have one goal: "chastity—which may be achieved at a cost of strong fears and negative attitudes toward sex, with such fears and attitudes causing sexual maladjustment and dissatisfaction in marriage." Additionally, he felt the impression was conveyed "that chastity alone will guarantee a fulfilling marriage." The philosophy of sex Cannon sought was one "which would help us not only to maintain chastity but to develop healthy attitudes toward sex," and he felt it "meaningless . . . to talk about some of the purposes of sex as being beyond procreation unless there is freedom to use contraception."[53]

In principle, given its doctrinal legacy, Mormonism might well have expounded a view of marital sexuality which was as positive as its view of nonmarital sexuality was negative. In practice, however, it was *reproductive* marital sexuality alone that church leaders approbated. As one turn-of-the-century leader put it, "married people who indulged their passions for any other purpose than to beget children, really committed adultery."[54] The same point later was made again (it put "the marriage relationship on a level with the panderer and the courtesan" [1916]) and again ("Remember the prime purpose of sex desire is to beget children. Sex gratification must be had at that hazard." [1949]).[55] The twentieth century was to be two-thirds over before any significant public indication was offered that leadership views had changed; even then the message was implicit rather than expressly articulated. By this time a substantial, though largely private, shift also had taken place in attitudes toward birth control.

While late-nineteenth-century church leaders occasionally spoke of "prevention" or "race suicide" as indicative of the depths to which the outside world had descended, they seemingly did not believe this to be a problem within the church. This perspective soon changed. The first formal statements on family limitation directed at church members came early in this century, during a period of societal ferment similar to that surrounding the abortion question a half-century later. The term *birth control* originated in this period, and initial LDS guidelines, as with the case of abortion, came rather early in what was a radical reform movement, and at a time when many aspects of contraception were illegal.

Joseph F. Smith was the first church president to address the question of what was then termed "prevention." Having heard as early as 1900 that "steps were being taken," even among Latter-day Saints, "to prevent . . . spirits being tabernacled . . . ," he spoke regularly on the subject for nearly two decades.[56]

One early response followed a physician's inquiry in 1908 about whether it was ever right "intentionally to prevent, by any means whatever, the spirits . . . from obtaining earthly tabernacles?" Smith's response was that "In a general way, and as a rule, the answer to this question is an emphatic negative. I do not hesitate to say that prevention is wrong." In addition to bringing in its wake selfishness, and a "host of social evils," it would also "disregard or annul the great commandment of God to men, 'Multiply and replenish the earth.'"[57]

While the tone and substance of much of Smith's early-twentieth-century counsel derived from the perspective of earlier years, he added a caveat reminiscent of the turn-of-the-century pragmatism with which the Mormons dealt with difficult medical questions: "I am now speaking of the normally healthy man and woman. But that there are weak and sickly people who in wisdom, discretion and common sense should be counted as exceptions, only strengthens the general rule." Believing, as church leaders did, that passion without reproduction was tantamount to adultery, Smith advised that in such exceptional cases the only legitimate preventive was "absolute abstinence."

Although Smith held to the same basic view throughout his presidency, which ended with his death in 1918, his last extensive commentary on the subject introduced another exception to the general condemnation. "I think that [curtailing the birth of children] is a crime whenever it occurs," he advised the women's Relief Society in 1917, "where husband and wife are in possession of health and vigor and are *free from impurities* that would be entailed upon their posterity. I believe that where people undertake to curtail or prevent the birth of their children that they are going to reap disappointment by and by. I have no hesitancy in saying that I believe this is one of the greatest crimes in the world today, this evil practice . . ." (emphasis added).[58]

Smith's successor, Heber J. Grant, presided over the church during Utah's depression years, which—unlike the nation's—began in the early twenties. During these years, the birth rate among Mormons declined precipitously, to levels not again reached until the advent of "modern" contraceptives in the sixties. Relatively little was said by the church leadership in response to this unprecedented evidence of intentional family limitation.

President Grant's advice, when finally given, was modified somewhat from that of his predecessor. In one now well-known private letter penned in 1939, he invoked Smith's counsel along the lines quoted above but then added, "Married couples who, by inheritance and proper living, have themselves been blessed with mental and physical vigor are recreant in their duty if they refuse to meet the natural and rightful responsibility of parenthood. Of course, in every ideal home the health of the mother, as well as the intelligence and health of the children should receive careful consideration."[59]

A continued evolution in leadership thinking was evident in the 1940s. The influential apostle John A. Widtsoe published an important essay on the subject in an official church magazine in 1942. Earlier that year he had written privately to a correspondent that "as far as I know the Church has not expressed itself as to birth control."[60] Widtsoe's published essay—forthrightly entitled "Should Birth Control Be Practiced?"—was a remarkably evenhanded treatment of the subject. It reflected clearly another phase in the liberalization of church guidance. Instead of rejecting economic arguments out of hand, he rather found them "seldom convincing." Equally interesting, he implicitly rejected total abstinence as the sole recourse open to those with legitimate grounds for controlling fertility. His advice was that "a careful recognition of the fertile and sterile periods of woman would prove effective in the great majority of cases."[61] Four years later, then-apostle David O. McKay was willing in private correspondence to carry this a step further in advising that "when the health of the mother demands it, the proper spacing of children may be determined by seeking medical counsel, by compliance with the processes of nature, or by continence. . . ."[62]

Through these years and on into the sixties, the public record was still dominated by the writings of Mormon authorities still willing to label birth control "gross wickedness," and popular (though "unofficial") compendiums of church teachings condemned this practice in the harshest terms.[63] Privately, the much more tolerant view of McKay, who became church president in 1951, was becoming more widely known, and in 1960 his counselor, Hugh B. Brown, published a book of personal advice on *You and Your Marriage* which advised that "the Latter-day Saints believe in large families wherever it is possible to provide for the necessities of life, for the health and education of their children, and when the physical and mental health of the mother permits."[64]

Ultimately, a formal statement was issued in 1969—the first and only such statement by the First Presidency specifically on the subject of birth control. In this McKay, Brown, and Nathan Tanner wrote:

> The First Presidency is being asked from time to time as to what the attitude of the Church is regarding birth control. . . .
>
> We seriously regret that there should exist a sentiment or feeling among any members of the Church to curtail the birth of their children. We have been commanded to multiply and replenish the earth that we may have joy and rejoicing in our posterity.
>
> Where husband and wife enjoy health and vigor and are free from impurities that would be entailed upon their posterity, it is contrary to the teachings of the Church artificially to curtail or prevent the birth of children. We believe those who practice birth control will reap disappointment by and by.
>
> However, we feel that men must be considerate of their wives who bear the greater responsibility not only of bearing children, but of caring for them through childhood. To this end the mother's health and strength should be conserved and the husband's consideration for his wife is his first duty, and self-control a dominant factor in all their relationships.
>
> It is our further feeling that married couples should seek inspiration and wisdom from the Lord that they may exercise discretion in solving their marital problems, and that they may be permitted to rear their children in accordance with the teachings of the gospel.[65]

This diplomatically combined the essence, if not the bottom lines, of guidance issued throughout the twentieth century. While reiterating the strong profamily tradition which has sustained nearly all Mormon commentary on the subject, the statement was notable for publicly shifting full responsibility on the question from the church to the individual member. It thereby placed the specifics of how family goals were achieved above ecclesiastical review.

In a larger sense, the church leadership also ratified the collective judgment of most of the rank-and-file of Mormonism. For years surveys of active Mormons had found a large majority either planning to use or currently using modern contraceptives, and by the late sixties, when the First Presidency statement was issued, the Mormon birthrate had fallen to a new low.[66]

Those who followed McKay (who died early in 1970) into the presidency of the church were both more outspoken and more negative on birth control. However, they chose not to formally revise the official guidance already issued on the subject. While the new emphasis frustrated some educators in the church, and apparently contributed to a brief rise in the birthrate of Mormons in Utah, it seems not to have influenced overall usage of contraceptives within the church. The most recent published study addressing LDS attitudes found, based on a small sample from the 1975 National Fertility Studies, that 96 percent of reporting Mormons made use of birth control.[67] By 1986 the birthrate among Mormons was lower by far than ever previously had been the case, and hovered at about 20 births per thousand.

Current guidance on birth control is, if anything, more open than even that of the late sixties. The most extensive recent commentary came in a thoughtful 1979 "Answer to Gospel Questions" essay in the official church magazine, the *Ensign*. Writing in support of "gospel family planning," prominent Mormon obstetrician Homer Ellsworth first rejoiced in "our spiritual obligation, to bear children and to have a family," and decried family limitation for "selfish" reasons. "But, on the other hand," he continued (in part), "we need not be afraid of studying the question from important angles—the physical and mental health of the mother and father, the parents' capacity to provide necessities, and so on. If for certain personal reasons a couple prayerfully decides that having another child immediately is unwise, the method of spacing children—discounting possible medical or physical effects—makes no difference. Abstinence, of course, is also a form of contraception, and like any other method it has side effects, some of which are harmful to the marriage relationship."[68]

Official guidance has passed through two more modest steps. The first, a statement on birth control published in the 1983 edition of the authoritative *General Handbook of Instructions* (and repeated in 1985), basically preserved only the second half of the 1969 statement:

> The Lord has commanded husbands and wives to multiply and replenish the earth that they might have joy in their posterity.
> Husbands must be considerate of their wives, who have the greater responsibility not only of bearing children but of caring for them through childhood, and should help them conserve their health and strength. Married couples should exercise self-control in all of their relationships. They should seek inspiration from the Lord in meeting their marital challenges and rearing their children according to the teachings of the gospel.[69]

This message was insured wide distribution through inclusion in a 1984 First Presidency talk telecast nationwide on "Cornerstones of a Happy Home," which subsequently was published as a brochure and delivered by home teachers to every LDS family. This further advised that God had not designated the number of children a family should have, "nor has the Church. That is a sacred matter left to the couple and the Lord."[70]

The final step came with the 1989 revision of the *General Handbook*. In restating the position on birth control, the 1983 text (quoted above) was shorn of the first and third sentences, referring to the commandment to "multiply and replenish the earth" and the obligation of married couples to "exercise self-control in all their relations." With this editing the last vestige of the initial LDS stance truly has been eliminated.

Understandably, the increased tolerance of the late sixties with regard to birth control was accompanied by somewhat greater openness on the subject of marital sexuality. Though unwilling to address the subject publicly, influential church leaders privately condoned publication by a leading Mormon physician of *"And They Shall Be One Flesh": A Sensible Sex Guide for the L.D.S. Bride and Groom* (1968). This landmark effort was unprecedented in both candor and perspective. Forthrightly (and supportively) discussing techniques of both coitus and contraception, the author unreservedly, though tastefully, argued for a full and satisfying sexual relationship in marriage.

Reflecting to some extent the national openness of the day, the contrast of the 1968 *Sex Guide* with the traditional Mormon perspective can hardly be overstated. Where the long-standing (and authoritatively supported) view held that coitus was to be not only reproductively oriented but clothed in the intentionally asexual traditional undergarment, the guide suggested (citing Genesis 2:25) a "sheer negligee" or nudity. Manual manipulation, when appropriate, to assist female orgasm was explained and encouraged. As to "what is normal and what is not in marriage, . . . there are few rules to go by in this very private relationship, . . . but one rule holds supreme: Nothing that appeals to the imagination of either partner and is not repulsive or unacceptable to the other should be considered abnormal. It is well to remember that nearly all variations attempted by the average couple have been tried before . . . by nearly every other couple. This applies to varieties of positions, types of caresses, and any other innovation."[71] The *Sex Guide*, which is still in print, in a sense is a continuing milestone in that it has not ushered in a comparably unrestrained attitude in LDS publications. While once again willing to acknowledge openly the intrinsic value of the sexual relationship in marriage, church periodicals (and most unofficial publications) almost always emphasize the "sacramental" rather than the celebratory or passionate aspects of the sexual act.[72]

In the two decades since the *Sex Guide* first appeared, a few LDS professionals have begun to offer the Mormon community counseling on marital sex, particularly since 1980. A University of Utah–based sex and marital therapy clinic (co-directed by an LDS therapist) now treats LDS patients— without official censure—in Salt Lake City. As elsewhere in the country, its treatment modalities include when appropriate the use of masturbation, typically "for a time-limited period toward a righteous goal and purpose"— that is, achieving a normal sexual relationship. Notably, the experience of this clinic to date suggests that notwithstanding their chastity code Mormons are no more sexually dysfunctional within marriage than are Americans in general.[73]

It may in fact be that Latter-day Saints are not really so much more inhibited within marriage than their contemporaries. As early as 1971 a private inquirer sought leadership counsel regarding "certain deviated sex practices" being used by married friends. Reflecting a previously expressed view that the church "was not going to follow anybody into their bedroom," the Secretary to the First Presidency, responding privately on their behalf, felt the question to be one which "should be answered by you and your husband in accordance with your own convictions. The Church has never believed it necessary to issue instructions pertaining to intimate relations between husband and wife."[74]

Similar inquiries continued over the next few years, asking more explicitly about the propriety of "oral sex." Though responses were all private, the guidance given made it clear that some leaders felt strongly enough to label such "perversions" as "abhorrent in the sight of the Lord." Even those who responded more gently felt that married couples should stay with the "normal process."[75] The first related public guidance, though perhaps clearer in retrospect, avoided specifics in cautioning against "questionable lectures on sex practices." Carried as authoritative guidance in a 1974 *Priesthood Bulletin,* this advised:

> Church leaders and members are cautioned against participating in classes, lectures, or seminars that advocate vulgar or other questionable sex practices between husbands and wives. Some of these hide behind the guise of increasing "masculinity" or "femininity" but actually encourage or even glorify deviant sexual conduct. Latter-day Saints should avoid any exposure to such teachings, the effect of which might lead them into unholy and impure conduct in the marital relationship.[76]

By the early 1980s the leadership had become sufficiently concerned to expand on the questions asked yearly of active members in interviews about their worthiness (for example, to enter the temple). Local leaders were instructed to ask, in language reflecting that of a temple vow, whether members were involved in any "unnatural, impure or unholy practice." This was interpreted explicitly by the First Presidency to include "oral sex."[77] Local leaders further were enjoined to "scrupulously avoid indelicate inquiries, which may be offensive to the sensibilities of those being interviewed," but in complying with the basic instructions some were found to delve "beyond the scope of what is appropriate." As a result, further instruction was issued a few months later that local leaders should "never inquire into personal, intimate matters involving marital relations between a man and his wife." Believing it best that interviews be conducted so as not to invite explicit inquiries from members, the Presidency advised that if there were a question about "the propriety of specific conduct, you should not pursue the matter but should merely suggest that if the member has enough anxiety about the propriety to ask about it, the best course would be to discontinue it."[78] This is where the subject now rests, with all judgments about and responsibility for marital relations now resident exclusively within the home.

One conclusion *not* to be drawn from this brief review is that the church succumbed to societal pressure on the issues of sexual relations and birth control. Rather, what has happened is that—as with the waltz—a change in societal context has been accompanied, eventually, by a related change within the church. In fact, the church has not abandoned its most fundamental viewpoint—that procreation and family life reside at the heart of a person's reason to be. The positive injunction given to Adam and Eve to multiply and replenish the earth was (and is) really the foundation of all Mormon commentary. While this is now interpreted in the context of a very broadly defined medical concern for the well-being of the total family, Mormons at large have responded to this challenge. Though influenced by societal and economic factors, much as are their non-Mormon contemporaries, LDS families still collectively have on the average one or more additional children than do Americans in general—as they have throughout the twentieth century.

ABORTION

Although there was no formal statement of church policy on abortion until very recently, the views of early church leaders were very clear: abortion to the nineteenth-century Mormon mind was synonymous with murder. Polemically, at least, no distinction was made between "foeticide," the "destruction of embryos," or abortion, on the one hand, and "infanticide" or "infant murder" on the other. President John Taylor (successor to Brigham Young), for example, spoke with some regularity of "pre-natal murders," or "murders . . . committed while the children are pre-natal"; of infants killed "either before or after they are born"; of murdering children "either before or after they come into the world." Similar language can be found in the related sermons of nearly all late-nineteenth-century Mormon leaders.[79]

Given this perspective, it is not surprising that the church viewed those involved in such "hellish" practices as under grave condemnation. George Q. Cannon of the First Presidency was perhaps the most graphic: "they will be damned with deepest damnation; because it is the damnation of shedding innocent blood, for which there is no forgiveness. . . . They are outside the pale of salvation. They are in a position that nothing can be done for them. They cut themselves off by such acts from all hopes of salvation. . . ."[80]

This early commentary was fueled largely by national agitation on the subject rather than a perceived problem within the Mormon community. With the passing of the general ferment, the subject largely disappeared from church commentary—for nearly a century. When abortion finally re-emerged as a common topic, the social and medical context was radically different.

The abortion reform movement reached Utah in 1969, and legislation was introduced to revise the state's century-old statute (allowing abortion only to save the mother's life). In accordance with a growing national consensus, it was proposed to allow abortions in cases where the mother's mental or physical health (not solely her life) was at stake, or where there had been rape or incest, or if the likely result was a child "with grave or permanent physical disability or mental retardation." A measure of the degree to which sentiment had shifted even within the Mormon community was the view of some Mormon physicians at the time that the church would not oppose the proposed legislation. (In fact, at the time a somewhat liberalized policy already was tacitly in effect in most major hospitals in Salt Lake City, including the Latter-day Saints Hospital itself. Although not nearly as commonplace as elsewhere in the U.S., abortions were being performed occasionally for the very indications the new legislation proposed to authorize.)[81]

Despite the precedent of nineteenth-century church discourse, mid-twentieth-century Mormon leaders did not view abortion in entirely the same doctrinal light as did their predecessors. Although nothing definitive had been stated publicly, as early as 1934 Apostle David O. McKay privately expressed his opinion that the church had not made an "authoritative answer" to the question of whether abortion should be "termed murder or not." Later, as church president, McKay and the First Presidency had affirmed that "as the matter stands, no definitive statement has been made by the Lord one way or another regarding the crime of abortion. So far as is known, he has not listed it alongside the crime of the unpardonable sin and shedding innocent blood. That he has not done so would suggest that it is not in that class of crime. . . ."[82] Given Mormonism's fundamental doctrine that where no law was given there can be no accountability, the First Presidency's judgment is certainly less tentative than this sounds.

Potential flexibility on the abortion question existed in part because Mormonism has no established doctrine on the timing of "ensoulment." (I have borrowed this expression; Mormons do not have a specific term for the point at which a spirit joins the physical body.) As biblical literalists early Mormons might have assumed, as did many of their contemporaries, that a prenatally present spirit animated fetal life, using as proof text the familiar passage in Luke (1:44) in which Elisabeth's fetal babe "leaped in [her] womb for joy" at the news of Mary's pregnancy. The problem with this as a firm scriptural guide was a *Book of Mormon* episode in which the voice of Christ was heard—presumably in the tones of an adult—the day prior to his birth.[83]

With both these scriptures as precedents, it is understandable that a variety of views had been espoused over the years on the timing of ensoulment. Brigham Young, accepting the conventional wisdom of his day, assumed the spirit arrived at the time of quickening.[84] A later First Presidency, in 1909, offered tangential support to Young's view in a statement which observed that "the body of man enters upon its career as a tiny germ or embryo, which becomes an infant, quickened at a certain stage by the spirit whose tabernacle it is, and the child, after being born, develops into a man."[85] Some influential mid-twentieth-century church writers have further promulgated this general understanding, on the basis on Brigham Young's early comments. Apostle Joseph Fielding Smith expressed a "personal opinion that these little [stillborn] ones will receive a resurrection and then belong to us," and most recently Apostle Bruce R. McConkie held the same view.[86]

An alternative to this position was expressed privately by members of the First Presidency for much of the twentieth century. David O. McKay, who eventually became church president, believed that the spirit joined the body at the time of birth. "[L]ife manifest in the body before that time would seem to be dependent upon the mother."[87] J. Reuben Clark, for over four decades an influential member of the First Presidency, believed similarly but also thought that the spirit periodically interacted with the fetus and influenced its development.[88] While McKay offered only the *Book of Mormon* reference to the prenatal Christ in support of his position, other proponents see the "breath of life" texts of Genesis and parallel Mormon scripture as confirming this viewpoint. This, with slight variation, is the familiar account of Adam coming to life only after God "breathed into his nostrils the breath of life; and man became a living soul. . . ."[89]

Despite their different understandings, Young and McKay seem to agree on the fundamental issue of the fate of a spirit in an unsuccessful pregnancy. Clearly McKay's view allows an alternative mortal experience, but Brigham also believed that "when some people have little children born at 6 & 7 months from pregnancy & they live a few hours then die . . . I think that such a spirit will have a Chance of occupying [*sic*] another Tabernacle and develop itself. . . ." Though it is not clear where he drew the line, that he did so is evident from his condemnation of a similar notion—held by one of his colleagues—that full-term babies who died were "resurrected" into new, mortal infant bodies.[90]

Ultimately the First Presidency, in 1970, wrote—though it was never formally published—that "there is no direct revelation upon the subject [of when the spirit takes possession of the body] . . . it has always been a moot question. That there is life in the child before birth is undoubted fact, but whether that life is the result of the affinity of the child in embryo with the life of its mother, or because the spirit has entered it remains an unsolved mystery."[91]

In practice Mormon ritual makes a fairly clear statement on this issue, in that it always has distinguished between miscarriages or stillborn deliveries, and neonatal deaths. The former are not formally recorded in church records; the latter are. Vicarious temple ordinances (that is, for the dead) are never performed in the case of a miscarriage or stillborn delivery; vicarious sealing ordinances (baptism being unnecessary below age eight) are performed for deceased infants.[92] In essence, whatever the doctrinal uncertainties, the church in practice deals with birth as though it were the time when an important spirit-body bond takes place. Parenthetically, the church has not taken any stand on the question of what constitutes a live birth, despite the obvious ecclesiastical implications. In practice it apparently follows the legal definition current in a given jurisdiction (which most often is contingent on a first breath).

All this notwithstanding, the church did issue a short statement on the abortion reform bill proposed in 1969, just over a week after it was introduced in the Utah legislature. In this, the First Presidency stated that after "careful consideration," they were opposed "to any modification, expansion, or liberalization of laws on these vital subjects."[93] And the bill was not enacted.

That the official view was not so categorical as this would suggest was evident in private guidance issued about the same time on behalf of the

First Presidency. After reiterating Mormon opposition to a liberalization in the laws, this added: "Nevertheless there may be conditions where abortion is justified, but such condition must be determined acting under the advice of competent, reliable physicians, preferably members of the church, and in accordance with the laws pertaining thereto."[94] Just under two years later, this latter statement was given much wider circulation when a new First Presidency published it in the official leadership newsletter, the *Priesthood Bulletin* (February 1971).

In June 1972 the Presidency's views on abortion were more fully elaborated in another issue of the *Bulletin*. Their statement at that time remains the most comprehensive official Mormon response to the question of abortion. It reads:

> The church opposes abortion and counsels its members not to submit to or perform an abortion except in the rare cases where, in the opinion of competent medical counsel, the life or good health of the mother is seriously endangered or where the pregnancy was caused by rape and produces serious emotional trauma in the mother. Even then it should be done only after counseling with the local presiding authority and after receiving divine confirmation through prayer.
>
> As the matter stands today, no definite statement has been made by the Lord one way or another regarding the crime of abortion. So far as is known, he has not listed it alongside the crime of the unpardonable sin and shedding of innocent human blood. That he has not done so would suggest that it is not in that class of crime and therefore that it will be amendable to the laws of repentance and forgiveness.
>
> These observations must not be interpreted to mean that acts of abortion, except under circumstances explained in a preceding paragraph, are not of a serious nature. To tamper or interfere with any of the processes in the procreation of offspring is to violate one of the most sacred of God's commandments—to multiply and replenish the earth. Abortion must be considered one of the most revolting and sinful practices in this day, when we are witnessing the frightening evidences of permissiveness leading to sexual immorality.
>
> Members of the Church guilty of being parties to the sin of abortion must be subjected to the disciplinary action of the councils of the Church as circumstances warrant. In dealing with this serious matter it would be well to keep in mind the word of the Lord stated in the 59th section of the Doctrine and Covenants, verse 6: "Thou shalt not steal; neither commit adultery, nor kill *nor do anything* like unto it."[95]

Several points should be made about this statement. It clearly stopped short of defining abortion as murder, finding it rather "like unto it." (Possibly in the sense that some might consider a fetus not to be identical with human life in the normal usage but like unto it.) As such abortion was usually to be viewed as a "most revolting and sinful practice." On the other hand, the statement was clearly more permissive than, for example, the existing Utah law at the time, and excepting the cases of fetal abnormalities and incest-related pregnancy was compatible with the unsuccessful legislative reform introduced three years earlier.

Although a panel of federal judges held in 1971 that Utah's abortion law was constitutional, the statute did not withstand the 1973 Supreme Court ruling which in essence struck down all state laws on the subject. In the wake of this development, abortion regained the prominence in LDS sermon and print it had achieved a century before, in large measure because of the strong concerns of Spencer W. Kimball, who had become church president soon after the Supreme Court decision. President Kimball regularly included abortion among a litany of grave sins besetting society. Eventually, in 1976, the church distributed to all Mormon congregations a very graphic filmstrip reinforcing its opposition to abortion. In addition to the proscriptions already outlined in the official statement, new counsel was included as part of an accompanying discourse by President Kimball entitled "A Visit With The Prophet": "Occasionally the question of pregnancy by rape will be asked. Medical evidence indicates that this is an extremely rare situation. But regardless of how the pregnancy was caused, abortion would greatly compound the wrong. An unborn baby must not be punished for the sins of his father. Letting the baby be born and placing him in an adoptive home would surely be a better solution for an unfortunate situation."[96]

Despite the extensive efforts involved in distributing the filmstrip and the explicit guidance of the accompanying talk, the church at this time did not officially depart from its former stand—a paradox that illustrates some of the problems in assessing an authoritative or authoritarian religion with few formal doctrines. That there had been no binding departure from previous guidance was clear within just a few weeks when the First Presidency reaffirmed its previous policy on abortion in an "official statement" that contained identical exceptions to those specified in 1972. Among these was "pregnancy . . . caused by forcible rape and produc[ing] serious emotional trauma in the victim." Eventually the controversial guidance was deleted from the filmstrip.[97]

The 1980s has seen some modest additional change in church counsel on abortion. The 1983 *General Handbook* for the first time added pregnancy resulting from incest to the list of published exceptional cases in which abortion might be justified. And in 1989 a fetal indication was first added, in cases in which "the fetus is known, by competent medical authority, to

have severe defects that will not allow the baby to survive beyond birth."
Official counsel on ecclesiastical discipline also finally stated clearly that in
this context "abortion is not defined as murder."[98]

Most recently, LDS views on abortion again received some national publicity, as Utah passed (in January 1991) what was at the time the strictest
state ban on abortion in the United States (though significantly more liberal
than the Utah state law struck down in 1973). During the legislative delibera-
tions prior to passage, a church spokesperson issued a statement reaffirming
LDS opposition to "elective abortion" and the "devastating practice of abortion for personal or social convenience" but also recognizing the "rare cases
in which abortion may be justified—cases involving pregnancy by incest or
rape; when the life or health of the woman is . . . in serious jeopardy or
when the fetus is known . . . to have serious defects that will not allow the
baby to survive beyond birth." To this the statement added that "as an
institution" the church "has not favored or opposed specific legislative proposals or public demonstrations concerning abortion" and that it would be
"impractical" for it "to take a position on specific legislative proposals."
Rather, members were encouraged "to let their voices be heard in appropriate and legal ways that will evidence their belief in the sacredness of
life."[99]

Not coincidentally, the law that passed two weeks later—said to have been
in part drafted by national antiabortion groups—matched almost precisely
the official church stand (allowing exceptions for rape, incest, "grave damage"
to the woman's "medical" health, and fetal defects "incompatible with sustained survival"). Its implementation has been delayed pending court challenges. If allowed to stand, this law will dramatically reduce the nearly
5,000 abortions performed annually in Utah. The impact, however, will be
substantially less than similar legislation would have elsewhere. Utah already
has abortion rates (per women of childbearing years) and ratios (in comparison to live births) half or less the national average—though, paradoxically,
state figures are somewhat *above* national averages for abortion rates and
ratios within the first eight weeks of pregnancy.[100]

As clear as is the present church stand, one area of lingering imprecision
remains. The First Presidency never has affirmatively condemned the termination of pregnancies involving viable but seriously defective fetuses.
Rather, they chose the indirect condemnation of not exempting such cases
from a general indictment of abortion. In his remarks accompanying the
1976 filmstrip, President Kimball did assert that "no one, save the Lord
himself, has the right to decide if a baby should or should not be permitted
to live." One can presume therefore that he personally would have counseled

strongly against intervening in such cases. Nonetheless, the First Presidency appears to have intentionally avoided singling out this issue for unequivocal condemnation, despite periodic inquiries from concerned physicians on this specific subject or on the related use of amniocentesis.

The church's quasi silence on this particularly difficult problem seems to coincide with a continuing evolution in perspective among both Mormon physicians and patients, an evolution of the sort previously seen under similar circumstances on the question of birth control. At the anecdotal level, for example, some local church leaders have availed themselves of amniocentesis when there were high-risk pregnancies within their own families. They say, at least, that they would have gravely abnormal pregnancies terminated. Their argument is that this option promotes *larger* families, for without it they would not risk further pregnancies. Similarly, some otherwise conservative, highly orthodox Mormon physicians also recommend or perform these studies with the same intent. The growing medico-legal obligation to at least discuss amniocentesis certainly accounts for some of this, but the motivation goes further.

So far as actual practice is concerned, very little is known. One LDS obstetrician estimated that in the general area where his practice was located, about half the LDS women pregnant after age forty now request amniocentesis. This was not in Utah, but it seems generally consistent with a Centers for Disease Control study which found that about 10 percent of Utah women pregnant after age thirty-five also sought amniocentesis—a figure about half the national average.[101] It is also compatible with the estimates given at a 1983 genetics symposium that in Utah about two-thirds of pregnancies found to have genetic abnormalities were terminated, versus about 80 percent nationally.[102] Although proportionately few amniocenteses reveal abnormalities, in some areas it apparently is not as rare as one might suppose for LDS women discovering significant fetal abnormalities to have these pregnancies terminated. Nor, so far as I have been able to ascertain, does this appear to bring on any church disciplinary action. It appears that agonizing personal problems such as these are now most frequently dealt with entirely within the family, or by local leaders who while counseling the family involved still indicate that the final moral judgment must reside within them.

So far as abortion for pregnancies in which rape, incest, fetal malformation, or maternal health are not involved, the record remains clear and consistent. Termination of pregnancy in the absence of these circumstances can lead to church discipline for both LDS doctor and patient. Unwed mothers are advised that if marriage is not possible, it is far better to carry an unwanted pregnancy to term and give the child up for adoption.[103] Family members who support an unwed teenager in a decision to terminate the pregnancy are themselves at risk for church disciplinary action, and there have been excommunications on this basis. Despite the evolutionary character of its doctrines—including that relating to abortion—it is likely that the church always will view a decision to terminate fetal life as a step with profound moral overtones, and when motivated by selfish or shallow motives as an eternally significant sin.

EUGENICS, GENETICS, AND STERILIZATION

For the past two decades or so, LDS commentary on sterilization has been principally in the context of the broader issue of birth control. Prior to this, however, the context was eugenics.

From the earliest years, Mormons were both race and lineage conscious. Accepting the nineteenth-century notion of an anthropological "chain of being," they saw the "white" race as the "pure" or Adamic ideal and, at the other extreme, black Africans as the race least mentally, physically, and morally gifted. Within the Adamic race, Mormons saw themselves as literally of the House of Israel, or at the least heirs to this lineage through both adoption and a subsequent physical transformation. They came to view their presence in this chosen line as premortally determined and saw themselves and their offspring as having been the valiant elite in the premoral spirit world. For these and other reasons, the Saints were encouraged to marry within the faith, and in Utah (as throughout the U.S.) interracial marriages were banned by law. In addition, civil restrictions initially were placed on blacks, and until recently blacks and their descendants were barred from the LDS priesthood.

Believing that undesirable physical, mental, and moral attributes were generally acquired through the debased actions of one generation (or race), and passed thereafter through heredity to succeeding generations, nineteenth-century Mormons were also sympathetic to strong societal controls on what might be termed "undesirables," regardless of race. Apostle Parley P. Pratt's early suggestion that "a wise legislation, or the law of God . . . would not suffer the idiot, the confirmed, irreclaimable drunkard, the man of hereditary disease, or of vicious habits, to possess or retain a wife" was echoed by another church leader, Dr. Seymour Young, a half-century later.[104]

Eventually, as noted in the preceding discussion on madness (Chapter 5), the predominantly Mormon state of Utah did take a step in this direction. In 1925, on the basis of a somewhat modified scientific understanding, a statute was passed in the wake of a national enthusiasm over eugenics which provided for the sterilization of institutionalized individuals (including infants) who were "habitually sexually criminal, . . . insane, mentally deficient, epileptic, or afflicted with degenerate sexual tendencies," if "by the laws of heredity [they were] the probable potential parent of socially inadequate offspring likewise afflicted." As a leading apostle, James Talmage, explained in a somewhat broader context, "a taint in the blood," if "known to be capable of transmission, should be hemmed in and not allowed further propagation."[105]

In practice few such sterilizations were performed after 1930 (and only 79 before). That year an LDS adult education manual nonetheless reaffirmed that sterilization had a legitimate, if more narrowly defined, "place in any plan of social control for the feebleminded." Since then the subject virtually disappeared from Mormon publications, until 1983 when an official policy statement once more affirmed the legitimacy of sterilizing the "mentally incompetent."[106]

A eugenic theme also can be traced in LDS guidance on birth control, which from the earliest years sanctioned marital abstinence when the husband or wife were not "free from impurities which would be entailed upon their posterity." This caveat can be traced throughout the twentieth century, right up to the First Presidency statement of 1969, which in fact quotes the earliest guidance verbatim on the point.

Aside from the narrowly defined exemptions for eugenic reasons, however, until recently Mormon Utah rejected all other grounds for sterilization. Even the tolerant McKay administration opposed an effort to liberalize a state law which as late as 1969 was interpreted as allowing only eugenic sterilizations. The same First Presidency statement that opposed any change in state laws on abortion also opposed a bill that would have authorized voluntary sterilizations "where medically necessary to preserve the life or prevent a serious impairment of the mental or physical health of the patient or spouse."[107] Although this legislative initiative failed, judicial review a few years later determined that no prohibition against such sterilization actually existed in Utah law. Unlike the case of abortion, this did not bring about a formal statement of guidance from the church.

Eventually, in 1976, the Church Commissioner of Health Services prepared a short statement on sterilization, patterned after guidance on birth control—and taken almost verbatim from privately issued First Presidency guidance, which stated, "The Lord's commandment imposed upon all Latter-day Saints is to 'multiply and replenish the earth.' Nevertheless there may be medical conditions related to the health of the mother where sterilization could be justified. But such conditions, rare as they may be, must be determined by competent medical judgment and in accordance with laws pertaining thereto."[108]

Two years later a Mormon authority warned that those submitting to vasectomy might be ineligible for participation in temple ordinances, but this guidance was never formally implemented. Nor have temple-recommend interviews ever officially included questions relating to sterilization (or birth control). Among other reasons, sterilization, like birth control, can be rationally justified in most cases. Moreover, the increasing frequency with which such procedures as hysterectomy are performed for non-pregnancy-related indications (for example, uterine prolapse and fibroids) has contributed coincidentally toward making the question of birth control moot for many women in their later childbearing years.

The first official public guidance on this subject dates from the 1983 *General Handbook,* which for the first time combined Utah's legal proviso with church counsel. A somewhat expanded version of the 1983 statement is found in the current *General Handbook,* which makes clearer the church's concern that to warrant sterilization, health risks must be substantial:

> The First Presidency has declared, "We seriously deplore the fact that members of the Church would voluntarily take measures to render themselves incapable of further procreation.
>
> Surgical sterilization should only be considered (1) where medical conditions seriously jeopardize life or health, or (2) where birth defects or serious trauma have rendered a person mentally incompetent and not responsible for his or her actions. Such conditions must be determined by competent medical judgment and in accordance with the law. Even then, the person or persons responsible for this decision should consult with each other and with their bishop (or branch president) and receive divine confirmation through prayer.[109]

Given the official record on birth control, in which family-planning decisions are now entrusted in very nonjudgmental language to husband and wife, it seems clear there will be at least one additional step in the official record on sterilization—cautiously acknowledging that sterilization may be justified later in the childbearing years when, with divine confirmation through prayer, it is concluded that the family size best for all concerned has been achieved.

INFERTILITY

Historically, the principal Mormon solution to the eugenics issue has been at the end of the spectrum opposite to that occupied by sterilization. Righteous (and, thereby, healthy) people should have more children. Or, as Brigham Young put it in a quotation not infrequently heard even today,

> I have told you many times that there are multitudes of pure and holy spirits waiting to take tabernacles, now what is our duty?—to prepare tabernacles for them; to take a course that will not tend to drive those spirits into the families of the wicked, where they will be trained in wickedness, debauchery, and every species of crime. It is the duty of every righteous man and woman to prepare tabernacles for all the spirits they can. . . . [110]

One might suppose, therefore, that the Church would look favorably on almost any technique that would lead to successful pregnancies in otherwise infertile LDS marriages. In fact, this almost is true, especially if only medication or surgical procedures are involved. For example, cases among Mormons of successful *in utero* procedures, or hormonally induced multiple births have been featured supportively in *Church News* articles.

When biological products such as ova or semen are involved, however, the subject has been more problematic. Despite a biblical and nineteenth-century Mormon precedent for "vicarious" insemination following a husband's death, artificial insemination in the modern sense was flatly rejected when it was first publicly addressed by the church in 1950. A *Church News* editorial that year reported that those inquiring about the "righteousness" of "artificial methods of insemination" have been told "to avoid such things, that the practice is not moral, and frequently would lead to family complications."[111] (Rather, infertile couples were advised to turn to adoption.)

The growing popularity, and success, of this procedure led to continued inquiries. Guidance consistent with that of 1950 was given privately in the sixties and early seventies: it was noted that the church was opposed specifically to insemination "with other than the semen of the husband." This was felt to "produce problems related to civil law, family harmony and eternal relationships." The latter concern notwithstanding, it was also held that "a child born under such conditions would be born in the covenant," that is, would be considered eternally sealed to parents who previously had themselves been sealed (in marriage) in the temple. (Although an adopted child must be formally sealed to his new parents, this ruling on artificially conceived children was consistent with previous church practice. Children born to a woman previously sealed, but now widowed or civilly divorced, and her second husband are considered sealed to the *first* marriage. Even the offspring of an adulterous relationship has been deemed sealed to the preexisting marriage.)[112]

The initial perspective has been tempered somewhat in the last decade and a half. In 1974, private counsel from the First Presidency, though still indicating that "the Church cannot approve of artificial insemination with other than the semen of the husband," included a recognition that "this is a personal matter which must ultimately be left to the determination of the husband and wife with the responsibility of the decision resting solely upon them." This perspective gained more visibility when it was included in a 1974 compilation of medical ethical guidelines prepared by the Church Commissioner of Health Services. These guidelines further advised, no doubt apropos sensitivity on the question of semen analysis, that regarding "sterility tests," "The Church believes that having children is a blessing and privilege and, that with any abnormal condition, it is appropriate to use medical science to diagnose and restore normal function."[113]

In 1976 official guidance recast "the Church does not approve" into the more positive counsel that "the Church approves of artificial insemination only in cases where the semen of the husband is used." The end point, to date, was reached in 1977, when the First Presidency, in their only formally published statement on the subject, softened the wording a little further in counseling that "the Church *discourages* artificial insemination with other than the semen of the husband." Their statement also made clear, for the first time publicly, that births through artificial insemination were to be viewed in the same ecclesiastical light regardless of whether the semen was that of the husband (that is, they were considered "born in the covenant").[114]

Within the past two years, one new development has brought forth related guidance. A small but growing national trend for single women to request artificial insemination led some LDS women to seek guidance on this issue. Following a reportedly nonjudgmental informal response, a clearly condemnatory public stance was ultimately adopted. A member of the First Presidency advised in General Conference that "artificial impregnation" in this setting "frustrates the eternal family plan." Not only did the church "strongly discourage" such action, but any "who do so may expect to be disciplined by the Church." This was followed up with new *General Handbook* (1985) guidance that succinctly reiterated the point: "The Church disapproves of artificial insemination of single sisters. Single sisters who deliberately refuse to follow the counsel of their priesthood leaders in this regard will be subject to disciplinary action."[115] Moreover, since the church will not allow a child to be sealed eternally to only one parent—regardless of whether adoption or divorce prior to conversion to Mormonism is involved—sealing the offspring of an artificially inseminated single mother also is barred.[116]

With the further advance of reproductive technology, *in vitro* fertilization

(IVF), with or without donated occytes (eggs) has joined artificial insemination as an option for infertile couples. The church did not publicly address this issue until 1989. Previous private guidance was generally nonjudgmental and again shifted full responsibility to the parties involved. An implied public assent was evident in the failure of the church to respond to the publicity surrounding the increasing use, during the 1980s, of *in vitro* techniques both by LDS physicians and patients. The guidance published on IVF in 1989 is very similar to that given on artificial insemination:

> In vitro fertilization using semen other than that of the husband or an egg other than that of the wife is strongly discouraged. However, this is a personal matter that ultimately must be left to the judgment of the husband and wife.
> A child conceived through in vitro fertilization after parents are sealed in the temple is born in the covenant [i.e., is automatically considered postmortally sealed to the parents]. Such a child born before parents are sealed in the temple may be sealed to them after they are sealed.

Certain issues set IVF apart from artificial insemination and could have drawn a more negative response. The reality that all fertilized eggs might not be implanted could easily have led to questions about abortion. Apparently, Mormonism's open theology on the timing of ensoulment has allowed personal discretion in this area. Additionally, scriptural precedents notwithstanding, LDS scientists working in this emerging field tend to understand the earliest phases of conception in the same biophysical terms as do their non-Mormon counterparts. Frozen embryos, chimeras (in which two early conceptions fuse into one), and twinning (in which one may divide into two) generally are believed by most to pose insurmountable philosophical obstacles to there being a prerequisite embryonal spirit presence. The subject nonetheless remains a sensitive one. A "pro-life" LDS physician on the staff of one of the first U.S. *in vitro* fertilization facilities (a Reno, Nevada clinic, begun in 1983) carefully explained that it followed "LDS standards" in refusing "to do experiments on left-over eggs" or to perform implants in either surrogate mothers or single women. [117]

A final emerging issue in the reproductive field is that of surrogate motherhood, a subject only recently addressed publicly by the church. In a surprisingly moderate statement modeled after (and cross-referenced to) guidance on artificial insemination and IVF, the 1989 *General Handbook* advised that "surrogate motherhood is discouraged. It might cause spiritual, emotional, and other difficulties." One might have expected a stronger condemnation than this, which as now written is somewhat less emphatic than the "strong" discouragement of IVF. Moreover, were the surrogate mother unmarried, she would seem to fall under the strong strictures against artificial insemination of single women (which is considered grounds for formal church discipline). Doctrinally a married surrogate mother could be more problematic still. As things now stand, an artificially inseminated LDS surrogate mother, for example, carrying a child for an infertile sister, would—if herself sealed in the temple to an LDS husband—be deemed sealed for eternity to the child, with no ecclesiastical provision for this bond to be broken through adoption (sealing) to the intended (infertile) mother.

For the moment this is, of course, not a pressing practical problem for the church. Surprisingly, though, a 1987 survey in Utah found Mormons only 58 percent opposed to the use of surrogate mothers, while 30 percent were in favor (with 46 percent of Utah non-Mormons opposed, and 35 percent in favor).[118] Unquestionably, there will be future modification in public LDS guidance on surrogate motherhood and, contrary to the record on other medical ethical issues, this will almost surely be more restrictive than the first published statement.

HOMOSEXUALITY AND SEX-CHANGE SURGERY

Perhaps the most emphatic of all doctrinal opinions within Mormonism, at least within the domain of human sexuality, are those relating to homosexuality. Although the subject was essentially absent from public commentary until 1968 (when it was felt necessary to add this to the list of offenses for which members could be excommunicated),[119] the previous silence undoubtedly reflects only the general attitude adopted by broader society, and not a nonjudgmental view. Two years later, in 1970, leadership concerns over an "apparent increase in homosexuality and other deviations" within the church led to a number of official actions, including the first of four different First Presidency statements (1970, 1973, 1975, 1978); creation of a program headed by two apostles, aimed at homosexuals within the church; a thirty-three-page pamphlet, "New Horizons for Homosexuals" (1971), designed to persuade homosexuals that their sexual activity was sinful but, with repentance, "curable"; a related publication, "Hope for Transgressors" (1973), to aid local leaders; a lengthier technical discussion of the subject, "Homosexuality" (1975, revised in 1981); and short pamphlets by Church President Kimball (1978) and Apostle Packer (1978), both to be used in counseling.[120]

All of these publications, as well as the First Presidency's letters, were distributed to local leaders throughout the church. In them, the Presidency made clear that the church viewed homosexuality "as sin in the same degree as adultery and fornication." Local leaders were warned to "be alert to this menace," to keep it in mind during official interviews, and "to counsel and direct" those involved "back to total normalcy and happiness." "Much understanding and sympathetic treatment" was needed, with the goal of convincing those involved that "a total continuing repentance could bring them forgiveness for the transgression." If, however, "after sincere and faithful and continuous efforts, . . . those persons are still belligerent, uncooperative and continuing in their transgressions, then, of course, they must be properly disciplined."[121]

This same basic message has been conveyed in all issued guidance. With time, there has been increased concern with handling cases confidentially and not overresponding to isolated episodes with premature labels. Instruction was also given that members who have "repented of homosexual problems" were to be allowed to serve in church assignments, but not in positions of "temptation." There has been no relaxation in the fundamental concern, however. Local leaders continue to be advised to "make special confidential inquiries into suspected behavior" and "to confront the accused candidly, to invite him to confess." One seeking forgiveness is expected to "disclose his sexual partners as an essential part of repentance." ("The purpose is to help save others.") Any who have not "totally repented and forsaken these evil practices" are excluded from attending (or working at) church schools and universities.[122]

Homosexuality is said by the church to be of "grave concern" for five reasons: it violates the Lord's eternal plan for humanity's progression by perverting the proper procreative powers and loving relationships; it deprives God's children of the happiness and fulfillment possible only in family life; it debases and demeans those involved; it is as sinful as heterosexual adultery and fornication; and it "may involve violent or criminal behavior." It is said to result from many factors, including disturbed family background, poor relationships with peers, unhealthy sexual attitudes, and early homosexual experiences; however, it is finally held to be a learned behavior that can be overcome.[123]

Local church leaders are widely believed capable of dealing successfully with homosexuality. When mental or emotional disturbances are also present, it is suggested that a professionally trained person (a social worker, counselor, or psychiatrist) also be utilized, though preferably a Latter-day Saint "with the necessary blend of gospel background and professional skills." Without this gospel background, it is feared that "the professional might not deal with homosexuality in a manner pleasing to the Lord."[124]

Most LDS counselors probably endorse the church perspective, even on the professional issues. Scientific arguments aside, they are disposed to accept what they view as prophetic guidance that homosexuality is both learned and amenable to "cure." (For a time in the late sixties, this led to the use of aversion therapy—pairing a negative stimulus with a depiction of unacceptable behavior—by some at Brigham Young University.) There is beginning concern, however, among some LDS professionals that the issues are much more complex than church guidance to date has acknowledged. A Mormon psychiatrist, for example, recently addressed this question in an essay titled "Sin and Sexuality," which presented the scientific case for a nonvolitional, nonlearned homosexuality tied to genetic or hormonal factors. Clearly uncomfortable with a doctrinaire solution to an extraordinary subject, he concluded with a rhetorical inquiry about who wished to shoulder the ultimate moral responsibility for dealing so summarily with such profound mysteries.[125]

In response to concerns of this sort, Mormon apostle Dallin Oaks, in a recent interview on national television, expressed a view now common within educated Mormon circles: "Those who have tendencies in that direction need not feel themselves to be outcasts. I should think they would be in no different position than those with heterosexual tendencies. They come under the injunction that Jesus had given to His followers, that they should not look upon a woman to lust after her, and I assume that includes a man looking on a man to lust after him." However, since there was "no scriptural warrant for homosexual marriages" and the "scriptural [commandment] is that men and women should refrain from any sexual relations outside the bonds of marriage," those with homosexual inclinations would have to remain celibate so far as their homosexuality was concerned.[126]

Another reaffirmation of current leadership views came in a 1988 First Presidency statement on AIDS. In conveying "compassion to those who are ill with AIDS," the Presidency expressed "great love and sympathy for all victims but particularly those who have received the virus through blood transfusions, babies afflicted from infected mothers, and innocent marriage partners who have been infected by a spouse." The greater part of the twelve-paragraph statement, however, was devoted to a restatement of the long-standing theme that "those who choose to violate the commandments of God put themselves at great spiritual and physical jeopardy. . . . We plead with people everywhere to live in accordance with the teachings of our Creator and rise above carnal attractions that often result in the tragedies that follow moral transgression. . . . The Lord has not left mankind without clear guidance on matters that affect our happiness. That guidance is chastity before marriage, total fidelity in marriage, abstinence from all homosexual relations, avoidance of illegal drugs, and reverence and care for the body, which is the 'temple of God.' (1 Cor. 3:16)." In sum, "We advocate the example of the Lord, who condemned the sin, yet loved the sinner."[127]

Though some Mormon homosexuals have attempted to work within the parameters established by the church, many have not. In 1978 a group of active, inactive, and excommunicated gay and lesbian Mormons founded Affirmation, a national organization "to help lessen the fear, guilt, self-oppression, and isolation that LDS homosexuals experience." Within five years they reportedly numbered 1,000 members, with an official publication, *Affinity*, and chapters in several cities. Reportedly very orthodox in most of their religious views, they have patterned support groups after LDS models and seek "to reconcile their sexual identity with traditional Mormon beliefs"—a formidable challenge indeed. Although a limited dialogue has taken place between midlevel church leaders and Affirmation leaders, it is not likely that this will ever influence the official Mormon view. In fact, until 1989 a public declaration of homosexuality almost surely resulted in excommunication. (Of the 13,500 persons reportedly excommunicated in 1981–82, nearly 800 were said to be on this basis.)[128] As with most other offenses for which excommunication has been a relatively common response, homosexuality in the future will likely not receive such ecclesiastically severe treatment. This, as in other instances, reflects more a change in the official view of the value of excommunication than a lessening of concern over homosexual activity.

At least one distinctively Mormon argument has accompanied discussions of homosexuality within the church. Most Mormons believe that the premortal spirits destined for earth already possessed gender (and, as well, that exalted souls will continue to have gender in the hereafter). Although Joseph Smith did not address the question directly, his contemporaries and successors were quite clear on this point.[129] This perspective has invited an argument that some homosexuality results from a spirit somehow being mismatched to the body. In fact this possibility was first rejected a half-century ago, when apostle James Talmage wrote that "there is no accident of chance due to purely physical conditions, by which the sex of the unborn is determined; the body takes form as male or female according to the sex of the spirit whose appointment it is to tenant that body."[130] Predictably, when the issue of spiritual misassignment was raised in recent years, it was rejected out of hand. Apostle Boyd K. Packer, one of those assigned to deal with issues relating to homosexuality, stated flatly in 1976, "there is no mismatching of bodies and spirits." A similar point was made by Gordon B. Hinckley, of the First Presidency, several years later.[131]

This understanding had particular relevance when medical advances made possible seemingly successful sex-change surgery. Though the church did not respond initially in a formal way to this development, church president Kimball early commented that "men and women who would change their sex status will answer to their Maker."[132] In fact, however, until 1979 the issue remained an unsettled one among the leadership. As late as 1978, a convert to Mormonism who had undergone sex-change surgery was allowed to be endowed and married in the temple to a Mormon husband—actions of transcendent doctrinal implications—despite the view of some church leaders that the case was one of "an eternal male spirit in a physically mutilated body."

When the issue was finally addressed publicly the following year, further deliberation clearly had taken place. At that time formal guidance was issued which not only reversed that previously given (though apparently not retroactively) but imposed on those associated with such procedures (patient *or* physician) the severest ecclesiastical sanctions in the history of the church: "In cases of . . . transsexual operations," local leaders were advised in 1980, "either received or performed, [excommunication is mandatory and] . . . no readmission to the Church is possible." Prospective converts who have had such surgery may be baptized only "on condition that an appropriate notation be made on the membership record so as to preclude [them] from either receiving the priesthood or temple recommends." (By comparison, although having or performing an abortion was also potential grounds for excommunication, local leaders were allowed discretion in even bringing offenders to trial. Nor were there any prescribed restrictions on readmission.)[133]

Notwithstanding this unequivocal stance, a subtle shift already has begun in guidance on even this subject. The 1983 *General Handbook* advised that "a change in a member's sex *ordinarily* justifies excommunication" (emphasis added). To this, the 1985 *General Handbook* further added, "After excommunication, such a person is not eligible again for baptism *unless approved by the First Presidency.*" Additionally, since 1983, local leaders have been advised that "difficult cases"—which, given the guidelines, might well have been all of them—could be forwarded directly to the First Presidency. In fact, exceptions to the required strictures have been granted under this First Presidency authority, in cases where the individual who had undergone sex-change surgery (male to female) was now in a healthy family situation (with adopted children). The most recently issued guidance, that of the 1989 *General Handbook,* is the most moderate to date:

> Church leaders counsel against elective transsexual operations. A bishop should inform a member contemplating such an operation of this counsel

and should advise the member that the operation may be cause for formal Church discipline. In questionable cases, a bishop should obtain the counsel of the First Presidency.[134]

A related group of implied exceptions also exists, acknowledged only in passing and never addressed doctrinally. These include cases (once termed by Kimball a "few accidents of nature")[135] in which hormonal "miscues" or surgical mishaps have left infants with ambiguous genitalia. In many instances, such cases are transformed for sound medical reasons from genotype males to phenotype females. While doctrinally perplexing, and technically involving "sex-change surgery," such cases seemingly do not fall under the general guidelines. Decisions on the best course of action apparently are based largely on what appears medically most reasonable.

The LDS record recounted in this chapter is notable for the insight it affords into the gestation and progress of Mormon doctrine, at least within the modern church. As one traces authoritative guidance on subject after subject, a remarkably clear and consistent pattern emerges in timing, content, and evolution. This pattern, best illustrated in guidance on birth control, sterilization, artificial insemination, and abortion, will be discussed more fully in the concluding section on authoritative guidance in Chapter 8.

·7·

On Caring

For their first century the Latter-day Saints constituted communities of both faith and geography. Isolated in belief and locale, Mormons in need were thrown almost exclusively upon Latter-day Saint resources—be they doctrinal, social, medical, legal, or economic. This circumstance—as well as a later "Americanization" process as Utah achieved statehood in 1896, the Great Depression of the thirties, and recent membership growth outside the western Great Basin—has shaped or reshaped LDS attitude and practice toward those in need. Much of the earliest philosophy remains, however, and continues to guide present-day developments.

This brief chapter will examine those facets of community "caring" among the Mormons that have direct relevance to the broader issues of health and medicine. These include inconspicuous but vital manifestations of congregational concern like fasting, prayer, and the delivery of compassionate service, as well as higher-profile activities like the provision of LDS hospitals and exploratory efforts in international health.

VISITING, TEACHING, FASTING, AND PRAYER

And now, for the sake of these things which I have spoken unto you—
that is, for the sake of retaining a remission of your sins from day to day,
that ye may walk guiltless before God—I would that ye should impart of
your substance to the poor, every man according to that which he hath,
such as feeding the hungry, clothing the naked, visiting the sick and administering to their relief, both spiritually and temporally, according to
their wants. (Mosiah 4:26)

Book of Mormon writers, like their New Testament counterparts, were clear about the responsibility of the Saints toward those less fortunate. Their message was reiterated in latter-day revelations, and the record shows that, within the community of the Saints, these admonitions have been followed faithfully. Community concern has been a prominent feature throughout the Mormon experience.

This caring response for the most part has been the province of—and dependent upon—the local congregation or ward, whose efforts can be both generalized and highly specific. At the broadest level are such practices as community fasting and prayer. In times of serious medical crisis within a ward, a special congregation-wide fast often will be held, which occasionally extends to several congregations or, during the illness of a church president, even to the church at large.

Prayer is an important part of the fast but as in nearly all religious communities may also stand alone. A distinctly Mormon manifestation of this near-universal response is a prayer associated with the temple endowment. Part of the endowment ceremony is a brief "prayer circle" in which a special blessing is invoked on individuals whose names have been submitted by friends and relatives, often because of a health-related problem. Although the prayer itself is not prescribed (indeed it follows the same free-form pattern of virtually all Mormon prayers), it is offered in a ritually rich setting believed to give added urgency and import to its message. (An analogous prayer circle—though without the attire worn in the temple—was conducted for those in need in some congregational meetings in the late-nineteenth-century church. This practice, like several others noted in the discussion of healing, was discontinued shortly after the turn of the century.)

Beyond this generalized response, Mormon communities long have been known for the extent to which they respond tangibly to the needs of "their own." This too has been principally a congregationally-based effort, involving several ward entities now under the direction of the local bishop, a lay leader who is the ecclesiastical father of the ward. The bishop, prior to Utah statehood, was often the dominant community leader, serving—through the church court system—as civil and sometimes criminal judge for members under his jurisdiction. During the brief early periods when the Mormons attempted to live as a communitarian society, he also was responsible for collecting and apportioning all community resources. The bishop's role in the twentieth century is much more circumscribed, though he continues to control access to LDS temple ordinances through "worthiness" interviews prior to the issuance of "temple recommends," and he is still the principal agent in the collection of tithes and offering within his congregation, a resource critical to the fulfillment of his welfare role.

(The practice of making offerings in conjunction with a monthly day of fasting—originally the first Thursday of the month, but now the first Sunday—was first introduced in the mid-1850s during a time of famine in pioneer Utah. Initially the food that would have been consumed was donated; now it is the cost of the meals missed during the fast. Tithing, also introduced very early in church history, is collected separately from fast offerings and presently is defined as an annual contribution of 10 percent of gross income. While fast offerings are used primarily to pay for the care of those in need, tithing funds support building construction and other centralized functions.)

The bishop, in seeing to the needs of his ward, has two main congregational resources. The first is "the priesthood" (that is, virtually all male members age twelve or older), which early revelatory guidance indicated bore broad responsibility for "the poor and the needy, the sick and afflicted" (*D&C* 52:40) and for "visit[ing] the house of each member, exhorting them to pray vocally and in secret and attend to all family duties" (*D&C* 20:51). In compliance with this instruction, priesthood representatives or "teachers" have been assigned from the earliest years to visit member families regularly. The purpose of the visits has been to insure the temporal and spiritual well-being of each family. Presently termed *home teachers* (and assigned in pairs), these individuals are expected to visit "their families" at least monthly to teach, to encourage, and, where warranted, to assess needs. It is to the home teachers that most families first turn (and are encouraged to turn) when in need of a priesthood administration because of illness. They also represent a formal contact with the institutional church in times of extended absence due to illness. During such times home teachers are expected to visit the homebound and on Sundays to administer the sacrament of bread and water.

The second major congregational resource is the Relief Society. Now comprising all adult LDS women, the society was first organized under Joseph Smith's wife Emma to "seek out and relieve the distressed." Especially in the years from about 1870 to 1930 the Relief Society administered a nearly autonomous relief program staffed by its own personnel and funded in significant measure by its own membership dues. For the last half-century, however, Relief Society efforts have been directed by (and all financial resources derived from) the bishop and other priesthood leaders.

Like their male priesthood counterparts, Relief Society "visiting teachers" are expected to be thoroughly familiar with their assigned families through a regular schedule of monthly visits to every woman in the ward. Although also an educational and social organization, the Relief Society strongly encourages its members to involve themselves with "compassionate service," which it explicitly defines as encompassing visits to the sick and homebound; care for the sick, including bedside nursing care and other services like bringing in food, assisting with housekeeping or caring for the children of a sister who is ill, and accompanying her to a doctor's office; and service at the time of death, including the preparation of food for the family of the bereaved and, when appropriate, assistance in the provision of temple clothing and dressing the dead for burial.[1]

In present-day LDS wards the Relief Society president generally takes the lead in assessing for the bishop the long-term food and clothing needs of those in economic distress. And as a practical matter Relief Society sisters are responsible for providing any needed domestic assistance. Their organizational efficiency in responding to such needs is remarkable, as anyone attempting to do something "on their own" soon learns. To be accommodated smoothly, a tangible caring response generally must be coordinated through the structured Relief Society effort. Priesthood members do occasionally still undertake special projects but are not directly involved in compassionate service to nearly the extent that the women are.

In sum, those with significant illnesses among the Latter-day Saints, be they in the hands of skilled physicians or under the hands of ministering elders (most often, both), are immersed also in a pervasive and well-organized congregational response which reflects both institutional and personal concern and provides practical support in a particular time of need.

HOSPITALS, SOCIAL SERVICE, AND THE WELFARE PLAN

In addition to congregationally-based help, Mormons over the years have been beneficiaries of several centrally directed initiatives. Beginning with its opening of a maternity hospital in 1882, the General Relief Society presidency (an overall presidency located in Salt Lake City) was for over five decades at the forefront of these efforts. Eventually their role was taken over by a general Welfare Department organized in 1936 under the auspices of the Office of the Presiding Bishopric (another priesthood-based central entity responsible for virtually all temporal church resources).

At this more central level Relief Society efforts were directed principally at the assurance of good medical care for all LDS communities and the promotion of what was termed *social welfare*. The medically related efforts were multifaceted and involved the dissemination of health care information through formal churchwide lesson manuals (an effort that continues to the present), the provision of training classes for practical nurses (1898 to 1921) with an incurred obligation to donate time to community service, an activist political role in support of maternal and child welfare initiatives and the reform of Utah state facilities for the mentally handicapped (both in the 1920s), volunteer work at sanitary milk depots (1913 to 1917) and maternity, infant, and preschool health clinics (in the 1920s), and on two occasions the establishment of hospitals (1882 and 1924).

The apogee came in the twenties, when the Relief Society marshalled its resources in support of the Federal Maternity and Infancy (Sheppard-Towner) Act of 1921. This program, the first social reform measure to involve federal matching funds, succeeded in Utah largely because of the efforts of LDS relief societies who supported state officials by distributing literature on proper prenatal care to expectant mothers, surveying community health facilities, organizing local clinics and classes (sometimes in Mormon meetinghouses), and assisting physicians in physical examinations. During the seven-year life of the program, nearly 4,000 Relief Society volunteers were involved. In response to this effort seventeen different stakes (dioceses) established maternity health centers for "hospital" deliveries, and virtually all LDS wards (congregations) developed "maternity closets" of instruments, bandages, and clothing to be made available for little or no charge to physicians, midwives, mothers, and babies at the time of delivery. The net effect was a substantial reduction in both maternal and infant mortality. Unfortunately repeal of the Sheppard-Towner Act nationally in 1928 essentially ended intensive Relief Society involvement in matters of community health. (Ironically, the filibuster of a Utah senator delivered the final blow to the act, which was opposed by conservative states' rights champions as being meddling and "Bolshevic.") Thereafter, however, expanded public resources were much more adequate to community needs.[2]

The Relief Society's "social welfare" program, while overlapping with the medical efforts, was for the most part a separate and distinct undertaking. Built on a long tradition of individual service within the community, this more formal effort derived from work during World War I in support of the Red Cross's home service program. This involved undertaking the role traditionally performed by Red Cross social workers in support of the families of absent servicemen whose pay was insufficient to make ends meet. The Relief Society accepted this role for all affected LDS families, obligating itself in the process to adhere to Red Cross methods and standards. A Relief Society Social Services Department grew out of this experience, with its own training program, which played a major role in the LDS community for the next two to three decades. Eventually its functions were replaced by the self-help LDS Welfare Plan begun during the Depression. Since then, the General (i.e., central) Relief Society leadership has directed its efforts primarily toward increasing the spiritual dimensions of LDS women through educational programs and promoting individual self-improvement and ward-based compassionate service.

Among the last programs to be transferred to what is now termed the Welfare Services Department was the care of unwed LDS mothers and, when necessary, the placement of infants in adoptive homes. As licensed services, adoptions and foster home placements were—and still are—legally beyond the authority of local ecclesiastical leaders. Until the recent expansion of LDS counseling services (discussed in Chapter 6), these licensed functions constituted most of what remained of the original Relief Society social service program. At present it is unclear whether the church per se will continue to provide licensed services. A major element of the program involving the voluntary, temporary placement of Native American children in LDS foster homes during school months already has been discontinued. It is very possible that a combination of liability concerns and the availability of competent, comprehensive services outside the church structure will lead to the transfer of licensed services to a private resource. As will be seen, this is an option already taken with regard to the direct provision of medical care.

Although the Relief Society opened the first Mormon hospital (in 1882), it was the priesthood-based Office of the Presiding Bishopric that oversaw the church's full-scale entry into the hospital business. The Relief Society's Deseret Hospital operated for less than a decade, but within a few years of its closing for financial reasons, church leaders agreed that the Presiding Bishopric should build a major general hospital for the LDS community. This culminated in the opening in 1905 of the Groves L.D.S. Hospital (discussed in Chapter 4). A growing desire that all members have access to sophisticated medical care led the church over the next several decades to assume, additionally, the operation of several faltering hospitals located in LDS communities and, in a few instances, to build entirely new "LDS" hospitals (the letters became part of the names of all these hospitals and were retained even after the church sold the hospitals). All together at one time or another the church has operated twenty different hospitals. Though several were not retained, others were expanded, modernized, or moved to new and larger facilities. Eventually an operating network of fifteen LDS hospitals made available to principally LDS communities in a three-state area some 2,000 inpatient beds—backed by over a thousand physicians. Collectively these hospitals cared for over 100,000 inpatients each year, in addition to an estimated 360,000 outpatient and emergency cases. Overall half the total membership of the church had more or less direct access to a Mormon hospital.

Though all these hospitals ultimately were administered by the Office of the Presiding Bishopric, not all entered the church system directly through this office. Cottonwood L.D.S. Hospital (1924) was the creation of the Cottonwood Stake Relief Society; Sanpete L.D.S. Hospital (1949) was built by the Sanpete North Stake (with help from two neighboring stakes). And Primary Children's Hospital (1911) was the culmination of efforts by the LDS children's auxiliary (the "Primary") to provide a facility for the convalescence of crippled children. Subsidized for years by Mormon children who donated "birthday pennies" each year, this Salt Lake City hospital has become a major full-service pediatric referral center.

When the Relief Society first opened its hospital in 1882, many mistakenly thought its services were without charge. Indeed charity cases were a sufficient strain that formal notices were issued emphasizing its "benevolent" rather than "charitable" role in the community. This notwithstanding, charity cases always have been a major part of the LDS hospital system, and from the outset perhaps 10 percent of all patients were "church services cases." Eventually, in 1938, the church created a Medical Welfare Department (under the Presiding Bishopric) to administer medical charity cases. As part of the larger LDS Welfare Plan introduced two years before, it adhered to principles designed to encourage self-sufficiency and first-line reliance on local congregational resources. As with the broader Welfare Plan it also prescribed a tight administrative structure and attentive oversight.

A 1956 Presiding Bishopric booklet, "Hospitalization and Medical Care of Church Services Cases," provided the fullest discussion of LDS practice and policy toward medical charity cases. As there explained, care was "confined to worthy church members only," and it was expected that those in need would turn first to family resources and any available health insurance. All patients receiving church support required a "hospital recommend"—Form 9A or 9B, depending on the urgency of the case—signed (as was a temple recommend) by both the local bishop and stake president. "Reoccuring cases" required repeated recommends. Both inpatient and outpatient care could be authorized, including psychiatric care. Under extraordinary circumstances dental work and optometry could be approved. Those seeking well-baby checkups, however, were referred to local public health facilities.

The care provided to "church services cases" was donated by LDS physicians, dentists, and optometrists. Hospital expenses (if, in 1956, they exceeded $10) were billed to the local bishop, who was to use fast offerings to meet the payment. Fast offerings also were available for the purchase of medicine and medical appliances. A parallel mechanism existed to reimburse non-LDS hospitals and physicians, though bishops were enjoined to use church-operated facilities whenever possible. If local resources fell short, the presiding bishop—that is, the hospital—absorbed the cost. (Patients who could pay physicians' bills but not hospital costs were, as a general rule, considered ineligible for free hospital care; it was assumed that if resources were available in the one instance, they probably were for both. On the other hand, individuals whose insurance paid hospital bills but not physicians' fees were eligible for admission to the church service. They were expected to bill their insurance company for covered hospital costs.)

After several decades' commitment to an LDS hospital system, the past two decades have seen a major shift in the LDS approach to health care provision. The change dates to 1970 when a new Health Services Corporation came into being, still under the auspices of the presiding bishop, but headed by a newly named Church Commissioner of Health Services. The first—and only—Church Commissioner of Health Services was Dr. James O. Mason, a respected infectious disease and public health specialist who had been deputy director of the National Center for Disease Control (and later returned there as director, before accepting his present position as Assistant Secretary for Health for the U.S. Department of Health and Human Services). Mason organized the Health Services Corporation into two divisions: the large existing Hospital System division and a small, nascent unit concentrating on worldwide health. The latter was responsible for the medical well-being of Mormonism's youthful worldwide missionary force, overall membership health education—especially in the international church—and, almost immediately, a new program of "health services missionaries."

In 1974, just four years after creation of the Health Services Corporation, the First Presidency announced a landmark decision to divest itself entirely of the hospital system. They explained:

> After a thorough study and consideration, the Council of the First Presidency and Quorum of the Twelve has decided to divert the full efforts of the Health Services of the church to the health needs of the worldwide church membership. As a result of that decision, and because the operation of hospitals is not central to the mission of the church, the church has also decided to divest itself of its extensive hospital holdings, including the 15 hospitals that have been operated in Utah, Idaho and Wyoming by the Health Services Corporation.
>
> The growing worldwide responsibility of the church makes it difficult to justify provision of curative services in a single, affluent, geographical locality. In past years, the church responded to the appeal of communities to save an existing facility or to build a hospital because their health needs seemingly could not be met in any other way. Today, however, there are other ways that these needs can be met. It is no longer necessary for the church to be involved in hospital ownership or management.

> This decision in no way signifies loss of interest or concern on the part of the church for the sick and afflicted. To the contrary, it provides greater flexibility as the church assists members and others everywhere with their temporal needs. Worldwide Health Services, which emphasizes disease prevention and assists people in various parts of the world to appropriately use local health facilities and personnel, is being expanded to a major degree. This will require a substantial increase in the number of Health Services missionaries.
>
> A new, nonprofit corporation is being created which will own and operate the hospitals and assume all current hospital indebtedness to the Church. The Church will turn over to the new corporation a vigorous and financially viable enterprise.[3]

Pragmatically speaking, the data behind the First Presidency's decision were persuasive. Church growth outside the intermountain West had been such that by then only a fourth of the membership was within geographic reach of an LDS hospital, and this shift away from the intermountain West was sure to continue. Even in the communities served it seemed that the presence of LDS hospitals at times retarded needed growth in alternative public and private facilities, the assumption being that the church eventually would expand its own resources. Although the existing system operated at a modest profit (3.5 percent against operating expenses of nearly $60 million, with only four of the hospitals showing losses), any meaningful expansion of the system would have been prohibitively expensive and would have drained sorely needed resources away from such high-priority programs as the construction of meetinghouses for the rapidly growing membership. Moreover the use of federal assistance was deemed generally unacceptable because it brought with it increased federal intervention in such sensitive areas as the provision of non-Mormon psychiatric services in LDS facilities.

Also fundamental, in a more theoretical sense, to the divestiture decision was a review of LDS scripture which failed to unearth any requirement to provide LDS-originated medical care to the faithful—so long as fast offerings were available to insure that needed care could be made available from non-LDS sources. This, therefore, is the practice today. Local wards (or stakes), through their fast offerings pay for necessary medical care for needy, worthy members of their congregations who are not otherwise covered by some public mechanism. If expenses are beyond local capabilities, the presiding bishop's Welfare Services Department will make the necessary funds available. Indeed, cases costing more than $5,000 must be reviewed by the central office, which works with physicians and facilities involved to obtain any reductions that may be possible.

Although it no longer directly subsidizes a hospital system, the church continues to encourage members to support such national efforts as the March of Dimes, and the American Cancer and Heart societies. By far the most ambitious private effort has been the Children's Miracle Network Telethon, originated in 1982 by two Mormons in Salt Lake City. Designed to raise money for children's hospitals—the first to subscribe being the city's Primary Children's Medical Center—and actively supported by LDS and other celebrities (Marie Osmond was a co-founder; Bob Hope has been an honorary chairman), this telethon by 1987 was carried by nearly 200 stations around the world. That year it raised $40.5 million, a record for an annual fund-raiser. The funds raised—$170 million in its first six years—help support 160 children's hospitals, all in the local television markets in which the money was raised.

HEALTH SERVICE MISSIONARIES AND HUMANITARIAN SERVICES

Other notable developments took place during Mason's tenure as Church Commissioner of Health Services, among which was assembling the first systematic collection of authoritative LDS guidance on medical ethical issues (see Chapter 8). Perhaps the most dramatic of Commissioner Mason's proposals was that the church for the first time send medical missionaries to serve alongside the traditional proselyting force. These new missionaries were to be "in the tradition of the Word of Wisdom" and have as their guiding principle an emphasis on health education and disease prevention. As originally conceived, the program envisioned the use of several kinds of specialists, including physicians, dentists, dental hygienists, nurses, nutritionists, social workers, and agricultural experts. They were to work primarily with members living in areas of limited medical sophistication and teach such things as sanitation, nutrition, and maternal and child care. The program was not intended to provide curative care, a later *Church News* editorial explained, but rather "to encourage wise utilization of existing local resources and health facilities in cooperation with local health officials."[4]

The basic proposal was adopted, and in the summer of 1971 the first two LDS medical missionaries began their work—a nurse in Tonga and a physician in Samoa. Several months later six more nurses went to the field, in pairs, to serve in Guatemala, Bolivia, and Peru. The following year forty-two additional health missionaries joined the work, including a dentist who established a pilot clinic on a Navaho reservation in Arizona. The first agricultural missionaries were added in 1973.

By this early date small but significant changes to the program were felt necessary. First it was decided that young single men should be excluded from consideration, primarily because of the nearly concurrent requirement for their service as proselyting missionaries, which was held to be a more spiritually rewarding experience. Next it was concluded that as a practical matter physicians and dentists were not well-suited to the program. As therapists they understandably had a tendency to become involved in curative rather than preventive work during their missions, which was not only a great deal more expensive to support than health but also was contrary to a stated goal to avoid the creation of enduring dependency on outside specialists. In 1975 all health and agricultural missionaries were redesignated "welfare services missionaries," and by decade's end this group was composed almost exclusively of young single women trained in nursing or an allied field and older married couples who served as agricultural specialists.

Another major program change came about in 1981, when the supervisory responsibility was transferred from the welfare services department to the church's Missionary Department. The organizational transfer led to an inevitable shift in emphasis. Welfare services missionaries soon were redesignated "missionaries with other responsibilities—welfare" (part of a larger body of "specialists" in such areas as genealogy and temple work).

The redirection was viewed as overcoming a number of problems. Paramount was the establishment of the local mission president as preeminent in the direction of all local missionary activities. Welfare missionaries, though assigned to specific missions, had at times been perceived as serving two masters, the local mission president and the central welfare services staff. There also had been some difficulty with program emphasis and program continuity. Welfare services missionaries typically served for only eighteen months, so continuity of effort depended on a succession of comparably trained specialists. As a practical matter this was not always possible. An obstetrically qualified nurse might be succeeded by someone trained in nutrition, or vice versa. While both had much to offer, neither could sustain a program built on the other's expertise. It was decided that a preferable approach was to emphasize less ambitious, less technically demanding projects of the sort that could more readily be overseen by the mission president.

The final area of concern involved community response to the presence of LDS welfare services missionaries in Mormon congregations. Paradoxically, rather than attract investigators to the Mormon gospel, the existing program sometimes caused resentment, as the notion that "the Mormons take care of their own" took on a negative overtone—as "only their own." A broader community-based program, even something as basic as a simple health fair, was seen as affording less opportunity for criticism.

In practice, therefore, the health (or welfare services) missionary program proved a greater challenge than expected. As a result church leaders chose to scale down and redirect their efforts into an area more readily administered and requiring less sophisticated and less continuous expertise. In retrospect the 1980–81 time frame was the high watermark in the LDS health-related missionary effort. At that time some 800 welfare services missionaries served in perhaps 35 countries worldwide (though principally in Latin America and the South Pacific). By the late 1980s there were only about 300 "missionaries with other responsibilities—welfare" in the field, and essentially no health missionary program.

Interestingly, despite the eclipse of this program, the last three years again have seen the advent of a small but growing cadre of true health missionaries. In 1988 concerns about an unexpectedly high incidence of disease among LDS missionaries led the missionary department to establish a Medical Advisory Committee to attack the problem of missionary health in the Third World. On the basis of recommendations made by this committee (which now is permanently established), nurses and physicians again were called to serve in the mission fields, though this time the primary goal was to protect the health of missionaries asigned to the region. By early 1991 twenty-two nurses had been assigned, predominantly to Latin America, to support individual missions; and three physicians to serve as multimission advisers, also in Latin America. Still primarily preventive in focus, this program already has achieved a 75-percent reduction in missionary illness rates.[5]

The advent of health missionaries was just one manifestation of a growing desire among Mormons to be more heavily involved in international service—an interest that continues to grow despite the fate of that program. Humanitarian concerns in combination with dramatic membership growth in developing countries led to several additional private and institutional LDS initiatives, some of which will extend well into the future. The first of these was the creation in 1968 of Ayuda, the private project of a number of LDS professionals to upgrade the health services available to Latin American Indians (believed by most Mormons to be the descendants of the "Lamanite" people of the *Book of Mormon*). Ayuda's first project was the 1969 opening of a medical clinic to serve a Mayan community in Guatemala. The staff of the clinic, for the most part LDS volunteers who came for two-week to twelve-month stints, soon opened an adjunct preschool which with assistance from CARE distributed nutritional supplements to community children. Later a dental unit was added.

While not a church-sponsored organization per se, Ayuda's board included such prominent leaders as apostle (and later church president) Spencer Kimball and Church Commissioner of Health Services James Mason. It probably served as part of the impetus for the health missionary program, which it supported actively. Ayuda members, for example, provided the equipment and materials used to outfit the first dentist sent on an LDS medical mission. The extent of Ayuda's activities has waxed and waned over the years, but the Guatemalan clinic remains a continuing success.

More recently, especially in the 1980s, LDS individuals and other private or semiprivate organizations have undertaken small international health projects, primarily in Latin America. These include, among a score or so efforts, the Andean Children's Foundation, which has worked to upgrade health education and water supplies in communities in Bolivia and Peru; activities of Brigham Young University's Academy of Dentists in communities in Mexico and the Caribbean; and some beginning work in Equador by the health committee of Brigham Young University's Ezra Taft Benson Agricultural and Food Institute. Additionally, a BYU-sponsored association of LDS physicians, Collegium Aesculapium, was founded in 1982 with expressed goals of fostering Mormon caring values within the medical community and serving as a clearinghouse for those physicians who would like to do international volunteer work. To this end it has sponsored conferences promoting this agenda, directly supported a health care prevention program among the Tarahumara Indians in Chihuahua, Mexico, and regularly listed opportunities for international service in its periodic newsletter.

Unique to date among these semiprivate LDS aid projects have been the activities of the Thrasher Research Fund. Built on a $17-million endowment from non-Mormon E. W. "Al" Thrasher, this program has been administered since 1977 by the LDS church. Sustained by the annual interest of $1–2 million, the Thrasher Fund awards grants for research and demonstration projects relating to pediatric problems in developing countries, with three specific areas of identified interest: infectious disease control, health promotion, and nutrition. The criteria against which grant proposals are evaluated can be said to be an idealized statement of the general LDS philosophy toward such endeavors: (1) self-reliance should be taught as an integral part of any project; (2) the technology involved should be appropriate to the level of understanding of those served; (3) workers should approach their projects as "helper-learners" rather than "teacher-experts" (In the words of executive director Val MacMurray, "we consider cultural humility rather than cultural chauvinism to be the appropriate attitude as we emphasize fitting interventions to the local culture"); (4) problems should be approached through a cooperative experience "that affirms the worth of both parties" and allows them to learn from each other; (5) volunteers should be a cornerstone of the program ("full humanity can be expressed only through loving service to others"); and (6) the efforts complement, cooperate with, and collaborate with the efforts of government agencies, private groups, and other foundations.[6]

To date, the Thrasher Fund has supported a wide spectrum of activities in a score of countries. Most grants have gone to university-based research efforts—on subjects such as diarrheal disease, nutritional deficiencies, and the development of resistance to malaria in children. One major field effort was managed directly by the fund, in part with LDS volunteers. This was a village health worker project in Nigeria which focused on "clean water and improved sanitation, nutrition, home gardening, general agricultural development, immunization, communicable disease control, and other basic health and treatment measures including control of diarrheal diseases at the village level"—in essence, all the elements of the original health/welfare services missionary program.[7]

A significant final development in the realm of LDS "caring" took place in 1985 when an unprecedented fast was called by the First Presidency in support of African famine victims. Involving all U.S. and Canadian congregations, this one-day fast yielded an offering of just under $7 million. A second fast later in the year, as part of a National Day of Fasting, brought another $3.5 million in offerings.

The resulting "fast aid fund" has been administered by a newly created LDS Humanitarian Services Committee. Two different types of aid have been dispensed. First, nearly $4 million almost immediately was given to organizations involved directly with famine relief, specifically Catholic Relief Services, the Red Cross, and CARE. Subsequently smaller contributions have been made, for example, to aid victims of the 1988 Armenian earthquake and to assist in the construction of homeless shelters in Salt Lake City and Ogden, Utah. The church has a long history of responding to acute community crises with tangible help, but these recent initiatives unquestionably were a milestone. Previous relief efforts—usually in response to widespread natural calamities such as earthquakes or floods—have relied heavily on LDS mechanisms and have been directed primarily at church members.[8] The present delivery of material aid almost exclusively to those outside the LDS community has necessitated the selection of non-LDS relief organizations "of unquestioned integrity." In the case of aid to Armenia, where there were no private voluntary organizations, funds were given directly to the Soviet government.

The second and—since the initial disbursement of monies—primary use of collected fast aid funds has been in support of humanitarian development projects. These have included construction of an irrigation system in Ethiopia and other water and agricultural development projects in Chad, Niger, Cameroon, Nigeria, Ghana, and Bolivia. Most activity has been carried out through the auspices of Africare, but to a lesser extent development funds have gone to CARE, Technoserve, and a few small LDS-based volunteer groups such as the Andean Children's Foundation and the Benson Institute. Between the Thrasher and fast aid funds, the church now dispenses some $3–4 million a year in support of research or development programs in the international health arena and apparently intends to continue this level of support into the future. Though these grants may take into consideration the specific needs of an emerging church membership—occasionally may even encourage community-based efforts in areas of LDS concentration—the sponsored programs are in no sense directed specifically at church members. The basic prerequisite for aid has been only that there be "chronic debilitating conditions brought about by poverty, poor health, or unsafe environments that may be improved by self-help development."[9]

In the foreseeable future official LDS involvement in the field of humanitarian international health will undoubtedly be a three-part extension of the most recent activity. First, while disaster relief will continue to be sent directly to LDS congregations involved in local crises, substantial assistance may also be sent via established relief organizations to assist in more widespread disasters. (For example, recently relief supplies were sent via the Red Crescent Society to Iranian earthquake victims and Kurdish refugees.) Second, there will continue to be a substantial emphasis on development aid, administered primarily through non-LDS organizations with established skills and experience. This may well be focused on geographic areas in which the church has a substantial or emerging presence. Third, an increasing effort will be made to incorporate the activities of private and semiprivate Mormon groups into a more symbiotic relationship with programs supported by LDS development grants. It is hoped thereby to provide both a resource to those directly administering these programs and an opportunity for individual Mormons to be more personally involved. While the church will not likely undertake any substantial development activity of its own, it is clear that Mormons now are committed to continued support in this arena.

·8·

On Morality and Dignity

Even this hurried review has revealed a remarkable diversity in the LDS perspective. A partial explanation of this variance, in a religion popularly viewed as single-minded if not frankly authoritarian, is found in the Mormon understanding of the roles of God and humans in the earthly sojourn. In Joseph Smith's developed view, the untrammeled right to make and accept responsibility for ethical decisions—"free agency" was as sacred an entitlement as any enjoyed by humankind. Indeed it was said to be a premortal rejection of this divine right that led to the downfall of the devil and his hosts in the great "war in heaven" spoken of in Revelation (12:7–9). The Lord's "plan" demanded that humankind be allowed the test of personal choice. It is in the application of this cherished doctrine that the Mormon record becomes complex. The degree to which the institution of the church has defined "correct" choices has varied considerably over time. Although the eternal consequences of wrong choices may have been constant, their earthly implications have varied.

A corollary to humankind's divine right—and responsibility—is a belief that the individual is entitled to personal revelation on issues that affect him or her directly. Though not as conspicuous in its influence on church practice and belief as institutional initiatives, the inspiration of the rank and file has had a profound impact on the direction taken by the church.

AUTHORITY, AGENCY, AND ACCOUNTABILITY

Confronted with difficult personal dilemmas, medical or otherwise, Mormons are taught to study church guidance, counsel with local church leaders, and seek inspiration through prayer. Those following this advice have a number of published resources available, of differing degrees of authority. Though in reality these potential references constitute a near seamless spectrum, for present purposes they may be grouped into three broad categories: (1) canonized scripture, (2) statements issued by the First Presidency, and (3) sermons and other published works.

The *LDS canon* consists of four "Standard Works": the *Book of Mormon*, the Bible, the *Doctrine and Covenants*, and the *Pearl of Great Price*. The first two, both foundational scriptures of the Mormon restoration, are held respectively to be "the word of God" and "the word of God as far as it is translated correctly." Both, and particularly the *Book of Mormon*, also are believed by the vast majority of Mormons to be authentic ancient history. The *Doctrine and Covenants* is almost entirely a collection of the revelations and inspired guidance of Joseph Smith. Its 138 "sections" are often specific about time and place, and they dwell on what originally were labeled the "covenants" between the Latter-day Saints and the Lord. A brief "doctrinal" catechism, which gave rise to the title *Doctrine and Covenants*, has since been dropped. The *Pearl of Great Price* is a short collection of Joseph Smith's renditions of ancient texts including portions of Genesis and the twenty-fourth chapter of Matthew. The most controversial of the LDS canon, it is not accepted as scripture by those who, choosing not to follow Brigham Young and the Twelve westward, later formed the Reorganized Church of Jesus Christ of Latter Day Saints.

To the extent that the LDS canon touches on issues of health and medicine, it at least initially shaped (or reinforced) Latter-day Saint belief and practice. Its influence on Mormon notions of death and the hereafter, faith healing, herbalism, and the role of devils in disease has been noted. The *Doctrine and Covenants*, of course, was also the source of important general instructions on personal health practices. From the narrow perspective of medicine, however, LDS scriptures offer relatively little of definitive relevance to the difficult questions of the late twentieth century. Where the implications of the scriptures, read literally, might be considered explicit—such as with regard to devils and herbalism—the progress of science has led most Mormons to consider the health-related specifics to be more relevant to history than to the present day. Latter-day Saints thus now tend to read their scriptures not so much in search of explicit answers as for broad principles that might relate to their particular problem. Generally church members hope that through this study they will reach a point at which they can receive inspiration on a matter of concern, either through some creative application of a scriptural text or through an inward sense of the will of the Lord.

The second general category of published guidance is *formal statements of official policy* issued by the First Presidency of the church (that is, the president and, most often, two counselors). Initially there was some reluctance within the church to set forth formally anything that might be construed as a church "creed." Joseph Smith believed that it was "too much like methodism" to have "creeds which a man must believe or be kicked out of their church." He wanted, he said, "the liberty of believing as I please, it feels so good not to be trammelled."[1] Even the *Doctrine and Covenants* when first published carried the introductory apologia to the anticreedal view that "it does not make a principle untrue to *print* it, neither does it make it true not to print it." Eventually Joseph Smith did write a fifteen-sentence summary of church beliefs—Mormonism's thirteen "Articles of Faith," but some reluctance to publish officially any detailed statement of church doctrine continues to the present. For example, a "Bible Dictionary" currently included as part of the official LDS Authorized ("King James") Version of the Bible is prefaced with the disclaimer that the dictionary was "not intended as an official or revealed endorsement of the doctrinal, historical, cultural, and other matters set forth."

Despite some lingering vestige of this philosophy, it has become increasingly common since Joseph Smith's day for the First Presidency to issue brief statements of guidance and policy on matters of general concern. For well over a century virtually all authoritative church guidance has been in the form of official circular letters—now totaling well over a thousand—released by the First Presidency. While the exact status of such guidance never has been addressed officially, either in scripture or by the Presidency itself, it is widely understood in the context of an early revelation which stated that "whatsoever they [those ordained to the priesthood] shall speak as they are moved upon by the Holy Ghost shall be scripture, shall be the will of the Lord, shall be the mind of the Lord, shall be the word of the Lord, shall be the voice of the Lord, and the power of God unto salvation" (*D&C* 68:4).

A number of the First Presidency's statements, cited throughout the present monograph, have addressed issues relating to health and medicine. Significantly, in no other published source will one find anything approaching a comprehensive review of official guidance on this subject—in large measure because the church has not maintained a publicly available compendium of First Presidency statements. Even though some statements are publicized through official periodicals at the time of release, several years later the average member probably would not be able to locate as many as a half-dozen of these sources. The only effort to date to collect and publish First Presidency statements proved much more of historical than current relevance. This was a project undertaken in 1965 by a team of Brigham Young University professors. Ultimately they published six volumes (some eight hundred statements) spanning the years 1833 to 1951. The vast majority of official guidance bearing on medical issues, however, was not issued until well after this period.

In addition to releasing periodic circular letters, the First Presidency also has supervised, at least nominally, a wide range of official church publications. Only one of these sources has achieved essentially the same status as formal First Presidency statements. A *General Handbook of Instructions* has been issued periodically to local leaders throughout the twentieth century. Primarily administrative or procedural in content, this key publication carried the caveat as recently as 1960 that it was "not to be construed as an official statement of Church doctrine. The revelations of the Lord as set forth in the Standard Words constitute the law and doctine of the Church."[2] Beginning in 1976, however, the First Presidency added a brief authoritative section on "policies" to the *Handbook*. Fifty-four items now are addressed in this section, twenty-four relating to issues of health and medicine. Where appropriate the texts of these brief policy statements have been discussed in the preceding chapters.

The exact status of First Presidency guidance has been the subject of some discussion. In principle the church rejects the notion of leadership infallibility, but practically speaking both the Prophet and the First Presidency are widely held to be incapable of leading the church astray. Brigham Young may have been the first church president to espouse this view, which continues to be widely affirmed to the present. Although individual members are encouraged to seek their own inspiration on issues formally addressed, for at least a century the goal has been to learn for oneself *that*— not *if*—the president's (or First Presidency's) counsel is inspired. As succinctly put by a recent member of the First Presidency, writing for the church's official adult magazine, "When the prophet speaks, the debate is over."[3]

Currently First Presidency guidance is accepted almost without question, a clear reflection of the high regard in which the First Presidency is held. Indeed, especially in the mid and late twentieth century, the extent of one's overall commitment to the gospel is measured in most congregations by one's willingness to conform to officially promulgated guidance. On a few subjects such acceptance is mandated formally. Before granting access to the temple or selecting a member for congregational assignments of even modest responsiblity, local and regional Mormon leaders are obligated to interview prospective candidates to insure conformity to the LDS health code and a few other behavior guidelines. Those violating First Presidency guidance on abortion or homosexual behavior are, as previously discussed, subject to ecclesiastical discipline.

Although widely accepted, First Presidency guidance has fallen far short of achieving the status of scripture. The absence of a lasting public repository mitigates against this ever happening, of course, but of equal importance is the reality that over time the Presidency's perspective often has changed. This is especially apparent in the history of several subjects of medical-ethical interest. Privately, this progression in thinking is recognized and occasionally acknowledged. A member of the First Presidency once explained, for example, that unless issued statements are formally ratified by the membership at large—an extremely rare occurrence which would confer canonical status, they are "matters of temporary policy only." Moreover, when conditions change, he said, "the First Presidency may wish to make a statement which may not be in harmony with a former statement."[4] While consistent with the actual record, such candor—published in a posthumous memoir—is rare. Rather there is an overriding concern, as once was explained with regard to a disputed doctrine, that "to admit that [a presiding power] can advance incorrect doctrine, is to lay the ax at the foot of the tree."[5] In practice, therefore, while official guidance does evolve over time, there is virtually no retrospective discussion of views that have been discarded in the process. This development, if noted at all, is simply understood in terms of a commitment to continuing revelation. On the basis of an early revelation in which the Lord promised to "give unto the faithful line upon line, precept upon precept,"[6] it long has been understood that even the official understanding eventually might become more refined.

First Presidency statements (including the *General Handbook* section on policies) and the LDS scriptures themselves, provide church members with a modest amount of official ethical and interpretive commentary. Although uniquely authoritative, these sources represent only a minuscule fraction of the materials available to church members seeking answers to questions of personal concern. Beyond these there is a vast array of materials including the sermons of church leaders, dozens of officially published periodicals and manuals, hundreds of books and articles published over the years by church leaders, and a much, much larger number of books and articles by lay members.

It is impossible to summarize briefly either the authority or influence—issues ofttimes bearing little relationship to one another—of the tens of thousands of items that have appeared bearing directly on LDS doctrine or practice. Over the years a wide range of views has been expressed in these sources, on virtually every LDS doctrine and belief—including the underlying question of the relative authority of these sources themselves. Even church-controlled publications, though editorially limited to a modest range of perspectives at any given time, have varied from a strongly progressive stance early in the century to a much more conservative tone in recent years.

In practice only one subset of these non–First Presidency writings appears to have had a major impact on LDS belief. The doctrinal sermons and writings of the few church authorities who have been willing to flesh out core doctrine can be shown to have shaped popular Mormon thinking—at least during the lifetime of the authors—from the very beginning.[7] By far the most influential recent addition to this body of literature is an 856-page work entitled *Mormon Doctrine*, which was published privately in 1958 by Bruce R. McConkie, then one of the most junior of the church leadership (though made an apostle in 1972), and revised in 1966. Though neither sponsored nor endorsed by the First Presidency, the author nonetheless was comfortable bringing a definitive style to his work which obviously filled a felt void among the rank and file. Popular as well among those in the church hierarchy holding similar views, this work ultimately became a major documentary source for dozens of influential church manuals and periodicals.

In theory, one key to expanding the scriptural core of LDS belief is direct personal inspiration. And in practice the cumulative impact on the church of the inspired judgments of the rank and file has been substantial. This has occurred in several ways. At the most obvious level, local—often individual—initiatives have been adopted churchwide. Such pervasive elements of everyday Mormon life as the Relief Society, Sunday school, Primary (the children's program), Young Adults (and before this, YMMIA and YWMIA—Young Men's and Young Women's Mutual Improvement Associations), Seminary (a program of religious education for high school students), Institutes of Religion (the college equivalent of Seminary), the Welfare Program, and Family Home Evening all were originally local—not central—solutions to perceived needs.

Individuals outside the ecclesiastical leadership also have influenced many policy issues over the years. The adoption, at the turn of the century, of individual cups for the sacrament was prompted by the concerns of an LDS physician that the communal cup could spread disease. More substantively, the first collection of medical-ethical guidelines assembled by the church came at the prompting, in 1974, of the Church Commissioner of Health Services. Based on both preexisting private guidance and the commissioner's personal recommendations, these guidelines eventually formed the basis of many of the relevant *General Handbook* policy statements. To the present day a small group of highly respected physicians serve as advisers to church leaders both in the identification of subjects requiring leadership attention and in the formulation of official First Presidency guidance.

Finally, and more subtly, on occasion the membership at large simply has reached such an overwhelming degree of consensus on a subject, individually and privately, that church leaders in essence ratify their judgment. Birth control may offer the best case study of this phenomenon, but it is apparent in the record on most medical-ethical issues. To some extent this is a manifestation of a healthy dose of common sense evident throughout the Mormon record, on issues of the here and now. Recall that these are the folks who (1) unapologetically noted with regard to deceased converts who anticipated that they would live to see Christ's return, that experience had taught them to the contrary; (2) rebuked the devil in a homicidal "lunatik" in a priesthood prayer circle held *just beyond* the length of his chain; (3) concluded that those who follow the precepts of the Word of Wisdom would, as promised, "run and not be weary" because they would have enough wisdom to stop and rest when they needed to; and (4) when one member was faced with a severe toothache despite priesthood administration, consecrated oil, and appropriate topical herbs, concluded that "faith without works is dead," reached in and pulled out the offending tooth, and "Praise be to God, it hasn't hurt me since."

Notably, one way in which individual Mormons, at any level, have *not* contributed appreciably to the development of church teachings is through an influential body of reflective medical-ethical literature. Very little has been attempted to date comparable in any sense to the theological discussions found in most other faiths. The guidance issued formally by the church is, as noted, typically very brief and explicitly behavioral, supported if at all by a few lines of scriptural proof text. Most other commentary on medical-ethical subjects has adopted a similar approach, that is, has used in LDS parlance the method of the "scriptorian" rather than of the theologian. Very recently there has been a modest increase in interest in medical ethics within the church, spurred to some extent by the efforts of a segment of LDS society who seek a return to herbalism and other early practices. The reliance of this latter group on the superseded guidance of early church leaders has forced a limited reexamination of the theological basis of present-day teachings.

AUTHORITATIVE GUIDANCE

LDS medical ethics is finally still largely limited to the everyday application of the First Presidency's succinct behavioral guidelines. As this is likely to remain the case for the foreseeable future, it is appropriate to conclude with a brief review of their past approach to issues of concern. The First Presidency record on medical-ethical issues is, in fact, unparalleled in the window it provides on doctrinal development within the church. It also may offer some insight into the future of authoritative Mormon thought.[8]

First, the Church of Jesus Christ of Latter-day Saints—and specifically the uniquely authoritative First Presidency—often chooses *not* to express itself on issues with obvious ethical or theological overtones. This is especially true when the issues are extraordinarily complex and when important scientific questions remain unanswered. Significantly the vast majority of the public guidance that has been issued on medical subjects has come only within the last two decades, and this principally in response to the prompting of leading LDS physicians. Even so, the First Presidency still generally declines to address publicly developing issues within the medical-ethical arena. LDS health professionals, by contrast, have begun to involve themselves a little more actively in the discussion of ethical issues.

Second, when the First Presidency does comment on such issues, the initial guidance is given privately, in response to questions from those most directly involved. For almost a half-century, in fact, the most complete and accurate current statement of LDS beliefs has been the Presidency's file of privately answered letters.[9] Carefully indexed to insure consistency over time, these private statements not infrequently have provided the text for statements formally published several years later.

Third, formal public statements on medical-ethical issues generally do not appear until relatively late in the public discussion (for example, birth control was first formally addressed in 1969, artificial insemination in 1976, and *in vitro* fertilization in 1989). By this time, it is not unusual for individual members and local leaders to have reached independent judgments on the questions involved. While inevitably leading to some confusion, given the Mormon notion of free agency, this basic process is not necessarily viewed as bad.

Fourth, with the passage of time there almost always is an evolution in the guidance issued by the church. The public phase of this evolution invariably has been in the direction of greater conformity to the general medical and social consensus on the subject. In recent years, at least, one can trace the progression in thinking most readily in the key words associated with formal guidance. These words define a clear spectrum of attitudes: "mandatory excommunication," "not approved"/"may be disciplined," "strongly discouraged," "discouraged," "not encouraged," and a variety of neutral terms. Although guidance on medical issues has begun at different points on this spectrum, in all cases the progression has been in the same direction.

A major part of this evolution has been an implied decision to allow the Lord rather than the institution of the church to render judgment about personal decisions on a number of private issues. This has been signaled by the addition to formal guidance of a phrase indicating that "this is a personal matter that ultimately must be left to the individual." This, or similar counsel, is now part of nine statements, including that on birth control, sterilization, artificial insemination, *in vitro* fertilization, abortion, organ transplants, and prolonging life. Surely this trend will continue.

Fifth, to some extent the evolution in official guidance is accompanied by the emergence of what in retrospect might be termed the core of ethical concern that motivated the guidance from the outset. This core generally is expressed in terms unambiguously tied to central tenets of the faith: the centrality of marriage and children; the overriding importance of maintaining family harmony and stability and protecting the health and well-being of mother, children, and "tabernacles-to-be"; the preservation of free agency and personal accountability; and the total unacceptability of decisions based on "selfish" rationales. Of these the notion of personal accountability has proved especially important, because in moderating its guidance on such issues as birth control, artificial insemination, and abortion, the institutional church has been able to underscore that an ultimate accounting remains for everything done in mortality. It seems likely that the church eventually will move further in this direction and substantially limit the circumstances in which it calls members to account in the here and now.

Sixth, guidance that eventually is discarded in this evolutionary process in retrospect generally falls into one of two categories. It may simply have been asserted by fiat, with no doctrinal rationale ever publicly offered. Or, alternatively, it may have been justified with sociocultural (often emotion-laden) rationales readily identifiable with societal values formerly current.

Seventh, where core beliefs themselves are modified, this generally reflects an accommodation to new knowledge simply unreconcilable with the previous view. This development does not pose as much a challenge to church authority as might be supposed. It is in fact a tenet of the Mormon faith that this sort of refinement periodically will take place. Nonetheless, such evolution typically finds some segment of LDS society unwilling to modify affected views and practices. As a result Mormon communities include, particularly among the so-called "splinter groups," living reminders— embryological vestiges, as it were—of the history through which Latter-day Saint thought has passed.

Notes

As with biblical references, citations from the *Book of Mormon* are given as "book," chapter, and verse (for example, Alma 32:18). Citations from the *Doctrine and Covenants* are by section and verse (for example, *D&C* 1:24).

Abbreviations for cited LDS periodicals:

IE	*Improvement Era* (Salt Lake City, 1897–1970)
JD	*Journal of Discourses*, 26 vols. (1854–86)
JI	*Juvenile Instructor* (1880–1902)
M&A	*Latter Day Saints Messenger and Advocate* (1834–37)
MS	*The Latter-day Saints Millennial Star* (1840–1970)
RSM	*Relief Society Magazine* (1914–70)
T&S	*Times and Seasons* (1839–46)
YWJ	*Young Women's Journal* (1889–1929)

Preface

1. Thomas F. O'Dea, *The Mormons* (Chicago: University of Chicago Press, 1957), p. 117.

2. Lawrence Foster, *Religion and Sexuality: Three American Communal Experiments of the Nineteenth Century* (New York: Oxford University Press, 1981).

3. In theory the church president is selected, for life, by the Quorum of the Twelve. In practice, he is the senior apostle at the time of a president's death. The president chooses his own counselors.

Chapter 1 / On the Mormon Context

1. The phrase is taken from the title of Whitney R. Cross's classic work *The Burned-over District: The Social and Intellectual History of Enthusiastic Religion in Western New York, 1800–1850* (Ithaca, N.Y.: Cornell University Press, 1950).

2. Jan Shipps, *Mormonism: The Story of a New Religious Tradition* (Urbana: University of Illinois Press, 1985).

Chapter 2 / On Death and Dying

1. Peter L. Berger, *The Sacred Canopy: Elements of a Sociological Theory of Religion*, quoted in M. Guy Bishop, "To Overcome the 'Last Enemy': Early Mormon Perceptions of Death," *Brigham Young University Studies* 26: 64. (Hereafter cited as *BYU Studies*.)
2. Klaus J. Hansen, *Mormonism and the American Experience* (Chicago: University of Chicago Press, 1981), p. 105.
3. Joseph Smith, *History of the Church of Jesus Christ of Latter-Day Saints, Period I*, ed. B. H. Roberts, 7 vols. (Salt Lake City: Deseret Book, 1902–32), 6:50.
4. Moroni 8:12, 22; 2 Nephi 9:25. After an 1832 revelation specified that there were three different degrees of heavenly glory, it was assumed that only those who actually joined the church and were baptized could achieve the highest or celestial degree of heaven. However, Smith modified this understanding following an 1836 vision he experienced while contemplating the death of his brother, Alvin, who had passed away before the Mormon restoration. He announced that those who died "without a knowledge of the Gospel, who would have received it if they had been permitted to tarry, shall be heirs of the celestial kingdom" and also that children dying before the age of accountability were saved in this highest kingdom as well. See Smith, *History of the Church* 2:380–81.
5. *D&C* 37:1, 38:32.
6. Donald Q. Cannon and Lyndon W. Cook, eds., *Far West Record* (Salt Lake City: Deseret Book, 1983) pp. 19–24.
7. *D&C* 88:138–40; Smith, *History of the Church* 1:323–24.
8. *D&C* 95:8.
9. Smith, *History of the Church* 2:379; Leonard J. Arrington, "Oliver Cowdery's Kirtland, Ohio, 'Sketch Book,'" *BYU Studies* 12, no. 4 (1972): 410–26.
10. Smith, *History of the Church* 2:197.
11. Smith, *History of the Church* 2:430–33.
12. Blake Ostler, "The Idea of Pre-existence in the Development of Mormon Thought," *Dialogue: A Journal of Mormon Thought* 15, no. 1 (Spring 1982): 59–78. (Hereafter cited as *Dialogue*.)
13. *D&C* 131:7.
14. Van Hale, "The Doctrinal Impact of the King Follett Discourse," *BYU Studies* 18 (1978): 209–25.
15. *JD* 2:31–32 (1853).
16. James E. Talmage, *The House of the Lord* (1912; Salt Lake City: Deseret Book, 1968), pp. 83–84.
17. Much of the associated symbolism was similar to that of Masonic ritual, which was believed by Smith to be of ancient origin albeit "degenerated" from its authentic priesthood origins. Masonry in fact afforded for a number of Mormon leaders "a Stepping Stone or Preparation for something else, the true Origin of Masonry." See Andrew F. Ehat, ed., "'They Might Have Known That He Was Not A Fallen

Prophet'—The Nauvoo Journal of Joseph Fielding," *BYU Studies* 19 (1979): 133–66, and David John Buerger, "The Development of the Mormon Temple Endowment Ceremony," *Dialogue* 20, no. 4 (Winter 1987): 33–76. Many of the most manifestly Masonic elements of the temple ritual were dropped in 1990, as part of a larger revision.

18. Talmage, *House of the Lord*, p. 84.

19. David John Buerger, "'The Fullness of the Priesthood': The Second Anointing in Latter-day Saint Theology and Practice," *Dialogue* 16, no. 1 (Spring 1983): 10–44; Buerger, "The Development of the Mormon Temple Endowment Ceremony."

20. Lisa A. Cannon-Albright et al., "Common Inheritance of Susceptibility to Colonic Adenomatous Polyps and Associated Colorectal Cancers," *New England Journal of Medicine* 319 (1 September 1988): 533–37.

21. See, for example, *Handbook of Instructions for Stake Presidencies, Bishops and Counselors, Stake and Ward Clerks*, no. 15 (Salt Lake City: Deseret News Press, 1934), p. 10; *The Church of Jesus Christ of Latter-day Saints General Handbook of Instructions*, no. 21 (Salt Lake City: Church of Jesus Christ of Latter-day Saints, 1976) p. 53; and First Presidency letters of 5 January and 15 October 1982. (After the first mention of each edition these will be cited respectively as *Handbook of Instructions* and *General Handbook of Instructions*, followed by the date of the edition.)

22. 2 Nephi 9:10–16; the language is close to that of the New Testament, but most of those identified for this fate in Revelation 21:8 eventually inherit, in LDS theology, a degree of heavenly glory.

23. *D&C* 19:1–12.

24. *D&C* 76, 88.

25. *D&C* 88:98–99, 100–101; 76: 105–7. My thanks to Anthony Hutchinson for this insight.

26. *D&C* 76:34–46 (see also John 17:12); although without reference to perdition, *D&C* 42:16 previously had indicated that there was no forgiveness for murder, and this point was reaffirmed several years later in *D&C* 132:19, 27.

27. A number of these accounts are collected in Craig R. Lundahl, "The Perceived Other World in Mormon Near-death Experiences: A Social and Physical Depiction," *Omega* 12, no. 4 (1981–82): 319–27, and Duane S. Crowther, *Life Everlasting* (Salt Lake City: Bookcraft, 1967).

28. *JD* 3:369 (1856); Crowther, *Life Everlasting*, pp. 12–14.

29. *Wilford Woodruff's Journal, 1833–1898 Typescript*, 9 vols. (Midvale, Utah: Signature Books, 1983–84), 2:163; *JD* 7:163, 8:28, 13:76.

30. The episode, recorded in 1954, took place about 1908. It is published in *The Ezekiel Johnson Bulletin* 14, no. 3 (September 1967), p. 3, and is still popularly circulated in typescript.

31. Crowther, *Life Everlasting*, pp. 83–86; *Wilford Woodruff's Journal* 6:363; *JD* 16:334–36 (1873).

32. *Wilford Woodruff's Journal* 2:163, 5:544; A. Karl Larson and Katherine Miles Carson, eds., *Diary of Charles Lowell Walker* (Logan: Utah State University Press, 1980), 2:561.

33. Ostler, "The Idea of Pre-existence," pp. 59–78.

34. James R. Clark, ed., *Messages of the First Presidency of the Church of Jesus*

Christ of Latter-day Saints, 6 vols. (Salt Lake City: Bookcraft, 1965–75), 3:229–31; see also D. Michael Quinn, "LDS Church Authority and New Plural Marriages, 1890–1904," *Dialogue* 18, no. 1 (1985): 24.

35. *Handbook of Instructions for Stake Presidencies, Bishops and Counselors, Stake and Ward Clerks and Other Church Officers,* no. 16 (Salt Lake City: Deseret News Press, 1940), pp. 131–32; *General Handbook of Instructions* (Salt Lake City: Church of Jesus Christ of Latter-day Saints, 1989), p. 6–2.

36. *D&C* 42:45–47 (1831).

37. Truman G. Madsen, "Distinctions in the Mormon Approach to Death and Dying," in *Deity and Death,* ed. Spencer J. Palmer (Salt Lake City: Publishers Press, 1978), pp. 61–76.

38. Juanita Brooks, ed., *On the Mormon Frontier: The Diary of Hosea Stout, 1844–1861,* 2 vols. (Salt Lake City: University of Utah Press, 1964), 1:171.

39. Journal of Orson W. Huntsman, 7 June 1880, Library of Congress WPA Collection.

40. *Wilford Woodruff's Journal* 2:180.

41. Larry M. Logue, "Belief and Behavior in a Mormon Town: Nineteenth-Century St. George, Utah" (Ph.D. diss., University of Pennsylvania, 1984), pp. 54–74. Recent illustrations include Carole C. Hansen, "The Death of a Son," *Dialogue* 2, no. 1 (1967): 90–96, and a book-length account of a young LDS AIDS victim entitled *Go Toward the Light* (New York: Harper and Row, 1988), also carried as a *Reader's Digest* book section and a made-for-television movie.

42. *Church News,* 30 December 1984, p. 14.

43. See, for example, *Diary of Charles Lowell Walker* 1:393, in which Walker is requested by Brigham Young "to sit up with his deceased Daughter Alice." See also entries on 1:370, 417, 477; 2:572, 674.

44. C. Paul Dredge, "What's in a Funeral? Korean, American-Mormon and Jewish Rites Compared," in *Deity and Death,* ed. Palmer, p. 25.

45. Leonard J. Arrington, *Brigham Young: American Moses* (New York: Alfred A. Knopf, 1985), pp. 399–400.

46. Matthias F. Cowley, *Wilford Woodruff: History of His Life and Labors* (1909; Salt Lake City: Bookcraft, 1964), p. 622.

47. *YWJ* 14:239 (1903).

48. Ibid.; *IE* 12:145–46 (1908).

49. *Handbook of Instructions,* no. 16 (1940), p. 127.

50. E. Gordon Ericksen, "A Sociological Study of Funeral Customs and Legal Burial Requirements in Utah" (Master's thesis, University of Utah, 1939), pp. 19–23; *General Handbook of Instructions* (Salt Lake City: Church of Jesus Christ of Latter-day Saints, 1985), p. 2-6.

51. Boyd K. Packer, "Funerals—A Time for Reverence," *Ensign,* November 1988, pp. 18–21.

52. Ibid.

53. Christine Croft Water, "Pioneering Physicians in Utah, 1847–1900" (Master's thesis, University of Utah, 1976), p. 4.

54. *General Handbook of Instructions* (Salt Lake City: Church of Jesus Christ of Latter-day Saints, 1983), p. 78; *General Handbook of Instructions* (1989), p. 11-5.

55. *Contributor* 4:58–61 (November 1884).

56. *Handbook of Instructions,* no. 16 (1940), p. 128.

57. *RSM* 16:362 (1929).

58. "Instructions for Making Temple Clothing and Clothing the Dead" (Salt Lake City: Church of Jesus Christ of Latter-day Saints, 1972), p. 13.

59. *The Church of Jesus Christ of Latter-day Saints General Handbook of Instructions,* no. 20 (Salt Lake City: Deseret News Press, 1968), p. 161; no. 19 (Salt Lake City: Deseret News Press, 1963), p. 87; no. 21 (1976), p. 87.

60. *General Handbook of Instructions* (1989), p. 11-5.

61. *Diary of Charles Lowell Walker* 1:465–66.

62. Clark, ed., *Messages of the First Presidency* 3:88–89.

63. *Contributor* 16:319–21 (1895); *JI* 28:352 (1893); 31:218 (1896).

64. *JI* 28:352 (1893).

65. Diary of George F. Richards, 13 December 1906, as quoted in Dale C. Mouritsen, "A Symbol of New Directions: George F. Richards and the Mormon Church, 1851–1950" (Ph.D. diss., Brigham Young University, 1982), p. 81; *JI* 31:219 (1899).

66. First Presidency letter of 15 August 1966, on "Temple Ordinances for Deceased Persons"; *General Handbook of Instructions* (1989), pp. 2-7, 11-5.

67. *JI* 41:112–13 (1906).

68. *T&S* 12:86–89 (1842).

69. *Wilford Woodruff's Journal* 6:224; diary of L. John Nuttal, 24 July 1887.

70. *IE* 25:1122 (1922).

71. One such case in which an incapacitated stroke victim was "sealed" to die is found in Val D. MacMurray and Kim Ventura, "Decision Models in Bioethics," in *Perspectives in Mormon Ethics: Personal, Social, Legal, and Medical,* ed. Donald G. Hill, Jr. (Salt Lake City: Publishers Press, 1983), p. 265.

72. *General Handbook of Instructions* (1985), p. 11-4 (this guidance was first issued by the Church Commissioner of Health Services in 1976 and has been included in the *General Handbook* since 1983); *General Handbook of Instructions* (1989), pp. 11-6, 11-5.

73. Lynn D. Wardle, "Passive Euthanasia: A Three-Dimensional View," in *Perspectives in Mormon Ethics,* ed. Hill, pp. 285–315.

74. Val D. MacMurray and Kim Ventura, "Decision Models in Bioethics," *Perspectives in Mormon Ethics,* ed. Hill, pp. 253–84.

Chapter 3 / On Being Well and Suffering

1. *JD* 11:132 (1865).

2. Unless otherwise indicated, observations on the early Mormon health record are based on my own study of Nauvoo, Winter Quarters, and Salt Lake City sextons' reports.

3. Larry M. Logue, "Belief and Behavior in a Mormon Town," p. 158.

4. *M&A* 1:23 (1834).

5. Orson F. Whitney, *Life of Heber C. Kimball* (1888; Salt Lake City, 1967), pp. 258–59; Oliver B. Huntington, "The Prophet on Old Houses," *YWJ* 2:467–68 (July 1891).

6. *Wilford Woodruff's Journal* 3:326.

7. 2 Nephi 2:11–13.

8. Smith, *History of the Church* 2:80, 114.

9. Smith, *History of the Church* 4:11.

10. *Church News*, 4 May 1974, 1 June 1974.

11. *Contributor* 11:477–78 (1890).

12. Arthur Bassett, "What the Scriptures Say About Suffering," *Ensign*, December 1972, pp. 64–65.

13. Sandra Ferrin Strange, "The Uses of Suffering," *Ensign*, March 1987, pp. 56–58.

14. For more detail on this context, see Lester E. Bush, Jr., "The Word of Wisdom in Early Nineteenth-Century Perspective," *Dialogue* 14, no. 3 (1981): 47–65. The best general history of the Word of Wisdom is Paul H. Peterson, "An Historical Analysis of the Word of Wisdom" (Master's thesis, Brigham Young University, 1972).

15. *D&C* 49:18–19.

16. Smith, *History of the Church* 2:369.

17. Minutes of the School of the Prophets at St. George, 23 December 1883, p. 3, at LDS Library/Archives, Salt Lake City, Utah.

18. Smith, *History of the Church* 2:35; Peterson, "Word of Wisdom," pp. 27–28.

19. *Wilford Woodruff's Journal* 1:111, 4 December 1836; Cannon and Cook, *Far West Record*, p. 106.

20. Smith, *History of the Church* 6:178.

21. *MS* 21:283 (1859); Smith, *History of the Church* 7:101.

22. *T&S* 4:316 (1843); Smith, *History of the Church* 4:445; diary of Samuel Richards, in Juanita Brooks, *John Doyle Lee: Zealot, Pioneer Builder, Scapegoat* (Glendale, Calif.: Arthur C. Clark, 1962), pp. 86–87.

23. Smith, *History of the Church* 7:454.

24. On this period, see Peterson, "Word of Wisdom"; Robert J. McCue, "Did the Word of Wisdom Become a Commandment in 1851?" *Dialogue* 14, no. 3 (1981): 66–77; and Leonard J. Arrington, "An Economic Interpretation of the Word of Wisdom," *BYU Studies* 1 (1959): 37–49.

25. Peterson, "Word of Wisdom," pp. 54–65.

26. Thomas G. Alexander, "The Word of Wisdom: From Principle to Requirement," *Dialogue* 14, no. 3 (1981): 78–88.

27. Thomas G. Alexander, *Mormonism in Transition: A History of Latter-day Saints, 1890–1930* (Urbana: University of Illinois, 1986), pp. 258–66.

28. See, for example, Gordon B. Hinckley, "Liquor by the Drink," *IE*, October 1968; *Church News*, 27 October 1973; *Church News*, 10 February 1985.

29. Gordon Shepherd and Gary Shepherd, *A Kingdom Transformed: Themes in the Development of Mormonism* (Salt Lake City: University of Utah Press, 1984), pp. 229–59.

30. Frederick J. Pack, *Tobacco and Human Efficiency* (Salt Lake City: Church of Jesus Christ of Latter-day Saints, 1918); L. Weston Oaks, *Medical Aspects of the Latter-day Saint Word of Wisdom* (Provo, Utah: Brigham Young University, 1929); John A. Widtsoe and Leah D. Widtsoe, *The Word of Wisdom: A Modern Interpretation* (Salt Lake City: Deseret Book,1937; 2d ed., 1950). The genre continues: David

D. Geddes, *Our Word of Wisdom* (Salt Lake City: Deseret Book, 1964); Roy W. Doxey, *The Word of Wisdom Today* (Salt Lake City: Deseret Book, 1975).

31. Alexander, *Mormonism in Transition*, pp. 267–68.

32. Copies of several of these letters are in my possession; see also "Word of Wisdom: From Counsel to Commandment," in *Seventh East Press*, 12 April 1983, p. 11.

33. *Priesthood Bulletin*, February 1972.

34. *General Handbook of Instructions* (1989), p. 11-6.

35. See, for example, James E. Enstrom, "Health Practices and Cancer Mortality Among Active California Mormons," *Journal of the National Cancer Institute* 81 (6 December 1989): 1807–14; Joseph L. Lyon and Steven Nelson, "Mormon Health," *Dialogue* 12, no. 3 (Autumn 1979): 84–96.

36. Smith, *History of the Church* 5:357.

37. Clark, ed., *Messages of the First Presidency* 2:191.

38. Gene A. Sessions, *Mormon Thunder: A Documentary History of Jedediah Morgan Grant* (Urbana: University of Illinois, 1982), p. 221; Journal of Phineas Cook, in LDS Library/Archives, Salt Lake City, Utah.

39. *Salt Lake Sanitarian* 2 (May 1889): 47–48.

40. "Report of Surgeon E. P. Vollum, USA," in John Shaw Billings, *War Department Surgeon General's Office Circular No. 8, "Report on the Hygiene of the United States Army,"* 1 May 1875 (Washington, D.C., 1875), pp. 344–45.

41. Clark, ed., *Messages of the First Presidency* 3:123–24.

42. For some general public health history of this period see Joseph R. Morrell, *Utah's Health and You: A History of Utah's Public Health* (Salt Lake City: Deseret Book, 1956).

43. See, for example, *Handbook for the Bee-hive Girls* (Salt Lake City: Y.L.M.I.A., 1916), p. 39.

44. See, for example, YWJ 10:76–80 (1879).

45. Lyman L. Daines and Arthur L. Beeley, *Community Health and Hygiene* (Salt Lake City: General Boards of the Y.M.M.I.A. and Y.L.M.I.A., 1930). This was an LDS young adult course manual.

46. First Presidency statement, 5 May 1978. Other recent First Presidency guidance has strongly supported appropriate prenatal care (1981) (see Chapter 4) and initiated a program to monitor and control tuberculosis and other health problems among LDS missionaries (1981, 1983).

47. First Presidency statement, 13 May 1972.

48. *MMWR (Morbidity and Mortality Weekly Report)* 38, no. 19 (19 May 1989): 347–50.

49. See, for example, *MMWR* 35, no. 16 (25 April 1986): 253–54.

50. Widtsoe and Widtsoe, *Word of Wisdom* (1937), p. 19.

51. Summaries of many of the findings can be found in Lyon and Nelson, "Mormon Health"; John W. Gardner, Joseph L. Lyon, and Dee W. West, "Cancer in Utah Mormons and Non-Mormons," *Journal of Collegium Aesculapium* 2, no. 1 (July 1984): 15–24. The first of the modern studies was James Enstrom, "Cancer Mortality among Mormons," *Cancer* 36 (1975): 825–41.

52. Gardner et al., "Cancer in Utah Mormons and Non-Mormons"; L. B. Jorde,

R. M. Fineman, and R. A. Martin, "Epidemiology of Neural Tube Defects in Utah, 1940–1979," *American Journal of Epidemiology* 119, no. 4 (1984): 489–95.

53. John W. Gardner and Joseph L. Lyon, "Cancer in Utah Mormon Men by Lay Priesthood," *American Journal of Epidemiology* 116, no. 2 (1982): 243–57; John W. Gardner and Joseph L. Lyon, "Cancer in Utah Mormon Women by Church Activity Level," *American Journal of Epidemiology* 116, no. 2 (1982): 258–65.

54. Enstrom, "Health Practices and Cancer Mortality Among Active California Mormons" (see n. 35 above).

55. Lyon and Nelson, "Mormon Health," p. 93; Edward Neil Robertson, "Life Table Analysis of Mormon and Non-Mormon Longevity Patterns in Utah, California, Idaho, and the United States" (Master's thesis, Ohio State University, 1977).

Chapter 4 / On Healing

1. Smith, *History of the Church* 1:83.
2. *D&C* 24:13–14 (July 1830).
3. *D&C* 35:8–9 (December 1830).
4. *D&C* 38:32 (2 January 1831).
5. *D&C* 42: 43–44, 48–52 (9 February 1831).
6. *D&C* 46:19–20 (8 March 1831); a similar message had been implied in the *Book of Mormon*, for example, in Alma 15:8–10.
7. *D&C* 84:67–72 (September 1832).
8. "Newell Knight Autobiography, 1800–1847," LDS Library/Archives, as quoted in Larry Porter, "The Joseph Knight Family," *Ensign* 8, no. 10 (October 1978): 39–46; quotation on p. 42.
9. "Hayde's History of the Disciples," pp. 250–51, in Smith, *History of the Church* 1:215–16; the episode apparently occurred in April 1831.
10. *Wilford Woodruff's Journal* 8:355.
11. Robert T. Divett, *Medicine and the Mormons* (Bountiful, Utah: Horizon Publishers, 1981), p. 43.
12. Wilford Woodruff, *Leaves From My Journal* (1881), reprinted in *Three Mormon Classics*, comp. Preston Nibley (Salt Lake City, 1944), pp. 71–75.
13. Smith, *History of the Church* 4:3–5; another popular account is found in Whitney, *Life of Heber C. Kimball*, pp. 262–64.
14. *Wilford Woodruff's Journal* 1:348.
15. *Wilford Woodruff's Journal* 5:53 (1857).
16. Diary of Mary Ellen Kimball, entry preceding 5 July 1857 entry, photocopy of holograph, original in LDS Library/Archives.
17. *MS* 10:158 (1848).
18. Dean C. Jessee, ed., *The Personal Writings of Joseph Smith* (Salt Lake City: Deseret Book, 1984), p. 82.
19. *M&A* 3:514 (1837).
20. *T&S* 4:325–26 (1843).
21. John Corrill, *Brief History of the Church of Christ of Latter Day Saints* (1839; Bountiful, Utah: Restoration Research, 1983), p. 38.
22. Smith, *History of the Church* 4:452 (1841).

23. *MS* 11:199 (1849).

24. Diary of L. John Nuttall, typescript, Brigham Young University Library, 25/ 26 June 1881.

25. *Wilford Woodruff's Journal* 4:347.

26. *D&C* 46 (8 March 1831).

27. Parley P. Pratt, ed., *Autobiography of Parley P. Pratt* (1873; Salt Lake City: Deseret Book, 1970), p. 325.

28. Smith, *History of the Church* 5:355 (1843).

29. *Wilford Woodruff's Journal* 1:348–51.

30. Ezra Booth to Ira Eddy, September 1831, in E. D. Howe, *Mormonism Unvailed* (1834; New York: AMS Press, 1977), p. 190. This may have been at the 1831 conference at which the new high priesthood was first bestowed.

31. See, for example, *M&A* 1:10–11 (1834).

32. F. Mark McKiernan and Roger D. Launius, eds., *An Early Latter Day Saint History: The Book of John Whitmer* (Independence, Mo.: Herald House, 1980), p. 95; *JD* 4:25 (1856).

33. *M&A* 3:514 (1837); Joseph Smith, *History of the Church* 2:379.

34. *JD* 2:276–77 (1855).

35. *Instructor* 83:325 (1948); *IE* 10:309 (1907).

36. Autobiography of John Lyman Smith, 12 November 1844, Library of Congress WPA Collection.

37. *JI* 21:186 (1886), 28:138–39 (1893), 30:613 (1895), 35:464 (1900); diary of J. D. T. McAllister, 4 January 1856, Huntington Library, San Marino, Calif.; journal of Andrew Sproul, 16 December 1846, and journal of James Farmer, 25 February 1851, both in Library of Congress WPA Collection; diary of L. John Nuttal, 25 February 1891.

38. Diary of J. D. T. McAllister, 11 January 1856.

39. *Wilford Woodruff's Journal* 7:32.

40. Diary of L. John Nuttal, 4 March 1877.

41. *JI* 14:174 (1879).

42. *Salt Lake Sanitarian* 1:5 (1888).

43. *Salt Lake Sanitarian* 1:4–5 (1888).

44. *Salt Lake Sanitarian* 1:4, 3:3, 38, 41–45 (1888, 1890).

45. Journal of Anthony W. Ivins, 29 August 1903, Utah Historical Society Library.

46. *JI* 37:307 (1902).

47. *YWJ* 5:493 (1893–94); *Relief Society Bulletin* 1, no. 8:7 (1914).

48. Autobiography of Flora Belnap, 12 June 1928, Library of Congress WPA Collection.

49. John A. Widtsoe, *Priesthood and Church Government* (Salt Lake City: Deseret Book, 1939), p. 374; *Handbook of Instructions*, no. 16 (1940), p. 126.

50. Andrew F. Ehat and Lyndon W. Cook, *The Words of Joseph Smith: The Contemporary Accounts of the Nauvoo Discourses of the Prophet Joseph* (Provo, Utah: Brigham Young University Religious Studies Center, 1980), p. 37. In this advice he apparently drew in part from Matthew 17:15–21.

51. See, for example, *Wilford Woodruff's Journal*, 31 January 1854, 3–4 August

1874; *Diary of Charles Lowell Walker* 2:597 (1882); diary of Abraham H. Cannon 12, 14 April 1888, Brigham Young University Library; *JI* 25:632–33 (1890).

52. *JI* 36:542 (1901), 37:42–43 (1902), 33:738 (1898).

53. *JI* 39:447 (1904).

54. *Diary of Charles Lowell Walker*, 1:477 (1879).

55. *JI* 38:327 (1903).

56. *Melchizedek Priesthood Handbook* (Salt Lake City: Church of Jesus Christ of Latter-day Saints, 1984), p. 28.

57. "An Epistle of the Twelve," 12 October 1841, in *T&S* 2:569 (1841).

58. Journal of William Clayton, 8 November 1841, as quoted in *JI* 21:60 (1886).

59. Smith, *History of the Church* 4:473 (1841).

60. Smith, *History of the Church* 4:586 (7 April 1842); 5:167–68 (5 October 1842).

61. D. Michael Quinn, "The Practice of Rebaptism at Nauvoo," *BYU Studies* 18 (Winter 1978): 226–32.

62. See, for example, Quinn, "The Practice of Rebaptism"; also Ogden Kraut, *A Brief History of Re-Baptism* (Dugway, Utah: Ogden Kraut, n.d.), pp. 8–10.

63. Hansen, *Mormonism and the American Experience*, p. 93; Quinn, "The Practice of Rebaptism," p. 230.

64. *T&S* 6:840 (1845).

65. Clark, ed., *Messages of the First Presidency* 1:247, 14 January 1845; *YWJ* 4:294–95, 299, 304 (1893); diary of Abraham H. Cannon, 8 November 1892; Melvin C. Merrill, ed., *Utah Pioneer and Apostle Marriner Wood Merrill and His Family* (Salt Lake City: Deseret News, 1937), p. 180.

66. See also Job 40:16 and Nahum 2:1.

67. *JI* 24:282–83 (1889).

68. See, for example, diary of Abraham H. Cannon, 11 February 1892; diary of L. John Nuttal, 10 March 1903; *JI* 41:351 (1906).

69. Quinn, "The Practice of Rebaptism," p. 232; *IE* 20:916–18 (1917); Alexander, *Mormonism in Transition*, p. 291.

70. First Presidency to Presidents of Temples, 15 December 1922, copy in my possession; Clark, ed., *Messages of the First Presidency* 5:223–24, 18 January 1923.

71. Clark, ed., *Messages of the First Presidency* 4:314–15, 3 October 1914.

72. Smith, *History of the Church* 4:602–4, 28 April 1842; Smith cites Mark 16:15–18.

73. Ibid.

74. Ibid. The quotation is from the official history of the church, but the actual minutes of the meeting state "Prest. S. then offered instruction respecting the propriety of females administering to the sick by the laying on of hands—said it was according to revelation." Possibly anointings by women did await their first participation in temple-related anointings a few weeks later. See Ehat and Cook, *The Words of Joseph Smith*, p. 119.

75. Linda King Newell, "Gifts of the Spirit: Women's Share," in *Sisters in Spirit: Mormon Women in Historical and Cultural Perspective*, ed. Maureen Ursenbach Beecher and Lavina Fielding Anderson (Urbana: University of Illinois Press, 1987), pp. 111–50.

76. Quoted in Linda King Newell, "A Gift Given: A Gift Taken: Washing, Anoint-

ing, and Blessing the Sick Among Mormon Women," *Sunstone* 6, no. 5 (September/ October 1981): 18.

77. Clark, ed., *Messages of the First Presidency* 4:313; *JI* 29:318 (1894).

78. Wilford Woodruff, 1888, quoted in Newell, "A Gift Given," p. 18.

79. Ibid.

80. *JI* 31:60 (1896); *JI* 31:102–3 (1896).

81. *JI* 29:241 (1894); *YWJ* 4:176 (1892–93).

82. *JI* 37:307 (1902).

83. Ibid. An illustration of this problem and the specificity of early Mormon health anointings is seen in this blessing given to women during pregnancy, as recorded in the minutes of a turn-of-the-century Relief Society record, and quoted in Newell, "Gifts of the Spirit," pp. 130–31: "We anoint your back, your spinal column that you might be strong and healthy no disease fasten upon it no accident belaff [befall] you, Your kidneys that they might be active and healthy and preform [*sic*] their proper functions, your bladder that it might be strong and protected from accident, your Hips that your system might relax and give way for the birth of your child, your sides that your liver, your lungs, and spleen that they might be strong and preform their proper functions, . . . your breasts that your milk may come freely and you need not be afflicted with sore nipples as many are, your heart that it might be comforted. . . . We anoint . . . your thighs that they might be healthy and strong that you might be exempt from cramps and from the bursting of veins. . . . That you might stand upon the earth [and] go in and out of the Temples of God."

84. *IE* 10:308 (February 1907).

85. Clark, ed., *Messages of the First Presidency* 4:315 (1914).

86. *Conference Reports*, April 1921, p. 199; Alexander, *Mormonism in Transition*, p. 293.

87. Widtsoe, *Priesthood and Church Government*, p. 375.

88. Newell, "A Gift Given," p. 23.

89. *IE* 58:559 (1955); *General Handbook of Instructions* (1989), p. 5-4.

90. *JI* 37:50–51 (1902).

91. *IE* 40:242 (April 1937); Widtsoe, *Priesthood and Church Government*, pp. 75–76.

92. *D&C* 42:43.

93. *D&C* 89:8, 10–11 (27 February 1833).

94. *T&S* 4:325–26 (1843).

95. Smith, *History of the Church* 4:414 (1841).

96. Ibid. 6:59 (1843).

97. Cannon and Cook, *Far West Record*, p. 96 (21 August 1834). Wight apparently took the counsel too much to heart, as he later became addicted to medicinal opium.

98. *T&S* 4:325–26 (1843).

99. *T&S* 4:325 (1843).

100. Smith, *History of the Church* 5:356–57 (1843).

101. Linda P. Wilcox, "The Imperfect Science: Brigham Young on Medical Doctors," *Dialogue* 12, no. 3 (Fall 1979): 30, 18.

102. *T&S* 4:325–26 (1843); Wilcox, "The Imperfect Science," p. 30.

103. *JD* 15:225–26 (1872).

104. Ezekiel 47:12; 2 Kings 20:7.

105. N. Lee Smith, "Herbal Remedies: God's Remedies?" *Dialogue* 12, no. 3 (Fall 1979): 39.

106. LeRoy S. Wirthlin, "Joseph Smith's Boyhood Operation: An 1813 Surgical Success," *BYU Studies* 21 (Spring 1981): 131–54.

107. Smith, *History of the Church* 5:366 (1843).

108. "Journal of Priddy Meeks," *Utah Historical Quarterly* 10 (1942): 199–200.

109. Examples of the early botanic influence could fill books. The many extant collections on Mormon "folk medicine," though drawn largely from pioneer or later years, clearly derive as well from this initial period. As an illustration, in one account known to many Mormons through its later inclusion in the church's official published history, Joseph Smith advises immigrants arriving in Illinois, "If you feel any inconvenience, take some mild physic two or three times, and follow that up with some good bitter. If you cannot get anything else, take a little salts and cayenne pepper. If you cannot get salts take ipecacuanha or gnaw down a butternut tree, or use boneset or horehound" (Smith, *History of the Church* 5:356–57 [1843]).

110. "Journal of Priddy Meeks," p. 178.

111. *Deseret News*, 15 June 1850.

112. Offenses Against Public Health; Acts, Resolutions and Memorials Passed at the Several Annual Sessions of the Legislative Assembly of the Territory of Utah (1850–1855), Chapter XXXII, Title IX, Sections 106, 107.

113. *Deseret News*, as reprinted in *MS* 14:215 (1852). Young added that he personally "would much prefer to die a natural death to being helped out of the world by the most intelligent graduate, new or old school, that ever scientifically flourished the wand of Esculapius or any of his followers."

114. *MS* 14:473 (1852).

115. *JD* 15:225 (1872).

116. *Wilford Woodruff's Journal* 1:348, 350.

117. *JD* 4:24 (1856).

118. Irene B. Woodford, "Nursing and Nurse Training in Relief Society," *RSM* 51:645–53 (1964).

119. *YWJ* 16:39–41 (1905); *A Tradition of Excellence: LDS Hospital 1905–1980* (Salt Lake City: LDS Hospital, 1980), pp. 21–29.

120. *Deseret News*, 6 January 1905.

121. Eugene Wood, "History of the Practice of Obstetrics in Utah," *Rocky Mountain Medical Journal*, April 1967, pp. 66–73.

122. Josephine M. Kasteler and Susan Hulme, "Attitudes toward Women Physicians in a Mormon Community," *Journal of the American Medical Women's Association* 35, no. 2 (February 1980): 37–41.

123. *IE* 5:626 (1902). The "quack" medicine of this day was the recommended fare of the 1840s, when an earlier generation of quacks was being condemned. The cycle, of course, is never-ending. Well into the twentieth century, church periodicals carried advertisements for Lifetime Radium Water Jars, the radioactive contents of which could cure about anything (See, for example, *RSM* 14:53 [1927].)

124. J. M. Morin, "An Investigation of Utilization of Herbs as Medication among a Selected LDS Population" (Master's thesis, Brigham Young University, 1979), as cited in Norman Lee Smith, "Why Are Mormons So Susceptible to Medical and

Nutritional Quackery?" *Journal of Collegium Aesculapium* 1:30 (1983); popular recent proherbalist books include John Heinerman, *Joseph Smith and Herbal Medicine: A Brief Study of the Botanical Arts in Mormonism* (Manti, Utah: Mountain Valley Publishers, 1972); LaDean Griffin, *"Is Any Sick Among You?"* (Provo, Utah: BiWorld Publishers, 1974); and LaDean Griffin, *No Side Effects: The Return to Herbal Medicine* (Provo, Utah: Bi-World Publishers, 1975).

125. *Church News*, 19 February 1977; *Bulletin*, no. 7, January 1981.

126. *General Handbook of Instructions* (1985), p. 11-4; (1989), p. 11-5.

127. Gene A. Sessions, ed., *Mormon Democrat: The Religious and Political Memoirs of James Henry Moyle*, (Salt Lake City: James Moyle Genealogical and Historical Association, 1975), p. 11.

128. *JI* 28:669–70 (1893).

129. *Deseret News*, 17 December 1921.

130. "Supplement to 'In the Realm of Quorum Activity,' Second Series," (Salt Lake City: Church of Jesus Christ of Latter-day Saints, 1932), p. 35.

131. *JI* 35, no. 2 (1900): 62–63. Recent concerns nationally over much less direct contact with AIDS victims—despite reasonable certainty that the risk of transmission under most circumstances is nil—offers an instructive context to sentiment nearly a century ago.

132. "Ward Teacher's Message for November, 1936," *IE* 39:626 (1936).

133. *MS* 9:49–54 (1847).

134. *JI* 31:450–51 (1896), 36:532–33 (1901), 45:406–8 (1910); *YWJ* 20:204–6 (1909); *IE* 21:902–4, 1065–68 (1918).

135. Bruce R. McConkie, *Mormon Doctrine* (Salt Lake City: Bookcraft, 1958), pp. 338–39; *Priesthood Bulletin*, August 1972; "Attitudes of the Church of Jesus Christ of Latter-day Saints Toward Certain Medical Problems," (1974), in "Mormon Medical Ethical Guidelines," ed. Lester E. Bush, Jr., *Dialogue* 12, no. 34 (Fall 1979): 100.

136. Diary of Abraham H. Cannon, 21–22 October 1889; *JI* 43:111–12 (1908).

137. See, for example, Russell Marion Nelson, *From Heart to Heart: An Autobiography* (USA: Quality Press, 1979), pp. 195–203; *Church News*, 20 June 1987, p. 4, and 29 August 1987, p. 11; *Ensign*, August 1985, pp. 65–67.

138. Louis A. Moench, "Mormon Forms of Psychopathology," paper presented at the second midyear meeting of Collegium Aesculapium, 20 January 1984; a modified version is reprinted in *AMCAP Journal*, March 1985, pp. 61–73.

139. Ibid.

140. Orson Scott Card, *Saintspeak: The Mormon Dictionary* (Salt Lake City: Orion Books, 1981), n.p.

141. The church never has made a serious effort to encourage the use of tobacco for bruises. Brigham Young University's athletic department did once announce that it had demonstrated the effectiveness of this revealed remedy (*Church News*, 4 September 1982).

142. *General Handbook of Instructions* (1989), p. 11-6; *Ensign*, February 1988, p. 50.

143. "Attitudes of the Church of Jesus Christ of Latter-day Saints Toward Certain Medical Problems" (1974), in Bush, ed., "Mormon Medical Ethical Guidelines," pp. 99–100.

144. *Utah Public Health Journal* 2, no. 1 (January–February 1922); 3.

218 : *Health and Medicine among the Latter-day Saints*

145. Quoted by Renée C. Fox in "'It's the Same, but Different': A Sociological Perspective on the Case of the Utah Artificial Heart," in *After Barney Clark,* ed. Margery W. Shaw (Austin: University of Texas Press, 1984), pp. 84–85.

Chapter 5 / On Madness

1. See, for example, Matthew 17:18; Mark 6:13, 9:38, 16:17–18; Luke 8:2, 9:49; Acts 8:7.
2. See, for example, 1 Nephi 11:31; Mosiah 3:5–6; 3 Nephi 7:19, 22; Mormon 9:24.
3. *D&C* 24:13, 35:8–9, 38:32, 84:67–72, and 124:98, extending from 1830 to 1841.
4. Smith, *History of the Church* 1:83.
5. *Autobiography of Parley P. Pratt,* pp. 154–55.
6. Parley P. Pratt, *Key to the Science of Theology* (Liverpool, 1855), pp. 120–21.
7. *JI* 24:282–83 (1889).
8. *JI* 16:366 (1882); for enhanced agitation, see *MS* 11:205 (1849).
9. *JI* 17:180–81 (1882).
10. *MS* 9:231–33 (1847).
11. *Autobiography of Andrew Jenson* (Salt Lake City, 1938), pp. 110–11.
12. *MS* 11:207 (1849).
13. See, for example, *Autobiography of Parley P. Pratt,* p. 61.
14. *D&C* 50:23 (1831).
15. Lucy Mack Smith, *Biographical Sketches* (Liverpool, 1853), pp. 171–72.
16. Among the several sources reporting this episode, see diary of Levi Ward Hancock, 4 June 1831, and Corrill, *Brief History of the Church,* pp. 13–14.
17. *JD* 11:7.
18. *JI* 29:577 (1894); 19:91 (1884).
19. *JI* 19:91, 102–3 (1884).
20. *Wilford Woodruff's Journal* 1:408 (1840).
21. *JI* 18:346 (1883). The illness probably was acute glomerulonephritis, an occasional complication of scarlet fever. The cerebral symptoms can be part of the disease, or they may have been induced by the doctor's use of diuretics to reduce swelling from fluid retention ("dropsy").
22. *Conference Reports,* April 1926, p. 125.
23. *IE* 1:154–55 (1898).
24. *JI* 37:563 (1902).
25. Daines and Beeley, *Community Health and Hygiene,* p. 135.
26. *Wilford Woodruff's Journal* 1:310 (1838).
27. Smith, *History of the Church* 1:265.
28. Arthur L. Beeley, "Insanity," *IE* 16:231–38 (1913).
29. *JI* 26:244 (1891).
30. *RSM* 7:78 (1920).
31. For example, see *JD* 2:10–11, 222–23; 13:70–75, 266–67, 280–81.

32. See, for example, *Biennial Report . . . of the Board of Directors . . . of the Insane Asylum of Utah Territory* (Salt Lake City, 1888), pp. 3, 45.

33. *Diary of Charles Lowell Walker,* p. 621 (1883).

34. Charles R. McKell, "The Utah State Hospital: A Study in the Care of the Mentally Ill," *Provo Papers,* 1 October 1976, pp. 6–28, originally published in *Utah Historical Quarterly* 23 (1955): 297–327.

35. McKell, "The Utah State Hospital," p. 9.

36. Ibid., p. 11; in 1879 Young bought the asylum outright.

37. Ibid., p. 12; YWJ 3:368–69.

38. McKell, "The Utah State Hospital," p. 15.

39. Ralph T. Richards, *Of Medicine, Hospitals, and Doctors* (Salt Lake City: University of Utah Press, 1953), p. 258.

40. Louis G. Moench, "Notes on the History of Psychiatry in Utah," *Utah State Medical Association Bulletin* 33, no. 5 (May 1985): 3–5.

41. From an 1899 publication for hospital administrators, quoted in Seymour P. Steed, "Utah State Hospital, 1885–1942," *Provo Papers,* 1 October 1976, p. 2.

42. Moench, "Notes on the History of Psychiatry in Utah."

43. Charles R. McKell, "The Problem of Mental Illness in Utah," *Provo Papers* 1, no. 4 (October 1957): 1–14.

44. *Guidebook for Parents and Guardians of Handicapped Children* (Salt Lake City: Church of Jesus Christ of Latter-day Saints, 1986), p. 13.

45. YWJ 3:422–24, 4:227–28, 366–71, 19:118–20.

46. Charles R. McKell, "History of the Utah State Hospital, Provo" (Master's thesis, University of Utah, 1948), pp. 154–57; Daines and Beeley, *Community Health and Hygiene,* pp. 148–49.

47. Pratt, *Key to the Science of Theology,* p. 167.

48. Daines and Beeley, *Community Health and Hygiene,* pp. 148–50.

49. *General Handbook of Instructions* (1983), p. 77.

50. *Guidebook for Parents and Guardians of Handicapped Children,* pp. 34–35.

51. Ibid., p. 3.

52. Joseph Fielding Smith, *Man: His Origin and Destiny* (Salt Lake City: Deseret Book, 1954), p. 487.

53. Wesley W. Craig, Jr., "Confrontation and Rejection of an Evil Spirit in a Therapy Session," *AMCAP Journal* 10, no. 1 (January 1984): 6–9, 23.

54. *AMCAP Newsletter,* Summer 1984, p. 3.

55. AMCAP Journal 10, no. 1 (January 1984): 5; *AMCAP Newsletter,* Summer 1984, p. 3.

56. Bruce R. McConkie, *Mormon Doctrine* (1958), p. 549, and 2d ed. (1966), pp. 610–11.

57. Louis G. Moench, "Religion and Psychiatry—Interface," (typescript, n.d.); Dr. Moench was the principal referral psychiatrist for the church at the time.

58. Louis G. Moench, letter to the author, 30 December 1985.

59. Spencer W. Kimball, as quoted in C. Jay Skidmore, "Mormonism and Psychotherapy," in *Religious Systems and Psychotherapy,* ed. Richard H. Cox and E. Mansell Pattison (Springfield, Ill.: Charles C. Thomas, 1973), p. 99.

60. As cited in *Bishop's Training Course and Self-Help Guide* (Salt Lake City:

Church of Jesus Christ of Latter-day Saints, n.d. [in use during the 1980s]), p. VI–13.

61. *General Handbook of Instruction* (1985), p. 11–2.

62. Genevieve De Hoyos and Arturo De Hoyos, "The Mormon Psychotherapists: A Synthesis," *AMCAP Journal* 7, no. 1 (July 1982): 21–28.

63. *Priesthood Bulletin*, August 1972.

64. "New Horizons for Homosexuals," (Salt Lake City: Church of Jesus Christ of Latter-day Saints, 1971), p. 28.

65. *Resource Manual for Helping Families with Alcohol Problems* (Salt Lake City: Church of Jesus Christ of Latter-day Saints, 1984), p. 24.

66. *Priesthood Bulletin*, August 1972.

67. Vern H. Jensen, "A History of the Association of Mormon Counselors and Psychotherapists (AMCAP)," *AMCAP Journal* 4, no. 2 (Fall 1978): 1–30.

68. De Hoyos and De Hoyos, "The Mormon Psychotherapists," pp. 21–22.

69. Gary James Bergera and Ronald Priddis, *Brigham Young University: A House of Faith* (Salt Lake City: Signature Books, 1985), pp. 82–83.

70. Quotations, p. 83.

71. Allen E. Bergin, "A Religious Framework for Personality and Psychotherapy," Brigham Young University, 8 April 1977.

72. Ibid.

73. Ibid.

74. Harold C. Brown, "New Developments in LDS Social Services," *AMCAP Journal* 7, no. 1 (January 1981): 11–13, 31–32.

75. *AMCAP Journal* 7, no. 2 (April 1981): 30.

76. *AMCAP Newsletter*, Winter 1982, pp. 5–7.

77. Victor L. Brown, Jr., *Human Intimacy: Illusion and Reality* (Salt Lake City: Parliament Publishers, 1981).

78. Jan Pinborough, "Mental Illness," *Ensign*, February 1989, pp. 51–58.

79. Louis G. Moench, "Notes on the History of Psychiatry in Utah," pp. 3–5.

80. "Which Path," in *JI* 27:586ff.

81. *JI* 31:325–26 (1896).

82. McConkie, *Mormon Doctrine* (1958), p. 696.

83. McConkie, *Mormon Doctrine*, 2d ed. (1966), p. 771.

84. *Identification and Prevention of Suicidal Behavior* (Salt Lake City: Church of Jesus Christ of Latter-day Saints, 1974), p. 2.

85. *General Handbook of Instructions* (1989), p. 11-5.

Chapter 6 / On Sexuality and Birth

1. Sterling Sill, *Church News*, 31 July 1965, quoted in O. Kendall White, "The Transformation of Mormon Theology," *Dialogue* 5, no. 2 (1970): 16; 2 Nephi 2:25.

2. *D&C* 76:24 (1832).

3. *The Seer* 1:37–39 (1853); Pratt, *Key to the Science of Theology*, p. 41.

4. *D&C* 132:19 (1843).

5. *The Seer* 1:155 (1853).

6. Pratt, *Key to the Science of Theology*, p. 173.

7. From "Intelligence and Affection," quoted in *Dialogue* 10, no. 2 (1976): 8.

8. *JD* 13:206–8 (1869).

9. *Journal History* of the Church of Jesus Christ of Latter-day Saints, 29 April 1849.

10. *Diary of Charles Lowell Walker* 2:620–21 (1883).

11. Lester E. Bush, Jr., "Mormon Elders' Wafers: Images of Mormon Virility in Patent Medicine Ads," *Dialogue* 10, no. 2 (1976): 89–93.

12. Charles A. Cannon, "The Awesome Power of Sex: The Polemical Campaign Against Mormon Polygamy," *Pacific Historical Review* 43 (February 1974): 61–81.

13. Lawrence Foster, *Religion and Sexuality: Three American Communal Experiments of the Nineteenth Century* (New York: Oxford University Press, 1981), p. 236.

14. *D&C* 59:6, 42:24–26 (1831).

15. Cannon, "The Awesome Power of Sex," pp. 70–73.

16. Richard S. Van Wagoner, "Mormon Polyandry in Nauvoo," *Dialogue* 18, no. 3 (1985): 67–83; Theodore Schroeder, "Incest in Mormonism," *American Journal of Urology and Sexology* 11:409–16 (1915).

17. Clark, ed., *Messages of the First Presidency* 5:12.

18. *YWJ* 2:229–32, 464–65, 561–62; 3:32–34 (1891–93).

19. See, for example, *YWJ* 13:61–64 (1912); Daines and Beeley, *Community Health and Hygiene*, pp. 214–19.

20. *RSM* 19:89–93 (1932).

21. *RSM* 14:89–94, 103–6, 629–30 (1927); 19:92 (1932); 20:760–61 (1933); 23:631–32 (1936); 24:684–87, 688–90 (1937).

22. Clark, ed., *Messages of the First Presidency* 5:12.

23. Carlfred B. Broderick, "The Core of My Belief," in *A Thoughtful Faith: Essays on Belief by Mormon Scholars*, ed. Philip L. Barlow (Centerville, Utah: Canon Press, 1986), pp. 93–96.

24. Lester E. Bush, Jr., "Excommunication and Church Courts: A Note from the General Handbook of Instructions," *Dialogue* 14, no. 2 (1981): 74–98; John Heinerman and Anson Shupe, *The Mormon Corporate Empire* (Boston: Beacon Press, 1985), p. 84.

25. *General Handbook of Instructions*, no. 21 (1976), p. 81.

26. *Ensign*, June 1975.

27. *Church News*, 29 June 1986, p. 7.

28. Wilford E. Smith, "Mormon Sex Standards on College Campuses, or Deal Us Out of the Sexual Revolution!" *Dialogue* 10, no. 2 (1976): 76–81; Tim B. Heaton, "Four Characteristics of the Mormon Family: Contemporary Research on Chastity, Conjugality, Children, and Chauvinism," *Dialogue* 20, no. 2 (1987): 101–14.

29. Tim B. Heaton, "Demographics of the Contemporary Mormon Family" (Paper presented at Sunstone Symposium XIII, Salt Lake CIty, Utah, August 1991. Heaton aggregated results from three Centers for Disease Control surveys, in which 60 percent of Mormon women reported premarital sex, and 13 percent cohabitation. In contrast, the national averages were 80 percent and 26 percent respectively.

30. *The Seer* 1:155 (1853); *JD* 13:3 (1869).

31. *JI* 27:480–83 (1892).

32. Lester E. Bush, Jr., "A Peculiar People: 'The Physiological Aspects of Mormonism' 1850–1875," *Dialogue* 12 (1979): 61–83.

33. *JD* 13:206–8 (1869).

34. Schroeder, "Incest in Mormonism," p. 410; J. E. Hickman, "The Offspring of the Mormon People," *Journal of Heredity* 15:55–68 (1924).

35. *Diary of Charles Lowell Walker* 2:621 (1883); "Insanity," *IE* 16:231–38 (1913); *Biennial Report . . . of the Insane Asylum of Utah Territory*, pp. 18, 45.

36. Daines and Beeley, *Community Health and Hygiene*, p. 138.

37. McConkie, *Mormon Doctrine* (1958), p. 549; 2d ed. (1966), pp. 610–11.

38. See, for example, Lindsay R. Curtis and Wayne J. Anderson, *Living, Loving, and Marrying* (Salt Lake City: Deseret Book, 1968), pp. 46–49, 221–24; Brown, *Human Intimacy*, pp.73–75.

39. "Homosexuality" (Welfare Services Packet 1 of the Church of Jesus Christ of Latter-day Saints, ca. 1976), pp. 16–17; "Homosexuality," 2d ed. (1981), pp. 6–7.

40. Smith, *History of the Church* 1:519 (1837).

41. *T&S*, 1 March 1884; *The Nauvoo Neighbor*, 6 September 1843; *D&C* 136:28 (1847); Nels Anderson, *Desert Saints*, p. 422.

42. Thomas Kane's description, in J. B. Jennings, "A Backward Glance at Dancing," *IE*, June 1936, p. 381.

43. Quoted in Davis Biton, "'These Licentious Days': Dancing Among the Mormons," *Sunstone* 2, no. 1 (1977): 16–27.

44. *JI* 11:42 (1876), 19:56 (1884), 29:449–50 (1894); Bitton, "Dancing Among the Mormons," p. 23; "Rules Which Should Be Observed in Dancing Parties in St. George Stake of Zion," 24 December 1887; Clark, ed., *Messages of the First Presidency* 3:122 (1887).

45. Merrill, ed., *Marriner Wood Merrill and His Family*, p. 136 (1891).

46. *Contributor* 16:115 (1887); *JI* 29:449–50 (1894).

47. *YWJ* 8:419–20 (1896–97).

48. Karl E. Wesson, "Dance in the Church of Jesus Christ of Latter-day Saints, 1830–1940," (Master's thesis, Brigham Young University, 1975), pp. 47, 49.

49. *YMMIA Handbook*, 2d ed. (Salt Lake City: General Board of the Y.M.M.I.A., 1915), pp. 106–7; *YMMIA Recreation Bulletin #3* (1924), pp. 91–99; *YMMIA Hand Book* (Salt Lake City: General Board of the Y.M.M.I.A., 1928), pp. 388–89; *M.I.A. Executive Guide* (Salt Lake City: General Boards of the Y.M.M.I.A. and Y.L.M.I.A., 1937), pp.196–210.

50. *JI* 48:291–93 (1913); Clark, ed., *Messages of the First Presidency* 4:218.

51. *JI* 48:291–93 (1913).

52. *MIA Executive Manual* (Salt Lake City: Church of Jesus Christ of Latter-day Saints, 1970), p. 191.

53. Kenneth L. Cannon, "Needed: An LDS Philosophy of Sex," *Dialogue* 10, no. 2 (1976): 57–61.

54. Apostle John Henry Smith, in diary of Abraham H. Cannon, 8 September 1890, Brigham Young University Library.

55. David O. McKay, in *RSM* 3:366 (1916); J. Reuben Clark in *Conference Reports*, 1 October 1949, pp. 194–95.

56. *Conference Reports* of the Church of Jesus Christ of Latter-day Saints 70A

(Annual): 39–40, 5 April 1900. See Lester E. Bush, Jr., "Birth Control Among the Mormons: Introduction to an Insistent Question," *Dialogue* 10, no. 2 (1976): 12–44.

57. *IE* 11:959–61 (October 1908).

58. *RSM* 4:317–18 (June 1917).

59. Heber J. Grant to Arnold Haymore, 1 May 1939, copy in my possession.

60. John A. Widtsoe to Cardon Klinger, 15 April 1942, copy in my possession. J. Reuben Clark, of the First Presidency, privately wrote to the same effect in 1933. See D. Michael Quinn, *J. Reuben Clark: The Church Years* (Salt Lake City: Brigham Young University Press, 1983), p. 158.

61. *IE* 45:801, 831 (1942).

62. Letter of 27 May 1946, from "files of LaMar Berrett, Professor of Religion, Brigham Young University," in "Statements of the General Authorities on Birth Control," Department of Religion, Brigham Young University, n.d.

63. McConkie, *Mormon Doctrine* (1958), p. 81; Bruce R. McConkie, comp., *Doctrines of Salvation* (Salt Lake City: Bookcraft, 1955), 2:86–89.

64. Hugh B. Brown, *You and Your Marriage* (Salt Lake City: Bookcraft, 1960), pp. 135–36.

65. First Presidency statement, 14 April 1969.

66. See Bush, "Birth Control Among the Mormons," pp. 23, 32.

67. Tim B. Heaton and Sandra Calkins, "Contraceptive Use Among Mormons: 1965–1975," *Dialogue* 16, no. 3 (Fall 1983): 106–9.

68. *Ensign* 9 (August 1979): 23–24.

69. *General Handbook of Instructions* (1983), p. 77.

70. Gordon B. Hinckley, "Cornerstones of a Happy Home," 29 January 1984 (published February 1984), p. 6.

71. Lindsay R. Curtis, *"And They Shall Be One Flesh": A Sensible Sex Guide for the L.D.S. Bride and Groom* (Salt Lake City: Publishers Press, 1968), p. 53.

72. See, for example, *Foundations for Temple Marriage* [an official LDS manual] (Salt Lake City: Church of Jesus Christ of Latter-day Saints, 1979), pp. 35–40; Brown, *Human Intimacy.* See also the related view of RLDS authors F. Glenn Goff and Anna Mae Goff, "Sexual Intercourse in Renewal of the Marriage Covenant," *Courage* 3, no. 1 (1973): 91–100.

73. "Some Thoughts on Sexual Dysfunction," *AMCAP Newsletter,* Winter 1983, pp. 5–7.

74. Joseph Anderson (Secretary to the First Presidency) to L.A., 23 March 1971; Eugene Campbell and Richard Poll, *Hugh B. Brown* (Salt Lake City: Bookcraft, 1975), p. 288.

75. As summarized in a letter from General Authority James A. Cullimore to L.R.H., 10 June 1977.

76. *Priesthood Bulletin,* First Quarter 1974.

77. First Presidency letter of 5 January 1982.

78. First Presidency letter of 15 October 1982.

79. Bush, "Birth Control Among the Mormons," pp. 14–16.

80. *JD* 26:14–15 (1884); see also *JD* 22:320 (1881).

81. Richard W. Lohner, "Therapeutic Abortion in Salt Lake City, 1954–1964," *Selected Writings by the Staff of Latter-day Saints Hospital* 6, no. 1 (Spring 1967): 9–19. Although the overall incidence was lower than the presumed national norm,

224: Health and Medicine among the Latter-day Saints

only the Roman Catholic Holy Cross Hospital had no therapeutic abortions during the eleven-year period of this study. Nine percent of the abortions had been for fetal indications, and 18 percent for psychiatric. The author judged many of the 73 percent labeled "medical" in fact to have been for other indications.

82. David O. McKay to Tiena Nate, 31 October 1934, copy in my possession; First Presidency statement, *Ensign*, March 1973, p. 64. In 1958 J. Reuben Clark, of the First Presidency, though generally strongly opposed to abortion, advised a woman concerned that she had contracted German measles while pregnant that on the question of terminating the pregnancy "she should seek the advice of her physicians . . . and also seek the Lord in prayer." See Quinn, *J. Reuben Clark*, p. 158.

83. 3 Nephi 1:12–13.

84. *JD* 17:143 (1874).

85. Clark, ed., *Messages of the First Presidency*, 4:205.

86. McConkie, comp., *Doctrine of Salvation* 2:280–81; McConkie, *Mormon Doctrine*, 2d ed. (1966), p. 768.

87. David O. McKay to Tiena Nate, 31 October 1934.

88. David H. Yarn, Jr., ed., *J. Reuben Clark: Selected Papers* (Provo, Utah: Brigham Young University Press, 1984), pp. 113–29.

89. Abraham 5:7 in the canonized *Pearl of Great Price* (Salt Lake City: Church of Jesus Christ of Latter-day Saints, 1962); LDS temple liturgy includes similar language.

90. *Wilford Woodruff's Journal* 5:109 (1857), 6:361–63 (1867); *JD* 12:66 (1867).

91. First Presidency letter of 12 February 1970.

92. *General Handbook of Instructions* (1983), p. 44.

93. "Church Opposes Abortion Bill," *Deseret News*, 23 January 1969.

94. Joseph Anderson (Secretary to the First Presidency) to unidentified correspondent, 16 May 1969.

95. *Priesthood Bulletin*, June 1972.

96. As reprinted in *Church News*, 27 March 1976, p. 6.

97. *Church News*, 5 June 1976, p. 3.

98. *General Handbook of Instructions* (1983), pp. 77–78; (1989), pp. 11-4, 10-3.

99. *Church News*, 19 June 1991, p. 5.

100. *MMWR* 40; SS-2 (July 1991): 25, 31. Eight-week comparisons calculated from data provided. National eight-week comparisons based on 34 reporting states, District of Columbia, and New York City.

101. Stephen J. Sepe et al., "Genetic Services in the United States, 1979–1980," *JAMA* 248 (October 8, 1982): 1733–35. Utah figures are not included but were provided by Stephen Sepe to the author via personal correspondence, 26 January 1983.

102. Robert Fineman, Fifth Annual Birth Defects, Mental Retardation, and Medical Genetics Symposium, University of Utah, 24–25 March 1983.

103. *General Handbook of Instructions* (1983), p. 52; "[LDS] Services for Unwed Parents" (1981).

104. Parley P. Pratt, *Key to the Science of Theology*, p. 167; *YWJ* 6:220 (1894–95).

105. *Utah Code Annotated* sec. 89-0-1, 1925; sec. 64-10-1 after 1953; John Widtsoe, *RSM* 13:82 (1913).

106. Daines and Beeley, *Community Health and Hygiene*, pp. 148–50; *General Handbook of Instructions* (1983), p. 77.

107. *Deseret News,* 23 January 1969.
108. Bush, ed., "Mormon Medical Ethical Guidelines," p. 100.
109. *General Handbook of Instructions* (1983), p. 77; (1989), p. 11-5.
110. *JD* 4:56 (1856).
111. "Childless Marriages," *Deseret News* Church Section, 25 October 1950, p. 16.
112. First Presidency guidance as quoted in private correspondence from a member of the Quorum of the Twelve, 12 April 1973, copy in my possession; *General Handbook of Instructions,* no. 21 (1976), p. 62.
113. Bush, ed., "Mormon Medical Ethical Guidelines," p. 97.
114. Ibid., pp. 97, 101.
115. *Ensign,* November 1985, p. 89; *General Handbook of Instructions* (1985), p. 11-3.
116. *General Handbook of Instructions* (1983), p. 43.
117. *Sunstone Review* 1, no. 3 (March 1983): 6.
118. *USA Today,* 22 June 1987, p. 8A.
119. *General Handbook of Instructions,* no. 20 (1968), p. 122.
120. First Presidency letters to local leaders were sent 19 March 1970, 30 May 1975, and 8 May 1978; an additional statement was carried in the *Priesthood Bulletin,* February 1973.
121. First Presidency letter of 19 March 1970; Priesthood Bulletin, February 1973.
122. "Homosexuality," Welfare Services Packet 1 (1975), pp. 12–14.
123. "Homosexuality," 2d ed. (1981), pp. 1–2.
124. "Homosexuality," (1975), p. 15.
125. Bergera and Priddis, *Brigham Young University,* pp. 82–83; R. Jan Stout, "Sin and Sexuality: Psychobiology and the Development of Homosexuality," *Dialogue* 20, no. 2 (1987): 29–41.
126. *Church News,* 14 February 1987.
127. *Ensign,* July 1988, p. 79.
128. Heinerman and Shupe, *The Mormon Corporate Empire,* p. 84.
129. See Jeffrey E. Keller, "Is Sexual Gender Eternal?" *Sunstone* 10, no. 11 (1986): 38–39.
130. *YWJ* 25:600 (1914).
131. *Conference Reports,* October 1976, p. 101.
132. *Ensign,* November 1974, p. 8.
133. Replacement chapter 8, "The Church Judicial System," for *General Handbook of Instructions,* no. 21 (1976), dated October 1980.
134. *General Handbook of Instructions* (1983), p. 53; (1985), p. 8-2; (1989), p. 10-4.
135. *Ensign,* November 1974, p. 8.

Chapter 7 / On Caring

1. General Board of the Relief Society, *Handbook of Instructions of the Relief Society of the Church of Jesus Christ of Latter-day Saints* (Salt Lake City: Church of Jesus Christ of Latter-day Saints, 1972), pp. 49–51.

226 :   *Health and Medicine among the Latter-day Saints*

2. Loretta L. Hefner, "The National Women's Relief Society and the U.S. Sheppard-Towner Act," *Utah Historical Quarterly* 50 (1982): 255–67.

3. *Deseret News 1975 Church Almanac* (Salt Lake City: Deseret News, 1975), p. A10.

4. *Ensign,* December 1971, pp. 107–8; *Church News,* 8 December 1973.

5. *Ensign,* February 1991, pp. 34–37; *Newsletter* of Collegium Aesculapium, November 1990, pp. 1–2.

6. Val D. MacMurray, "Priorities and Perspectives: The View of One Private Voluntary Organization," speech at the Annual Congressional Luncheon sponsored by the National Council of International Health, 27 February 1985.

7. "Thrasher Research Fund Annual Report 1984," pp. 12–13; Thrasher Research Fund, "A Proposal to the Nigerian Government for a Village Health Worker Project," 2 September 1983.

8. *Church News,* 14 April 1985, p. 19.

9. Isaac C. Ferguson, "Freely Given," *Ensign,* August 1988, pp. 10–15.

Chapter 8 / On Morality and Dignity

1. Ehat and Cook, *Words of Joseph Smith,* pp. 183–84.

2. *General Handbook of Instructions,* no. 18 (1960), pp. 1, 3.

3. N. Eldon Tanner, "The Debate Is Over," *Ensign,* August 1979, pp. 2–3.

4. Edwin B. Firmage, *An Abundant Life: The Memoirs of Hugh B. Brown* (Salt Lake City: Signature Books, 1988), p. 124.

5. Gary James Bergera, "The Orson Pratt–Brigham Young Controversies: Conflict within The Quorums, 1853 to 1868," *Dialogue* 18, no. 2 (1980): 29.

6. *D&C* 98:12.

7. Peter Crawley, "Parley P. Pratt: Father of Mormon Pamphleteering," *Dialogue* 15, no. 3 (1982): 13–26; esp. p. 21 and 23.

8. Sources for official First Presidency guidance include the following:

1. Church periodicals and newspapers, including especially the *Deseret News* (1850–present) with its weekly *Church News* supplement (1933–present); the *Millennial Star* (1840–1970); the *Improvement Era* (1897–1970); and *Ensign* (1970–present).
2. *The General Handbook of Instructions* (1899–present), which has evolved from annual instructions on financial matters into a definitive guidebook for local and regional leaders on church administration and policy. It currently is in its twenty-fourth edition (1989).
3. The *Priesthood Bulletin* (1965–74), a brief monthly begun by the First Presidency "to provide information concerning the policies, administration, and organization of all the Priesthood programs of the Church."
4. *Messages* (1974–80) from the Offices of the First Presidency, Council of the Twelve, First Council of the Seventy, Presiding Bishopric, and General Departments of the church to stake/district presidents, bishops, and branch presidents, which was an abbreviated successor to the *Priesthood Bulletin.*
5. *Bulletin* (1980–present), the successor to *Messages.*
See also James R. Clark, ed., *Messages of the First Presidency of the Church of Jesus Christ of Latter-day Saints, 1833–1964,* 6 vols. (through 1951) (Salt Lake City, 1965–75), a useful though not comprehensive compilation of statements issued over the years;

and "Attitudes of the Church of Jesus Christ of Latter-day Saints toward Certain Medical Problems" (1974), a short summary prepared with First Presidency approval by then–Church Commissioner of Health Services James O. Mason and available through the Church Public Communications Department as an accurate statement of LDS beliefs.

9. *Church News,* 19 November 1988, p. 5.

Index

Health/Medicine and the Faith Traditions

HEALTH AND MEDICINE AMONG THE LATTER-DAY SAINTS
Lester E. Bush, Jr.

HEALTH AND MEDICINE IN THE ANGLICAN TRADITION
David H. Smith

HEALTH AND MEDICINE IN THE CATHOLIC TRADITION
Richard A. McCormick

HEALTH AND MEDICINE IN THE CHRISTIAN SCIENCE TRADITION
Robert Peel

HEALTH AND MEDICINE IN THE EASTERN ORTHODOX TRADITION
Stanley Samuel Harakas

HEALTH AND MEDICINE IN THE HINDU TRADITION
Prakash N. Desai

HEALTH AND MEDICINE IN THE ISLAMIC TRADITION
Fazlur Rahman

HEALTH AND MEDICINE IN THE JEWISH TRADITION
David M. Feldman

HEALTH AND MEDICINE IN THE LUTHERAN TRADITION
Martin E. Marty

HEALTH AND MEDICINE IN THE METHODIST TRADITION
E. Brooks Holifield

HEALTH AND MEDICINE IN THE REFORMED TRADITION
Kenneth L. Vaux

SHAMANIC HEALING AND RITUAL DRAMA:
HEALTH AND MEDICINE
IN NATIVE NORTH AMERICAN RELIGIOUS TRADITIONS
Åke Hultkrantz